SPACE LAW
TREATIES AND PRINCIPLES
- notes and commentaries-

THIRD EDITION

Edited by Daniel-Eduard Rociu

© 2013, 2014, 2015 Daniel-Eduard Rociu
All rights reserved.

ISBN: 1490995498
ISBN-13: 978-1490995496

Cover and book design by AGORA BOOKS

Printed in the United States of America

Revised on May 2014, November 2015
First Printing: July 2013

DEDICATION

This book is dedicated to my wife, Eliza-Roxana

SPACE LAW
TREATIES AND PRINCIPLES
- notes and commentaries-

THIRD EDITION

CONTENTS

INTRODUCTORY NOTES 24

UNITED NATIONS TREATIES - INTRODUCTORY COMMENTARIES..26

TREATY ON PRINCIPLES GOVERNING THE ACTIVITIES OF STATES IN THE EXPLORATION AND USE OF OUTER SPACE, INCLUDING THE MOON AND OTHER CELESTIAL BODIES (OUTER SPACE TREATY) 31

    ARTICLE I 32
    ARTICLE II...33
    ARTICLE III 33
    ARTICLE IV 33
    ARTICLE V 34
    ARTICLE VI...36
    ARTICLE VII 37
    ARTICLE VIII 37
    ARTICLE X...38
    ARTICLE XI 38
    ARTICLE XII 39
    ARTICLE XIII..39
    ARTICLE XIV 39
    ARTICLE XVI..40
    ARTICLE XVII 40
    NOTES ON THE EXPLORATION AND USE OF OUTER SPACE, INCLUDING THE MOON AND OTHER CELESTIAL BODIES TREATY......42

AGREEMENT ON THE RESCUE OF ASTRONAUTS, THE RETURN OF ASTRONAUTS AND THE RETURN OF OBJECTS LAUNCHED INTO OUTER SPACE (RESCUE AGREEMENT)..44

    ARTICLE 1 45

- ARTICLE 2 46
- ARTICLE 3 47
- ARTICLE 4 47
- ARTICLE 5 48
- ARTICLE 6 49
- ARTICLE 7 49
- ARTICLE 8 50
- ARTICLE 9 50
- ARTICLE 10 51
- NOTES ON AGREEMENT ON THE RESCUE OF ASTRONAUTS, THE RETURN OF ASTRONAUTS AND THE RETURN OF OBJECTS LAUNCHED INTO OUTER SPACE 52

CONVENTION ON INTERNATIONAL LIABILITY FOR DAMAGE CAUSED BY SPACE OBJECTS (LIABILITY CONVENTION) 54

- ARTICLE I 55
- ARTICLE II 56
- ARTICLE III 57
- ARTICLE IV 58
- ARTICLE V 59
- ARTICLE VI 59
- ARTICLE VII 60
- ARTICLE VIII 60
- ARTICLE IX 61
- ARTICLE X 61
- ARTICLE XI 62
- ARTICLE XII 62
- ARTICLE XIII 63
- ARTICLE XIV 63
- ARTICLE XV 63
- ARTICLE XVI 64
- ARTICLE XVII 64
- ARTICLE XVIII 65
- ARTICLE XIX 65
- ARTICLE XX 65
- ARTICLE XXI 66

ARTICLE XXII	66
ARTICLE XXIII	67
ARTICLE XXIV	67
ARTICLE XXV	68
ARTICLE XXVI	68
ARTICLE XXVII	69
ARTICLE XXVIII	69
NOTES ON THE CONVENTION ON INTERNATIONAL LIABILITY FOR DAMAGE CAUSED BY SPACE OBJECTS	70

CONVENTION ON REGISTRATION OF OBJECTS LAUNCHED INTO OUTER SPACE (REGISTRATION CONVENTION) 73

ARTICLE I	74
ARTICLE II	75
ARTICLE III	75
ARTICLE IV	75
ARTICLE V	76
ARTICLE V	76
ARTICLE VII	77
ARTICLE VIII	77
ARTICLE IX	78
ARTICLE X	78
ARTICLE XI	78
ARTICLE XII	78
NOTES ON THE CONVENTION ON REGISTRATION OF OBJECTS LAUNCHED INTO OUTER SPACE (REGISTRATION CONVENTION)	80

AGREEMENT GOVERNING THE ACTIVITIES OF STATES ON THE MOON AND OTHER CELESTIAL BODIES (MOON AGREEMENT) 83

ARTICLE 1	84
ARTICLE 2	84
ARTICLE 3	85
ARTICLE 4	85
ARTICLE 5	86
ARTICLE 6	87
ARTICLE 7	87

 Article 8 88
 Article 9 89
 Article 10 89
 Article 11 90
 Article 12 92
 Article 13 92
 Article 14 92
 Article 15 93
 Article 16 94
 Article 17 94
 Article 18 95
 Article 19 95
 Article 20 96
 Article 21 96
 Notes on the Moon Agreement 98

PART II: PRINCIPLES ADOPTED BY THE GENERAL ASSEMBLY 99

DECLARATION OF LEGAL PRINCIPLES GOVERNING THE ACTIVITIES OF STATES IN THE EXPLORATION AND USE OF OUTER SPACE 100

PRINCIPLES GOVERNING THE USE BY STATES OF ARTIFICIAL EARTH SATELLITES FOR INTERNATIONAL DIRECT TELEVISION BROADCASTING 103

 Annex 104
 A. Purposes and objectives 104
 B. Applicability of international law 105
 C. Rights and benefits 105
 D. International cooperation 106
 E. Peaceful settlement of disputes 106
 F. State responsibility 106
 G. Duty and right to consult 106
 H. Copyright and neighbouring rights 107
 I. Notification to the United Nations 107
 J. Consultations and agreements between States 107

PRINCIPLES RELATING TO REMOTE SENSING OF THE EARTH FROM OUTER SPACE 108

Annex..109
Principle I 109
Principle II 110
Principle III..110
Principle IV..111
Principle V 111
Principle VI..111
Principle VII 112
Principle VIII 112
Principle IX 112
Principle X 112
Principle XI..113
Principle XII 113
Principle XIII 113
Principle XIV...114
Principle XV 114

PRINCIPLES RELEVANT TO THE USE OF NUCLEAR POWER SOURCES IN OUTER SPACE 115

Principle 1. Applicability of international law 116
Principle 2. Use of terms...116
Principle 3. Guidelines and criteria for safe use..................117
   1. General goals for radiation protection and nuclear safety 117
   2. Nuclear reactors..118
   3. Radioisotope generators 120
Principle 4. Safety assessment 120
Principle 5. Notification of re-entry 121
Principle 6. Consultations...122
Principle 7. Assistance to States 122
Principle 8. Responsibility 123
Principle 9. Liability and compensation............................124
Principle 10. Settlement of disputes 125
Principle 11. Review and revision 125

DECLARATION ON INTERNATIONAL COOPERATION IN THE EXPLORATION AND USE OF OUTER SPACE FOR

THE BENEFIT AND IN THE INTEREST OF ALL STATES, TAKING INTO PARTICULAR ACCOUNT THE NEEDS OF DEVELOPING COUNTRIES 126

ANNEX 127

PART III: NATIONAL LEGISLATION 131

FRANCE 132

LOW NO. 2008-518 OF 3ʳᴰ JUNE 2008 REGARDING THE SPACE OPERATIONS 132

REPUBLIC OF KOREA... 148

LAW NO.8852 OF 8852 OF DEC. 21, 2007 - SPACE LIABILITY ACT . 148
Article 1 (Purpose) 148
Article 2 (Definitions) 148
Article 3 (Relation to International Treaties) 148
Article 4 (Absolute liability and waiver of liability) 149
Article 5 (limit on compensation)... 149
Article 6 (Third-party liability insurance) 149
Article 7 (governmental measures).. 150
Article 8 (Lapse of right) 150
Additional Clauses 150
SPACE DEVELOPMENT PROMOTION ACT 151
Article 1 (Purpose) 151
Article 2 (Definitions) 151
Article 3 (Government Responsibilities) 152
Article 4 (Relation to Other Acts) 152
Article 5 (Establishing Basic Plan for Promoting Space Development) 152
Article 7 (Designation as a Space Development Institute)..... 154
Article 8 (Domestic Registration of Space Objects)................ 154
Article 9 (International Registration of Space Objects)......... 155
Article 10 (Management of Space Objects Registry).............. 156
Article 11 (A Launch permit of a Space Launch Vehicle)........ 156
Article 12 (Disqualification).. 157
Article 13 (Cancellation of Launch Permit and the Hearing) 157
Article 14 (Liability for Damages due to Space Accidents).... 158
Article 15 (Third-Party Liability Insurance) 158

Article 16 (Formation of a Space Accident Inquiry Committee)
...158
Article 17 (Utilization of Satellite Information).....................159
Article 18 (Support of Civil Space Development Activities) ...159
Article 19 (Suspension and Modification of Space Development Activities)..159
Article 20 (Requesting and Cooperation for Space Development)..160
Article 21 (Implementation of Space Development Activities Relevant to National Security) 160
Article 22 (Rescue of Astronauts) 160
Article 23 (Return of Space Objects).......................................161
Article 24 (Collection of information and fact-finding surveys on Space Development Activities) 161
Article 25 (Confidentiality) 161
Article 26 (Consignment of Power) 161
Article 27 (Penalty Clauses) 162
Article 28 (Dual Penalization)...162
Additional Clauses 163

ITALY 165

LAW 23, 25 JANUARY 1983 - NORMS FOR THE IMPLEMENTATION FOR THE CONVENTION ON INTERNATIONAL LIABILITY FOR DAMAGE CAUSED BY SPACE OBJECTS, SIGNED IN LONDON, MOSCOW AND WASHINGTON MARCH 29, 1972 165

NETHERLANDS...167

RULES CONCERNING SPACE ACTIVITIES AND THE ESTABLISHMENT OF A REGISTRY OF SPACE OBJECTS (SPACE ACTIVITIES ACT) 167
    CHAPTER 1. GENERAL PROVISIONS 167
    CHAPTER 2. LICENCES...168
        § 3. Disasters...171
    CHAPTER 3. REGISTRY OF SPACE OBJECTS 172
    CHAPTER 4. REDRESS 172
    CHAPTER 5. ENFORCEMENT 173
    CHAPTER 6. AMENDMENTS TO OTHER LEGISLATION....177
    CHAPTER 7. CONCLUDING PROVISIONS 177

AUSTRALIA 179

SPACE ACTIVITIES ACT - 1998 179
Part 1—Introduction 179
1 Short title 179
2 Commencement 179
3 Objects of Act 179
4 Simplified outline of Act..180
5 Act binds the Crown 180
6 External Territories 180
7 Application of *Criminal Code*..................................180
Part 2—Definitions 180
8 Definitions 180
8A Approved scientific or educational organisations.........186
8B Guidelines for making a declaration..............................186
8C Applying for a declaration...186
9 Related party..186
Part 3—Regulation of space activities 187
10 Simplified outline...187
Division 1—Certain space activities require approvals etc. ..189
11 Launch in Australia requires a launch permit or exemption certificate 189
12 Overseas launch requires an overseas launch certificate 189
13 Return to Australia of Australian-launched space object requires a launch permit or exemption certificate 190
14 Return to Australia of overseas-launched space object requires authorisation 190
15 Space licence required to operate a launch facility in Australia 191
16 Commonwealth not bound 192
17 Activities of international space organisations...............192
Division 2—Space licences 193
18 Granting a space licence 193
19 Terms of space licence 194
20 Standard space licence conditions 194
21 Breaching a space licence condition 194
22 Transfer of space licence..195

 23 Applying for the grant, variation or transfer of a space licence 195
 24 Procedure etc. 195
 25 Suspending a space licence..196
 25A Annual review of space licence 196
Division 3—Launch permits *196*
 26 Granting a launch permit 196
 27 Australian launches: continuing requirement for space licence 198
 28 Terms of launch permit...198
 29 Standard launch permit conditions 199
 30 Breaching a launch permit condition............................199
 31 Transfer of launch permit 200
 32 Applying for the grant, variation or transfer of a launch permit 201
 33 Procedure etc. 201
 34 Suspending a launch permit..201
Division 4—Overseas launch certificates *202*
 35 Granting an overseas launch certificate 202
 37 Breaching a condition 204
 38 Transfer of overseas launch certificate.........................204
 39 Applying for the grant, variation or transfer of an overseas launch certificate...205
 40 Procedure etc. 205
 41 Suspending an overseas launch certificate 205
Division 5—Authorisation of return of overseas-launched space objects *206*
 42 Scope of Division...206
 43 Returns may be authorised by permission or by agreement..207
 44 Offences relating to returns...208
 45 Breaching a condition 209
 45A Applying for an authorisation or for the variation of an authorisation 209
 45B Procedure etc. 209
 45C Suspending an authorisation under section 43...........210
Division 6—Exemption certificates *212*

46   Exemption certificates 212
46A Terms of exemption certificate 212
46B Breaching a condition 213
Division 7—Insurance/financial requirements 213
   47 Satisfying the insurance/financial requirements 213
   48 Insurance requirements 213
   49 Additional insurance not precluded 215
Division 8—Launch Safety Officer 215
   50 Launch Safety Officer 215
   51 Functions of Launch Safety Officer 215
   52 Powers of Launch Safety Officer 216
   53 Offence of failing to comply with directions 217
   54 Procedure for giving and complying with directions 217
   55 Launch Safety Officer to comply with Minister's instructions 218
   56 Seizures in emergency situations 218
   57 Launch Safety Officer may obtain assistance 218
   58 Identity cards 218
Division 9—Administration etc. 221
   59 Fees 221
   60 Request for information 222
   61 Review of decisions 222
   62 Notice of decisions 223
Part 4—Liability for damage by space objects 223
Division 1—Scope of Part 223
   63 Damage covered 223
   64 Compensation for third party damage by space objects to be determined solely under this Part 224
   65 Regulations about waivers 224
Division 2—Liability for third party damage 225
Subdivision A—Rules for damage caused by launches and most returns 225
   66 Scope of Subdivision 225
   67 Damage on Earth or in the air 225
   68 Damage to other space objects 226
   69 Limit on amount of permit or certificate holder's liability 226

Subdivision B—Rules for certain returns conducted by overseas nationals 227
  70 Scope of Subdivision 227
  71 Liability 228
Division 3—Procedure etc. 229
  72 Federal Court has jurisdiction.................................229
  73 Action for compensation 229
Division 4—Compensation claims by foreign countries 231
  74 Responsible party's liability to the Commonwealth.......231
  75 Claims Commission 231
Part 5—Register of space objects 233
  76 Minister to keep Register 233
  77 Registration number..233
  78 Register may be kept on computer 234
  79 Inspection of Register 234
Part 5A—Implementation of space cooperation agreements 234
  79A Implementation of intergovernmental agreement with Russia 234
  79B Regulations may amend Schedule..........................234
Part 6—Civil penalties..236
  80 Civil penalty provisions 236
  81 *Fines for contravening civil penalty provisions*................236
  82 Procedure..237
  83 Not an offence to contravene civil penalty provision 237
Part 7—Investigation of accidents.............................238
Division 1—Scope of Part 238
  84 Scope of Part 238
  85 Meaning of *accident*...238
  86 Meaning of *incident* 238
Division 2—Investigations 238
  87 Object of Division 238
  88 Appointing an Investigator......................................239
  89 Investigator to investigate accident or incident 239
  90 Investigator may invite assistance.................239
  91 Investigator's powers to gather information................239
  92 Offences relating to section 91 requirements..........240
  93 Report of investigation..242

    94 Custody of space object etc. 242
    95 Automatic suspension of launch permit etc. after accident
    243
    96 Disclosure of safety records 243
    97 Relationship with other powers 245
    Division 3—Accident site powers 245
    98 Accident sites and accident site premises 246
    99 Power of entry to accident site 246
    100 Procedure before entry 247
    101 Identity cards 248
    102 Availability of assistance and use of force in entering
    accident site premises 248
    103 Offence of entering etc. an accident site without
    permission 249
Part 8—Miscellaneous 249
    104 Delegation 249
    105 Operation of other laws 249
    106 Immunity 249
    107 Compensation—constitutional safety net 249
    108 Severability: additional effect of Act 250
    109 Application of Act: pre-existing agreement 251
    110 Regulations 253

AUSTRIA 254

AUSTRIAN FEDERAL LAW ON THE AUTHORIZATION OF SPACE ACTIVITIES AND THE ESTABLISHMENT OF A NATIONAL SPACE REGISTRY (AUSTRIAN OUTER SPACE ACT, ADOPTED BY THE NATIONAL COUNCIL ON 6 DECEMBER 2011, ENTERED INTO FORCE ON 28 DECEMBER 2011) 254

THE RUSSIAN FEDERATION 264

LAW OF THE RUSSIAN FEDERATION ABOUT SPACE ACTIVITY
.... 264

UKRAINE 296

ORDINANCE OF THE SUPREME SOVIET OF UKRAINE, ON SPACE ACTIVITY LAW OF UKRAINE OF 15 NOVEMBER 1996 296

On The Amendment Of Particular Legislative Acts Of Ukraine Regarding The Activities Of Communications Enterprises ...311

JAPAN ...315

Law Concerning The National Space Development Agency Of Japan ...315

NORWAY ...338

Act on launching objects from Norwegian territory etc. into outer space ...338

REPUBLIC OF KAZAKHSTAN ...339

Law of the Republic of Kazakhstan on Space Activities 6 January, 2012 No. 528-IV ...339

Article 2. Legislation of the Republic of Kazakhstan in the Ficld of Space Activities ...342

Article 3. Principles of implementation of space activities ...342

Article 4. Directions of space activities ...343

Article 5. Types of space activities for creation and use of space infrastructure ...343

Article 6. Material and human resource bases of space activities ...344

Article 7. Financing space activities ...344

Article 8. Competence of the Government of the Republic of Kazakhstan in the field of space activities ...344

Article 9. Competence of an authorized body in the field of space activities ...346

Article 10. Sectoral expertise of projects in the field of space activities ...349

Article 11. State registration of space objects and rights for them ...349

Article 12. State control in the field of space activities ...352

Article 13. Licensing activities in the field of use of outer space ...352

Article 14. Scientific researches in the field of the space activities ...353

Article 15. Creation of space systems and space rocket complexes 353
Article 16. Usage of space communication system 354
Article 17. Usage of Earth remote sensing space system.... 354
Article 18. Usage of high-accuracy satellite navigation system 355
Article 19. Usage of space-rocket complexes 355
Article 20. Objects of space infrastructure of the Republic of Kazakhstan 356
Article 21. The objects of ground space infrastructure.... 356
Article 22. Facilities for space engineering production.... 356
Article 23. «Baikonur» cosmodrome 357
Article 24. Marking of space objects of the Republic of Kazakhstan 357
Article 25. Utilization of space objects and technical facilities 357
Article 26. Lend-lease of space sector object 358
Article 27. Safety assurance of space activities 358
Article 28. Investigation of accidents during the implementation of space activities.. 359
Article 29. Ecological control of the environment and level of health of population in regions, subject to influence of space activities 360
Article 30. Interdictions and restrictions in the space activities 360
Article 31. Status of cosmonaut candidate, the cosmonaut. Preparation of cosmonaut candidate, cosmonaut 361
Article 32. Guarantees in case of reception of mutilation, diseases or destructions (death) of cosmonaut candidates, cosmonaut 362
Article 33. Indemnification of expenses on burial 363
Article 34. Medical and sanatorium service to cosmonaut candidate, cosmonaut 363
Article 35. Endowment of cosmonauts awarded a title of honor "The pilot-cosmonaut of Kazakhstan" 364

Article 36. Liability for infringement of the legislation of the Republic of Kazakhstan in the field of space activities 364

Article 37. Corning into force procedure of the present Law 364

SWEDEN 366
Act on Space Activities 366
SPAIN 368
Royal Decree No. 278/1995 of 24 February 1995 368
UNITED KINGDOM OF GREAT BRITAIN AND NORTHERN IRELAND 373
Outer Space Act 1986 373
INDEX 384
DEFINITIONS 391
NATIONAL REGULATORY FRAMEWORKS FOR SPACE ACTIVITIES 416
BIBLIOGRAPHY 420

ABOUT THIS BOOK

This work offers a general & systematic collection of basic legal documents
that will be a required tool for researchers & practitioners.
First part contains principal legal instruments--the so-called 'classical
instruments'--elaborated within the United Nations,
Principles adopted by the General Assembly & notes and commentaries.
Second part deals with national legislation specifically
concerning outer space issues.
Each treaty & convention is followed by notes and
commentaries on each subject.
We provided a comprehensive index
and definitions section as well.

Status As Of November 2015

INTRODUCTORY NOTES

The space age has brought with it the excitement and drama of exploration and compelling tales about the people and technology that have made it possible. From the advent of space flight beginning with Sputnik, then with flights to the moon and the continuing use of the International Space Station, spaceflight has taken the center stage on many occasions. Less obvious is that there is a legal environment in which these activities take place.

Space law is a creature of international law, which is a combination of customs and treaties. An example of customary space law is the principle of free passage in space established when the USSR launched Sputnik into orbit and crossed over territories other than its own without protest from those countries.

Most of the fundamentals of international space law were devised by the Legal Sub-Committee of the UN Committee for the Peaceful Uses of Outer Space (UNCOPUS). Those fundamentals are that no nation can make territorial claims to outer space and celestial bodies within it; that nations have free access to space; that all nations are free to conduct scientific investigation in space; that national rights to space objects launched by them are preserved; and that nations will cooperate in rendering assistance to crews of spaceships in emergencies. These principles form the basis of the founding five treaties that are the framework of international space law. These treaties are:

1. *The Treaty on Principles Governing the Activities of States in the Exploration and Use of Outer Space, including the Moon and Other Celestial Bodies* (the "Outer Space Treaty"), adopted by the General Assembly in its resolution 2222 (XXI), opened for signature on 27 January 1967, entered into force on 10 October 1967;

2. *The Agreement on the Rescue of Astronauts, the Return of Astronauts and the Return of Objects Launched into Outer Space* (the "Rescue Agreement"), adopted by the General Assembly in its resolution 2345 (XXII), opened for signature on 22 April 1968, entered into force on 3 December 1968;

3. *The Convention on International Liability for Damage Caused by Space Objects* (the "Liability Convention"), adopted by the General Assembly in its resolution 2777 (XXVI), opened for

signature on 29 March 1972, entered into force on 1 September 1972;

4. *The Convention on Registration of Objects Launched into Outer Space (the "Registration Convention")*, adopted by the General Assembly in its resolution 3235 (XXIX), opened for signature on 14 January 1975, entered into force on 15 September 1976;

5. *The Agreement Governing the Activities of States on the Moon and Other Celestial Bodies* (the "Moon Agreement"), adopted by the General Assembly in its resolution 34/68, opened for signature on 18 December 1979, entered into force on 11 July 1984.

This book puts together UN official texts on the space law, national legislation and a comprehensive index and definitions section.

PART I

UNITED NATIONS TREATIES - INTRODUCTORY COMMENTARIES

The progressive development and codification of international law constitutes one of the principal responsibilities of the United Nations in the legal field. An important area for the exercise of such responsibilities is the new environment of outer space and, through the efforts of the United Nations Committee on the Peaceful Uses of Outer Space and its Legal Subcommittee, a number of significant contributions to the law of outer space have been made. The United Nations has, indeed, become a focal point for international cooperation in outer space and for the formulation of necessary international rules. Outer space, extraordinary in many respects, is, in addition, unique from the legal point of view.

It is only recently that human activities and international interaction in outer space have become realities and that beginnings have been made in the formulation of international rules to facilitate international relations in outer space.

As is appropriate to an environment whose nature is so extraordinary, the extension of international law to outer space has been gradual and evolutionary—commencing with the study of questions relating to legal aspects, proceeding to the formulation of principles of a legal nature and, then, incorporating such principles in general multilateral treaties.

A significant first step was the adoption by the General Assembly A significant first step was the adoption by the General

Assembly in 1963 of the Declaration of Legal Principles Governing the Activities of States in the Exploration and Use of Outer Space.

The years that followed saw the elaboration within the United Nations of five general multilateral treaties, which incorporated and developed concepts included in the Declaration of Legal Principles:

- The Treaty on Principles Governing the Activities of States in the Exploration and Use of Outer Space, including the Moon and Other Celestial Bodies (General Assembly resolution 2222 (XXI), annex)—adopted on 19 December 1966, opened for signature on 27 January 1967, entered into force on 10 October 1967;

- The Agreement on the Rescue of Astronauts, the Return of Astronauts and the Return of Objects Launched into Outer Space (resolution 2345 (XXII), annex)—adopted on 19 December 1967, opened for signature on 22 April 1968, entered into force on 3 December 1968;

- The Convention on International Liability for Damage Caused by Space Objects (resolution 2777 (XXVI), annex)—adopted on 29 November 1971, opened for signature on 29 March 1972, entered into force on 1 September 1972;

- The Convention on Registration of Objects Launched into Outer Space (resolution 3235 (XXIX), annex)—adopted on 12 November 1974, opened for signature on 14 January 1975, entered into force on 15 September 1976;

- The Agreement Governing the Activities of States on the Moon and Other Celestial Bodies (resolution 34/68, annex)—adopted on 5 December 1979, opened for signature on 18 December 1979, entered into force on 11 July 1984.

- The United Nations oversaw the drafting, formulation and adoption of five General Assembly resolutions, including the Declaration of Legal Principles. These are:

- The Declaration of Legal Principles Governing the Activities of States in the Exploration and Use of Outer Space, adopted on 13 December 1963 (resolution 1962 (XVIII));

- The Principles Governing the Use by States of Artificial Earth Satellites for International Direct Television Broadcasting, adopted on 10 December 1982 (resolution 37/92);

- The Principles Relating to Remote Sensing of the Earth from Outer Space, adopted on 3 December 1986 (resolution 41/65);

- The Principles Relevant to the Use of Nuclear Power Sources in Outer Space, adopted on 14 December 1992 (resolution 47/68);

- The Declaration on International Cooperation in the Exploration and Use of Outer Space for the Benefit and in the Interest of All States, Taking into Particular Account the Needs of Developing Countries, adopted on 13 December 1996 (resolution 51/122).

The 1967 Treaty on Principles Governing the Activities of States in the Exploration and Use of Outer Space, including the Moon and Other Celestial Bodies, could be viewed as furnishing a general legal basis for the peaceful uses of outer space and providing a framework for the developing law of outer space. The four other treaties may be said to deal specifically with certain concepts included in the 1967 Treaty. The space treaties have been ratified by many Governments and many others abide by their principles. In view of the importance of international cooperation in developing the norms of space law and their important role in promoting international cooperation in the use of outer space for peaceful purposes, the General Assembly and the Secretary-General of the United Nations have called upon all Member States of the United Nations not yet parties to the international treaties governing the uses of outer space to ratify or accede to those treaties as soon as feasible

TREATY ON PRINCIPLES GOVERNING THE ACTIVITIES OF STATES IN THE EXPLORATION AND USE OF OUTER SPACE, INCLUDING THE MOON AND OTHER CELESTIAL BODIES (OUTER SPACE TREATY)[1]

Adopted by the General Assembly in its resolution 2222 (XXI) of 19 December 1966[2]

The States Parties to this Treaty,

Inspired by the great prospects opening up before mankind as a result of man's entry into outer space,

Recognizing the common interest of all mankind in the progress of the exploration and use of outer space for peaceful purposes,

Believing that the exploration and use of outer space should be carried on for the benefit of all peoples irrespective of the degree of their economic or scientific development,

---

[1] *The Treaty on Principles Governing the Activities of States in the Exploration and Use of Outer Space, Including the Moon and Other Celestial Bodies*, which is usually called *the Outer Space Treaty*, is one of the most significant law-making treaties concluded in the second half of the twentieth century. It was adopted by the United Nations General Assembly on 19 December 1966 (resolution 2222 (XXI)), opened for signature at London, Moscow and Washington on 27 January 1967, and entered into force on 10 October 1967. The Outer Space Treaty laid down the foundations of international regulation of space activities and thus established the framework of the present legal regime of outer space and celestial bodies. The Outer Space Treaty provides the basic framework on international space law, including the following principles: the exploration and use of outer space shall be carried out for the benefit and in the interests of all countries and shall be the province of all mankind, outer space shall be free for exploration and use by all States, outer space is not subject to national appropriation by claim of sovereignty, by means of use or occupation, or by any other means, States shall not place nuclear weapons or other weapons of mass destruction in orbit or on celestial bodies or station them in outer space in any other manner, the Moon and other celestial bodies shall be used exclusively for peaceful purposes, astronauts shall be regarded as the envoys of mankind, States shall be responsible for national space activities whether carried out by governmental or non-governmental entities, States shall be liable for damage caused by their space objects; a States shall avoid harmful contamination of space and celestial bodies.

[2] Sources: 18 UST 2410; TIAS 6347; 610 UNTS 205

Desiring to contribute to broad international cooperation in the scientific as well as the legal aspects of the exploration and use of outer space for peaceful purposes,

Believing that such cooperation will contribute to the development of mutual understanding and to the strengthening of friendly relations between States and peoples,

Recalling resolution 1962 (XVIII), entitled "Declaration of Legal Principles Governing the Activities of States in the Exploration and Use of Outer Space", which was adopted unanimously by the United Nations General Assembly on 13 December 1963,

Recalling resolution 1884 (XVIII), calling upon States to refrain from placing in orbit around the Earth any objects carrying nuclear weapons or any other kinds of weapons of mass destruction or from installing such weapons on celestial bodies, which was adopted unanimously by the United Nations General Assembly on 17 October 1963,

Taking account of United Nations General Assembly resolution 110 (II) of 3 November 1947, which condemned propaganda designed or likely to provoke or encourage any threat to the peace, breach of the peace or act of aggression, and considering that the aforementioned resolution is applicable to outer space,

Convinced that a Treaty on Principles Governing the Activities of States in the Exploration and Use of Outer Space, including the Moon and Other Celestial Bodies, will further the purposes and principles of the Charter of the United Nations,

Have agreed on the following:

Article I

The exploration and use of outer space, including the Moon and other celestial bodies, shall be carried out for the benefit and in the interests of all countries, irrespective of their degree of economic or scientific development, and shall be the province of all mankind.

Outer space, including the Moon and other celestial bodies, shall be free for exploration and use by all States without discrimination of any kind, on a basis of equality and in accordance with international law, and there shall be free access to all areas of celestial bodies.

There shall be freedom of scientific investigation in outer space, including the Moon and other celestial bodies, and States shall facilitate and encourage international cooperation in such investigation.

Article II

Outer space[3], including the Moon and other celestial bodies, is not subject to national appropriation by claim of sovereignty, by means of use or occupation, or by any other means[4].

Article III

States Parties to the Treaty shall carry on activities in the exploration and use of outer space, including the Moon and other celestial bodies, in accordance with international law, including the Charter of the United Nations, in the interest of maintaining international peace and security and promoting international cooperation and understanding.

Article IV

States Parties to the Treaty undertake not to place in orbit around the Earth any objects carrying nuclear weapons or any other kinds of weapons of mass destruction, install such weapons on celestial bodies, or station such weapons in outer space in any other manner.

The Moon and other celestial bodies shall be used by all States Parties to the Treaty exclusively for peaceful purposes[5]. The

---

[3] The Treaty is silent on the question of what is outer space, what it encompasses or what its boundaries are in relation to airspace. Therefore, more questions arise: What is the definition of outer space? Or, more specifically, what is the difference between national air space and outer space? How is one to be distinguished from the other? Or probably not necessary as US representatives stated some time ago: *"Our position continues to be that defining or delimiting outer space is not necessary. No legal or practical problems have arisen in the absence of such a definition. On the contrary, the differing legal regimes applicable in respect of airspace and outer space have operated well in their respective spheres"* (US Gov, 2001)

[4] Despite this clear wording, some try to dispute this principle. In our time of general private appropriation, they cannot accept a common domain for humanity. Some argue that the limitation is for "national appropriation" and thus does not apply to private persons. It is a misunderstanding of the word "national," which is not synonym with "state". If we consider the context, i.e., Article VI of the same treaty, "national activities" expressly include governmental and nongovernmental entities. In American English the word "nation" is often used instead of "state," but, in fact, the "nation" is both the government and the people having the nationality of a state

[5] The meaning of peaceful use may be disputed; given the common practice of states, it is difficult to see there a ban of any military activity and anything more than the obligation not to be aggressive. Currently, satellites, whether civilian or military, are used by the military for remote sensing/intelligence, communication, and positioning. Many of these activities are dual use. It may also be considered that remote sensing/ intelligence satellites may help tracking every activity and are therefore a necessity to preserve peace

There are conflicting interpretations of what of the phrase "peaceful purposes." The prevailing interpretation is that "peaceful purposes" does not exclude the presence of the

establishment of military bases, installations and fortifications, the testing of any type of weapons and the conduct of military manoeuvres on celestial bodies shall be forbidden. The use of military personnel for scientific research or for any other peaceful purposes shall not be prohibited. The use of any equipment or facility necessary for peaceful exploration of the Moon and other celestial bodies shall also not be prohibited.

Article V[6]

States Parties to the Treaty shall regard astronauts[7] as envoys of mankind in outer space and shall render to them all possible assistance in the event of accident, distress, or emergency landing on the territory of another State Party or on the high seas. When astronauts make such a landing, they shall be safely and promptly returned to the State of registry of their space vehicle.

In carrying on activities in outer space and on celestial bodies, the astronauts of one State Party shall render all possible assistance to the astronauts of other States Parties.

States Parties to the Treaty shall immediately inform the other States Parties to the Treaty or the Secretary-General of the United Nations of any phenomenathey discover in outer space, including the Moon and other celestial bodies, which could constitute a danger to the life or health of astronauts.

---

military or military activity in outer space so long as it is non-aggressive. Conversely, there are signatories of the Treaty who interpret "peaceful purposes" to mean that any military activity is excluded, regardless of whether it is non-aggressive.

[6] Article IV of the Outer Space Treaty confirmed the undertaking, which had already been made in United Nations General Assembly resolution 1884 (XVIII) of 17 October 1963, not to place in orbit around the Earth any objects carrying nuclear weapons or any other kinds of weapons of mass destruction, install such weapons on celestial bodies, or station them in outer space in any other manner. This principle relates to outer space as a whole, i.e., including the Moon and other celestial bodies

[7] There already discussions if the orbital tourists are astronauts or not. See the last part of this book for the multiple definitions for this term.

Article VI[8]

States Parties to the Treaty shall bear international responsibility[9] for national activities in outer space, including the Moon and other celestial bodies, whether such activities are carried on by governmental agencies or by non-governmental entities[10], and for assuring that national activities are carried out in conformity with the provisions set forth in the present Treaty. The activities of non-governmental entities in outer space, including the Moon and other celestial bodies, shall require authorization and continuing supervision by the appropriate State Party to the Treaty. When activities are carried on in outer space, including the Moon and other celestial bodies, by an international organization, responsibility for compliance with this Treaty shall be borne both by the international organization and by the States Parties to the Treaty participating in such organization.

Article VII[11]

---

[8] This principle, which had already appeared in the 1963 Declaration, was a compromise formula that reconciled the controversial views of those wishing to reserve space activities only for States and intergovernmental organizations, and those advocating access to outer space also for non-governmental entities. By adopting this principle, the negotiating States paved the way for the private sector to conduct space activities side by side with States and international intergovernmental organizations. At the same time, however, the respective States assumed responsibility not only for their own space activities, but also for the activities of private legal persons of their nationality. States parties have also become responsible for assuring that all national activities of this nature would be carried out in conformity with the provisions of the Outer Space Treaty. The activities of non-governmental entities in outer space, including the Moon and other celestial bodies, require authorization and continuing supervision by the respective States parties to the Outer Space Treaty

[9] The term 'responsibility' derived from the Latin word respondere (to answer) meaning primarily answerability and accountability. The notion of the term 'responsibility' appears to signify a general moral and legal State responsibility to be invoked by any activity in outer space, which may be considered a national endeavour, whether performed by a governmental agency or a private entity.

As far as international law is concerned, State responsibility is ordinarily divided into direct State responsibility and the so-called indirect State responsibility. Let's see some examples: *Direct State responsibility* refers to responsibility for its own acts through its servants and agents, in their official capacity, which are thus imputable to it as its own acts. *The Indirect State Responsibility* is an international legal obligation to protect foreign States and their nationals, as well as their property within its jurisdiction, particularly within its territorial jurisdiction

[10] An increasing number of private corporations and other forms of less explicitly government dominated enterprises participate in actual space venture.

[11] Article VII imposes liability upon a State for any damages on earth or to another State's

Each State Party to the Treaty that launches or procures the launching of an object into outer space, including the Moon and other celestial bodies, and each State Party from whose territory or facility an object is launched, is internationally liable for damage to another State Party to the Treaty or to its natural or juridical persons by such object or its component parts on the Earth, in air space or in outer space, including the Moon and other celestial bodies.

Article VIII[12]

A State Party to the Treaty on whose registry an object launched into outer space is carried shall retain jurisdiction and control over such object, and over any personnel thereof, while in outer space or on a celestial body. Ownership of objects launched into outer space, including objects landed or constructed on a celestial body, and of their component parts, is not affected by their presence in outer space or on a celestial body or by their return to the Earth. Such objects or component parts found beyond the limits of the State Party to the Treaty on whose registry they are carried shall be returned to that State Party, which shall, upon request, furnish identifying data prior to their return

In the exploration and use of outer space, including the Moon and other celestial bodies, States Parties to the Treaty shall be guided by the principle of cooperation and mutual assistance and shall conduct all their activities in outer space, including the Moon and other celestial bodies, with due regard to the corresponding interests of all other States Parties to the Treaty. States Parties to the Treaty shall pursue studies of outer space, including the Moon and other celestial bodies, and conduct exploration of them so as to avoid their harmful contamination and also adverse changes in the environment of the Earth resulting from the introduction of extraterrestrial matter and, where necessary, shall adopt appropriate measures for this purpose. If a State Party to the Treaty has reason to believe that an activity or experiment planned by it or its nationals in outer space, including the Moon and other celestial

property in the course of any space activity. This provision serves as the basis for the Liability Convention of 1972

[12] Article VIII of the Outer Space Treaty established the principle that the State on whose registry an object launched into outer space is carried shall retain jurisdiction and control over such object, and over any personnel thereof, while in outer space or on a celestial body. By analogy with air and maritime law, this principle provided a basis for registration of space objects and established a link between the registration and the exercise of jurisdiction of the State of registry over the respective object. Therefore, for a foreign country to remove or otherwise interfere with a defunct satellite belonging to another state it would have to receive permission from that state to do so.

bodies, would cause potentially harmful interference with activities of other States Parties in the peaceful exploration and use of outer space, including the Moon and other celestial bodies, it shall undertake appropriate international consultations before proceeding with any such activity or experiment. A State Party to the Treaty which has reason to believe that an activity or experiment planned by another State Party in outer space, including the Moon and other celestial bodies, would cause potentially harmful interference with activities in the peaceful exploration and use of outer space, including the Moon and other celestial bodies, may request consultation concerning the activity or experiment.

Article X

In order to promote international cooperation in the exploration and use of outer space, including the Moon and other celestial bodies, in conformity with the purposes of this Treaty, the States Parties to the Treaty shall consider on a basis of equality any requests by other States Parties to the Treaty to be afforded an opportunity to observe the flight of space objects launched by those States.

The nature of such an opportunity for observation and the conditions under which it could be afforded shall be determined by agreement between the States concerned.

Article XI

In order to promote international cooperation in the peaceful exploration and use of outer space, States Parties to the Treaty conducting activities in outer space, including the Moon and other celestial bodies, agree to inform the Secretary-General of the United Nations as well as the public and the international scientific community, to the greatest extent feasible and practicable[13], of the nature, conduct, locations and results of such activities. On receiving the said information, the Secretary-General of the United Nations should be prepared to disseminate it immediately and effectively.

Article XII

All stations, installations, equipment and space vehicles on the Moon and other celestial bodies shall be open to representatives of

---

[13] It seems that another problematic issue appeared during the negotiations. The core of the problem was whether providing such information should be obligatory or voluntary. Therefore, the negotiating partners agreed that such information *on the nature, conduct, locations and results of space activities by States parties* was to be provided "to the greatest extent feasible and practicable" and that the Secretary-General "should be prepared to disseminate it immediately and effectively"

other States Parties to the Treaty on a basis of reciprocity. Such representatives shall give reasonable advance notice of a projected visit, in order that appropriate consultations may be held and that maximum precautions may be taken to assure safety and to avoid interference with normal operations in the facility to be visited.

Article XIII

The provisions of this Treaty shall apply to the activities of States Parties to the Treaty in the exploration and use of outer space, including the Moon and other celestial bodies, whether such activities are carried on by a single State Party to the Treaty or jointly with other States, including cases where they are carried on within the framework of international intergovernmental organizations.

Any practical questions arising in connection with activities carried on by international intergovernmental organizations in the exploration and use of outer space, including the Moon and other celestial bodies, shall be resolved by the States Parties to the Treaty either with the appropriate international organization or with one or more States members of that international organization, which are Parties to this Treaty.

Article XIV

This Treaty shall be open to all States for signature. Any State which does not sign this Treaty before its entry into force in accordance with paragraph 3 of this article may accede to it at any time.

This Treaty shall be subject to ratification by signatory States. Instruments of ratification and instruments of accession shall be deposited with the Governments of the Union of Soviet Socialist Republics, the United Kingdom of Great Britain and Northern Ireland and the United States of America, which are hereby designated the Depositary Governments.

This Treaty shall enter into force upon the deposit of instruments of ratification by five Governments including the Governments designated as Depositary Governments under this Treaty.

For States whose instruments of ratification or accession are deposited subsequent to the entry into force of this Treaty, it shall enter into force on the date of the deposit of their instruments of ratification or accession.

The Depositary Governments shall promptly inform all signatory and acceding States of the date of each signature, the date of deposit of each instrument of ratification of and accession to this Treaty, the date of its entry into force and other notices.

This Treaty shall be registered by the Depositary Governments pursuant to Article 102 of the Charter of the United Nations.

Any State Party to the Treaty may propose amendments to this Treaty. Amendments shall enter into force for each State Party to the Treaty accepting the amendments upon their acceptance by a majority of the States Parties to the Treaty and thereafter for each remaining State Party to the Treaty on the date of acceptance by it.

Article XVI

Any State Party to the Treaty may give notice of its withdrawal from the Treaty one year after its entry into force by written notification to the Depositary Governments. Such withdrawal shall take effect one year from the date of receipt of this notification.

Article XVII

This Treaty, of which the Chinese, English, French, Russian and Spanish texts are equally authentic, shall be deposited in the archives of the Depositary Governments. Duly certified copies of this Treaty shall be transmitted by the Depositary Governments to the Governments of the signatory and acceding States.

IN WITNESS WHEREOF the undersigned, duly authorized, have signed this Treaty.

DONE in triplicate, at the cities of London, Moscow and Washington, D.C., the twenty-seventh day of January, one thousand nine hundred and sixty-seven.

NOTES ON the Exploration and Use of Outer Space, including the Moon and Other Celestial Bodies Treaty

From among several paragraphs the preamble of the Treaty, two paragraphs should in particular be recalled since they reveal the purposes for concluding the Outer Space Treaty in an outstanding manner: the desire *"to contribute to broad international cooperation in the scientific as well as the legal aspects of the exploration and use of outer space for peaceful purposes"*; and the belief *"that such cooperation will contribute to the development of mutual understanding and to the strengthening of friendly relations between States and peoples"*. Both adequately reflect the historical conditions of the origin of the Outer Space Treaty, which was not only a response to the scientific and technical needs of that epoch, but also a substantive contribution to a détente in the cold war.

From the language of the first three articles of the Outer Space Treaty the following elements can be derived:

(a) Recognition of the common interest of mankind in the exploration and use of outer space, including the Moon and other celestial bodies, as an area for space activities of all countries, without any difference in their economic and scientific development; such exploration and use having become *"the province of all mankind"*;

(b) Recognition of the freedom of outer space, including the Moon and other celestial bodies, for exploration and use by all States, on a basis of equality and in accordance with international law;

(c) Stipulation of free access to all areas of celestial bodies;

(d) Recognition of the freedom of scientific investigation in outer space, including the Moon and other celestial bodies, and promotion of international cooperation in such investigation;

(e) Renunciation of national appropriation of outer space, including the Moon and other celestial bodies, by any means; and

(f) Confirmation of the applicability of international law, including the Charter of the United Nations, to activities in the exploration and use of outer space, the Moon and other celestial bodies, in the interest of maintaining peace and security and promoting international cooperation and understanding.

The Treaty embodies the following principles:

1. *The exploration and use of outer space* shall be carried out for the benefit and in the interests of all countries and shall be the province of all mankind, and that outer space shall be free for exploration and use by all States, which is codified under Article I;
2. *Outer space,* including the moon another celestial bodies is not subject to national appropriation, which is codified under Article II;
3. *Nuclear weapons or other weapons of mass destruction* shall not be placed in orbit or on celestial bodies or stationed in outer space in any other manner, and the Moon and other celestial bodies shall be used exclusively for peaceful purposes, which is codified under Article IV;
4. *Astronauts* shall be regarded as the envoys of mankind and that assistance shall be rendered to them in case of emergency, which is codified under Article V;
5. *States* shall be responsible for national space activities whether carried out by governmental or non-governmental entities, which is codified in Article VI;
6. *States* shall be liable for damage caused by their activities in outer space and/or space objects registered to them, which is codified in Article VII;
7. *That States* will retain jurisdiction over objects launched into space (Article VIII);
8. *States* shall avoid harmful contamination of space and celestial bodies alert other States to dangers encountered in space codified in Article IX.

AGREEMENT ON THE RESCUE OF ASTRONAUTS, THE RETURN OF ASTRONAUTS AND THE RETURN OF OBJECTS LAUNCHED INTO OUTER SPACE (RESCUE AGREEMENT)[14]

Adopted by the General Assembly in its resolution 2345 (XXII) of 19 December 1967[15]

The Contracting Parties[16],

Noting the great importance of the Treaty on Principles Governing the Activities of States in the Exploration and Use of Outer Space, including the Moon and Other Celestial Bodies, which calls for the rendering of all possible assistance to astronauts[17] in the event of accident, distress or emergency landing, the prompt and safe return of astronauts, and the return of objects launched into outer space,

---

[14] Consensus agreement was reached in the General Assembly in 1967 (resolution 2345 (XXII)), and the Agreement entered into force in December 1968, dominated enterprises develop their duties of assistance in the event of accident distress or emergency landing and of prompt and safe return of astronauts and objects launched into outer space. Article 5 § 4 specifies that if a Contracting Party has reason to believe that astronauts, said the return of objects launched into outer space, the launching authority which must immediately take effective steps to eliminate possible danger or harm. It is often called the Rescue Agreement.

[15] Source: 19 UST 7570; TIAS 6599; 672 UNTS 119. Adoption by the United Nations General Assembly: 19 December 1967 ; Entry into force: 3 December 1968;

[16] The 1968 Rescue Agreement contains no provisions setting out any procedure for the settlement of disputes that arise between Contracting Parties with respect to the interpretation or application of this Agreement. Any dispute would therefore be subject to the general provisions on dispute settlement that are set out in Article 33 of the United Nations Charter.

[17] According to the Soviet Encyclopedia, *"Kosmonavtika"*, a cosmonaut is a person who was specially trained in medical, biological, scientific and technical field and who participated in a space flight as a pilot-commander or a member of the crew.

Desiring to develop and give further concrete expression[18] to these duties,

Wishing to promote international co-operation in the peaceful exploration and use of outer space,

Prompted by sentiments of humanity[19],

Have agreed on the following:

Article 1

Each Contracting Party which receives information or discovers that the personnel of a spacecraft have suffered accident

or are experiencing conditions of distress or have made an emergency or unintended landing in territory under its jurisdiction[20] or on the high seas or in any other place not under the jurisdiction of any State[21] shall immediately:

(a) notify the launching authority[22] or, if it cannot identify and immediately communicate with the launching authority, immediately make a public announcement by all appropriate means of communication at its disposal;

(b) notify the Secretary-General of the United Nations, who should disseminate the information without delay by all appropriate means of communication at his disposal.

---

[18] The 1968 Rescue Agreement was to develop and give further expression to the duties set out in the 1967 Outer Space Treaty.

[19] This expression is also consistent with one of the basic principles of outer space law, which is to promote international cooperation in the peaceful exploration and use of outer space.

[20] The territory under the jurisdiction of a Contracting State would include not only the land territory of a state, but also its territorial sea, because under the United Nations Convention on the Law of the Sea, 1982 (1982 LOS Convention), the sovereignty of a State extends to its territorial sea.

[21] By "*the high seas or in any other place not under the jurisdiction*" we understand Exclusive Economic Zone or the Continental Shelf. These provisions would have been clearer if the term "sovereignty" had been used rather than jurisdiction. The phrase "any other place not under the jurisdiction of any State" would also include Antarctica.

[22] The term *Launching Authority* would refer to the launching State on whose registry the space vehicle or space object is launched, as that State would be responsible for the launch.

Article 2

If, owing to accident, distress, emergency or unintended landing, the personnel of a spacecraft[23] land in territory under the jurisdiction of a Contracting Party, it shall immediately take all possible steps to rescue them and render them all necessary assistance. It shall inform the launching authority and also the Secretary-General of the United Nations of the steps it is taking and of their progress. If assistance by the launching authority would help to effect a prompt rescue or would contribute substantially to the effectiveness of search and rescue operations, the launching authority shall co-operate with the Contracting Party with a view to the effective conduct of search and rescue operations[24]. Such operations shall be subject to the direction and control of the Contracting Party, which shall act in close and continuing consultation with the launching authority.

Article 3

If information is received or it is discovered that the personnel of a spacecraft have alighted[25] on the high seas or in any other place not under the jurisdiction of any State, those Contracting Parties which are in a position to do so shall, if necessary, extend assistance in search and rescue operations for such personnel to assure their speedy rescue. They shall inform the launching authority and the Secretary-General of the United Nations of the steps they are taking and of their progress.

[23] The phrase "personnel of a spacecraft" is intended to be wider than astronauts, and would include any crewmembers or scientists that have responsibility under the mission. This is one possible meaning. What about the "space tourists" or "passengers" who have no responsibility under the mission ? Are they included ? As per "sentiments of humanity" it seems logical to include them under the category of "personnel of a spacecraft".

[24] There is no provision providing that the Launching Authority will bear the expenses incurred by the Contracting Party in the search and rescue operations.

[25] The phrase "have alighted" suggests that this article is not intended to place an obligation on Contracting Parties to assist in search and rescue operations in outer space or on the moon or other celestial bodies.

Article 4

If, owing to accident, distress, emergency or unintended landing, the personnel of a spacecraft land in territory under the jurisdiction of a Contracting Party or have been found on the high seas or in any other place not under the jurisdiction of any State, they shall be safely and promptly returned[26] to representatives of the launching authority.

Article 5[27]

1. Each Contracting Party which receives information or discovers that a space object or its component parts has returned to Earth in territory under its jurisdiction or on the high seas or in any other place not under the jurisdiction of any State, shall notify the launching authority and the Secretary- General of the United Nations.

2. Each Contracting Party having jurisdiction over the territory on which a space object or its component parts has been discovered shall, upon the request of the launching authority and with assistance from that authority if requested, take such steps as it finds practicable to recover the object or component parts.

3. Upon request of the launching authority, objects launched into outer space or their component parts found beyond the territorial limits of the launching authority shall be returned to or held at the disposal of representatives of the launching authority, which shall, upon request, furnish identifying data prior to their return.

[26]. What if an astronaut will ask for asylum? What about the right of a State to grant political asylum to anyone in its territory? In this case the general principles of international law should apply.

[27] This is strong evidence in support of the argument that Article 5 of the 1968 Rescue Agreement has become customary international law, especially if there is no State practice by non-parties that is contrary to Article 5. For instance, Saudi Arabia invoqued the provisions of Aricle 5, even though this state is not a party to the Agreement, so must have done so believing that it is under a legal obligation to do so under customary international law. In this respect, see A/AC.105/762 (COPUOS, 3 April 2001) - Note verbale dated 8 March 2001 from the Permanent Mission of SAUDI ARABIA to the United Nations (Vienna) addressed to the Secretary-General

4. Notwithstanding paragraphs 2 and 3 of this article, a Contracting Party which has reason to believe that a space object or its component parts discovered in territory under its jurisdiction, or recovered by it elsewhere, is of a hazardous or deleterious nature may so notify the launching authority, which shall immediately take effective steps[28], under the direction and control of the said Contracting Party, to eliminate possible danger of harm.

5. Expenses incurred in fulfilling obligations to recover and return a space object or its component parts under paragraphs 2 and 3 of this article shall be borne by the launching authority.

Article 6

For the purposes of this Agreement, the term "launching authority" shall refer to the State responsible for launching, or, where an international intergovernmental organization is responsible for launching, that organization, provided that organization declares its acceptance of the rights and obligations provided for in this Agreement and a majority of the States members of that organization are Contracting Parties to this Agreement and to the Treaty on Principles Governing the Activities of States in the Exploration and Use of Outer Space, including the Moon and Other Celestial Bodies.

Article 7

1. This Agreement shall be open to all States for signature. Any State which does not sign this Agreement before its entry into force in accordance with paragraph 3 of this article may accede to it at any time.

2. This Agreement shall be subject to ratification by signatory States. Instruments of ratification and instruments of accession shall be deposited with the Governments of the United Kingdom of Great Britain and Northern Ireland, the Union of Soviet Socialist

---

[28] The States not parties to the 1968 Rescue Agreement should consider becoming parties to the Agreement as otherwise they cannot ask for the respect of this article.

Republics and the United States of America, which are hereby designated the Depositary Governments.

3. This Agreement shall enter into force upon the deposit of instruments of ratification by five Governments including the Governments designated as Depositary Governments under this Agreement.

4. For States whose instruments of ratification or accession are deposited subsequent to the entry into force of this Agreement, it shall enter into force on the date of the deposit of their instruments of ratification or accession.

5. The Depositary Governments shall promptly inform all signatory and acceding States of the date of each signature, the date of deposit of each instrument of ratification of and accession to this Agreement, the date of its entry into force and other notices.

6. This Agreement shall be registered by the Depositary Governments pursuant to Article 102 of the Charter of the United Nations.

Article 8

Any State Party to the Agreement may propose amendments to this Agreement. Amendments shall enter into force for each State Party to the Agreement accepting the amendments upon their acceptance by a majority of the States Parties to the Agreement and thereafter for each remaining State Party to the Agreement on the date of acceptance by it.

Article 9

Any State Party to the Agreement may give notice of its withdrawal from the Agreement one year after its entry into force by written notification to the Depositary Governments. Such withdrawal shall take effect one year from the date of receipt of this notification.

Article 10[29]

This Agreement, of which the English, Russian, French, Spanish and Chinese texts are equally authentic, shall be deposited in the archives of the Depositary Governments. Duly certified copies of this Agreement shall be transmitted by the Depositary Governments to the Governments of the signatory and acceding States.

IN WITNESS WHEREOF the undersigned, duly authorized, have signed this Agreement.

DONE in triplicate, at the cities of London, Moscow and Washington, the twenty-second day of April, one thousand nine hundred and sixty-eight.

---

[29] This agreement gives significant benefits to Contracting Parties. First, if a Contracting Party incurs expenses in recovering and returning a space object that has landed in its territory, the Launching Authority will be obliged to bear those expenses. Second, if a space object that lands in the territory of a Contracting Party is found to be of a hazardous or deleterious nature, the Launching Authority will be under an obligation to immediately take effective steps to eliminate possible danger or harm

NOTES ON Agreement on the Rescue of Astronauts, the Return of Astronauts and the Return of Objects Launched into Outer Space

The Agreement develops the duties of assistance to astronauts in the event of accident, distress or emergency landing and of prompt and safe return of astronauts and objects launched into outer space. Article 5.4 specifies that if a Contracting Party has reason to believe that a recovered space object or its component parts are hazardous, it may notify the launching authority which must immediately take effective steps to eliminate possible danger or harm.
It is often called the Rescue Agreement.
Currently, to be an astronaut in space law, the following three conditions have to be fulfilled - they must be:
- in an object located in space;
- conducting their activities for the benefit and in the interests of all countries;
- regarded as an envoy of mankind in outer space.

These conditions are backed up by the fact that the majority of space activities have been done mainly by nations for scientific or national security purposes with a sense of mission and pioneer spirit. Under the above conditions, astronauts are given a special status by the Outer Space Treaty and other international regulations. For example, the Rescue Agreement provides immediate notification, search and rescue by all countries even if the astronauts in an accident, distress, emergency or unintended landing are on the high seas or in any other place not under t the jurisdiction of any nation

The overriding intent of the Rescue Agreement is to persuade greater cooperation in space between nations. The Rescue Agreement articulates two principles:
1. States, or Contracting Parties as they are called, must take all possible steps to rescue and assist astronauts in distress and promptly return them to the their State of origin, i.e. launching authority; and
2. States, upon request, provide assistance to launching authority in recovering space objects that return to Earth outside the territory of the Launching State.

CONVENTION ON INTERNATIONAL LIABILITY FOR DAMAGE CAUSED BY SPACE OBJECTS (LIABILITY CONVENTION)

Adopted by the General Assembly in its resolution 2777 (XXVI) of 29 November 1971[30]

The States Parties to this Convention,

Recognizing the common interest of all mankind in furthering the exploration and use of outer space for peaceful purposes,

Recalling the Treaty on Principles Governing the Activities of States in the Exploration and Use of Outer Space, including the Moon and Other Celestial Bodies,

Taking into consideration that, notwithstanding the precautionary measures to be taken by States and international intergovernmental organizations involved in the launching of space objects, damage may on occasion be caused by such objects,

Recognizing the need to elaborate effective international rules and procedures concerning liability for damage caused by space objects and to ensure, in particular, the prompt payment under the terms of this Convention of a full and equitable measure of compensation to victims of such damage,

[30] The Liability Convention was considered and negotiated by the Legal Subcommittee from 1963 to 1972. Agreement was reached in the General Assembly in 1971 (resolution 2777 (XXVI)), and the Convention entered into force in September 1972. Elaborating on Article 7 of the Outer Space Treaty, the Liability Convention provides that a launching State shall be absolutely liable to pay compensation for damage caused by its space objects on the surface of the Earth or to aircraft, and liable for damage due to its faults in space. The Convention also provides for procedures for the settlement of claims for damages. Sources: 24 UST 2389; TIAS 7762; 961 UNTS 187

Believing that the establishment of such rules and procedures will contribute to the strengthening of international co-operation in the field of the exploration and use of outer space for peaceful purposes,

Have agreed on the following:

Article I

For the purposes of this Convention:

(a) The term "damage[31]" means loss of life, personal injury or other impairment of health; or loss of or damage to property of States or of persons, natural or juridical, or property of international intergovernmental organizations;

(b) The term "launching" includes attempted launching;

(c) The term "launching State[32]" means:
(i) A State which launches or procures the launching of a space object;
(ii) A State from whose territory or facility a space object is launched;

(d) The term "space object[33]" includes component parts of a space object as well as its launch vehicle and parts thereof.

[33] Bin Cheng suggested that "space objects" covers "any object launched by humans into outer space, as well as any component part thereof, together with its launch vehicle and parts thereof" and so objects launched into Earth orbit and beyond are ipso facto regarded as space objects. *See:* "Space Objects", "Astronauts" and Related Expressions (1991) 34 PROC. COLL. L. OUTER SPACE 17. What about the case of a space object launched by a rocket deployed. Some authors suggest that as the aircraft may be considered the first stage of the launch vehicle, the take-off of the aircraft would be considered the start of the launch procedure and therefore the State from whose territory the aircraft took off would be considered a launching Statefrom an aircraft in airspace. *See: Karl-Heinz Böckstiegel, The Terms*

Article II

A launching State[34] shall be absolutely liable to pay compensation[35] for damage caused by its space object on the surface of the earth or to aircraft flight.

Article III

In the event of damage being caused elsewhere than on the surface of the earth to a space object of one launching State or to persons or property on board such a space object by a space object of another launching State, the latter shall be liable only if the damage is due to its fault[36] or the fault of persons for whom it is responsible.

---

[34] We should extend the meaning of "launching State" as follows: a launching State is not required to be an original launching State. This will solve the situations when a satellite for instance is sold to a State, which is not an original launching State, as defined by the registration Convention. The new State, while not a launching State, shall be on the list of launching States. Otherwise, the fact that it shall cause unfair results that only launching States will bear liability.

[35] "Appropriate State" and "Launching State" in the Space Treaties: Indications of State Responsibility and Liability for State and Private Space Activities (1992) 35 PROC. COLL. L. OUTER SPACE 15

Some authors (Carl Christol) propose these as an appropriate way to "weight" the "direct" damages:
1. Lost time and earnings and impaired earning capacity;
2. Destruction or deprivation of the use of property, including where the property has been rendered unfit for its intended purposes;
3. Loss of profits resulting from business interruption;
4. Loss of rents;
5. Reasonable medical, hospital and nursing costs associated with injuries sustained by natural persons;
6. Physical and mental impairment;
7. Pain and suffering;
8. Humiliation;
9. Reasonable costs for the repair of property; and
10. Costs incurred in acts taken to mitigate the damage caused by the space object.

[36] The concept of "fault" as used in Article III of the Liability Convention has different meanings in different legal systems. Therefore, we need to pay attention of the correct meaning. For instance, a satellite operator may be considered to be at fault if it placed the satellite in an orbit known to be already occupied by another

Article IV

1. In the event of damage being caused elsewhere than on the surface of the earth to a space object of one launching State[37] or to persons or property on board such a space object by a space object of another launching State, and of damage thereby being caused to a third State or to its natural or juridical persons, the first two States shall be jointly and severally liable to the third State, to the extent indicated by the following:

(a) If the damage has been caused to the third State on the surface of the earth or to aircraft in flight, their liability to the third State shall be absolute;

(b) If the damage has been caused to a space object of the third State or to persons or property on board that space object elsewhere than on the surface of the earth, their liability to the third State shall be based on the fault of either of the first two States or on the fault of persons for whom either is responsible.

2. In all cases of joint and several liability referred to in paragraph 1 of this article, the burden of compensation for the damage shall be apportioned between the first two States in accordance with the extent to which they were at fault; if the extent of the fault of each of these States cannot be established, the burden of compensation shall be apportioned equally between them. Such apportionment shall be without prejudice to the right of the third State to seek the entire compensation due under this Convention from any or all of the launching States which are jointly and severally liable the launching States.

[37] It should be noted that some States today conclude bilateral agreements pursuant to Article V (2) of the Liability Convention to require the "operating States" to indemnify the "launching States" for any damage caused after orbital insertion. There is a reson for it: nowadays the commercial reality in the launch industry is that the launch operator is generally not the entity that will operate and control the satellite once it has been inserted into orbit.

Article V

1. Whenever two or more States jointly launch a space object, they shall be jointly and severally liable for any damage caused.

2. A launching State which has paid compensation for damage shall have the right to present a claim for indemnification to other participants in the joint launching. The participants in a joint launching may conclude agreements regarding the apportioning among themselves of the financial obligation in respect of which they are jointly and severally liable. Such agreements shall be without prejudice to the right of a State sustaining damage to seek the entire compensation due under this Convention from any or all of the launching States which are jointly and severally liable.

3. A State from whose territory or facility a space object is launched shall be regarded as a participant in a joint launching.

Article VI

1. Subject to the provisions of paragraph 2 of this Article, exoneration from absolute liability[38] shall be granted to the extent that a launching State establishes that the damage has resulted either wholly or partially from gross negligence or from an act or omission done with intent to cause damage on the part of a claimant State or of natural or juridical persons it represents.

2. No exoneration whatever shall be granted in cases where the damage has resulted from activities conducted by a launching State which are not in conformity with international law including, in particular, the Charter of the United Nations and the Treaty on Principles Governing the Activities of States in the Exploration and Use of Outer Space, including the Moon and Other Celestial Bodies.

Article VII

---

[38] The simple definition of the term *liability*: Liability (i.e., a legal obligation to pay claims for bodily injury or property damage) imposed without regard to fault (Derived From Definition of Strict Liability, Merriam-Webster Online Dictionary)

The provisions of this Convention shall not apply to damage caused by a space object of a launching State to:

(a) nationals of that launching State;

(b) foreign nationals during such time as they are participating in the operation of that space object from the time of its launching or at any stage thereafter until its descent, or during such time as they are in the immediate vicinity of a planned launching or recovery area as the result of an invitation by that launching State.

Article VIII

1. A State which suffers damage, or whose natural or juridical persons suffer damage, may present to a launching State a claim for compensation for such damage.

2. If the State of nationality has not presented a claim, another State may, in respect of damage sustained in its territory by any natural or juridical person, present a claim to a launching State.

3. If neither the State of nationality nor the State in whose territory the damage was sustained has presented a claim or notified its intention of presenting a claim, another State may, in respect of damage sustained by its permanent residents, present a claim to a launching State.

Article IX

A claim for compensation for damage shall be presented to a launching State through diplomatic channels. If a State does not maintain diplomatic relations with the launching State concerned, it may request another State to present its claim to that launching State or otherwise represent its interests under this Convention. It may also present its claim through the Secretary-General of the United Nations, provided the claimant State and the launching State are both Members of the United Nations.

Article X

1. A claim for compensation for damage may be presented to a launching State not later than one year following the date of the occurrence of the damage or the identification of the launching State which is liable.

2. If, however, a State does not know of the occurrence of the damage or has not been able to identify the launching State which is liable, it may present a claim within one year following the date on which it learned of the aforementioned facts; however, this period shall in no event exceed one year following the date on which the State could reasonably be expected to have learned of the facts through the exercise of due diligence.

3. The time-limits specified in paragraphs 1 and 2 of this Article shall apply even if the full extent of the damage may not be known. In this event, however, the claimant State shall be entitled to revise the claim and submit additional documentation after the expiration of such time-limits until one year after the full extent of the damage is known.

Article XI

1. Presentation of a claim to a launching State for compensation for damage under this Convention shall not require the prior exhaustion of any local remedies which may be available to a claimant State or to natural or juridical persons it represents.

2. Nothing in this Convention shall prevent a State, or natural or juridical persons it might represent, from pursuing a claim in the courts or administrative tribunals or agencies of a launching State. A State shall not, however, be entitled to present a claim under this Convention in respect of the same damage for which a claim is being pursued in the courts or administrative tribunals or agencies of a launching State or under another international agreement which is binding on the States concerned.

Article XII

The compensation which the launching State shall be liable to pay for damage under this Convention shall be determined in accordance with international law and the principles of justice and equity, in order to provide such reparation in respect of the damage as will restore the person, natural or juridical, State or international organization on whose behalf the claim is presented to the condition which would have existed if the damage had not occurred.

Article XIII

Unless the claimant State and the State from which compensation is due under this Convention agree on another form of compensation, the compensation shall be paid in the currency of the claimant State or, if that State so requests, in the currency of the State from which compensation is due.

Article XIV

If no settlement of a claim is arrived at through diplomatic negotiations as provided for in Article IX, within one year from the date on which the claimant State notifies the launching State that it has submitted the documentation of its claim, the parties concerned shall establish a Claims Commission at the request of either party.

Article XV

1. The Claims Commission shall be composed of three members: one appointed by the claimant State, one appointed by the launching State and the third member, the Chairman, to be chosen by both

parties jointly. Each party shall make its appointment within two months of the request for the establishment of the Claims Commission.

2. If no agreement is reached on the choice of the Chairman within four months of the request for the establishment of the Commission, either party may request the Secretary-General of the United Nations to appoint the Chairman within a further period of two months.

Article XVI

1. If one of the parties does not make its appointment within the stipulated period, the Chairman shall, at the request of the other party, constitute a single-member Claims Commission.

2. Any vacancy which may arise in the Commission for whatever reason shall be filled by the same procedure adopted for the original appointment.

3. The Commission shall determine its own procedure.

4. The Commission shall determine the place or places where it shall sit and all other administrative matters.

5. Except in the case of decisions and awards by a single-member Commission, all decisions and awards of the Commission shall be by majority vote.

Article XVII

No increase in the membership of the Claims Commission shall take place by reason of two or more claimant States or launching States being joined in any one proceeding before the Commission. The claimant States so joined shall collectively appoint one member of the Commission in the same manner and subject to the same conditions as would be the case for a single claimant State. When two or more launching States are so joined, they shall collectively appoint one member of the Commission in the same way. If the claimant States or the launching States do not make the appointment within the stipulated period, the Chairman shall constitute a single-member Commission.

Article XVIII

The Claims Commission shall decide the merits of the claim for compensation and determine the amount of compensation payable, if any.

Article XIX

1. The Claims Commission shall act in accordance with the provisions of Article XII.

2. The decision of the Commission shall be final and binding if the parties have so agreed; otherwise the Commission shall render a final and recommendatory award, which the parties shall consider in good faith. The Commission shall state the reasons for its decision or award.

3. The Commission shall give its decision or award as promptly as possible and no later than one year from the date of its establishment, unless an extension of this period is found necessary by the Commission.

4. The Commission shall make its decision or award public. It shall deliver a certified copy of its decision or award to each of the parties and to the Secretary-General of the United Nations.

Article XX

The expenses in regard to the Claims Commission shall be borne equally by the parties, unless otherwise decided by the Commission.

Article XXI

If the damage caused by a space object presents a large-scale danger to human life or seriously interferes with the living conditions of the population or the functioning of vital centres, the States Parties, and in particular the launching State, shall examine the possibility of rendering appropriate and rapid assistance to the State which has suffered the damage, when it so requests. However, nothing in this article shall affect the rights or obligations of the States Parties under this Convention.

Article XXII

1. In this Convention, with the exception of Articles XXIV to Articles XXVII, references to States shall be deemed to apply to any international intergovernmental organization which conducts space activities if the organization declares its acceptance of the rights and obligations provided for in this Convention and if a majority of the States members of the organization are States Parties to this Convention and to the Treaty on Principles Governing the Activities of States in the Exploration and Use of Outer Space, including the Moon and Other Celestial Bodies.

2. States members of any such organization which are States Parties to this Convention shall take all appropriate steps to ensure that the organization makes a declaration in accordance with the preceding paragraph.

3. If an international intergovernmental organization is liable for damage by virtue of the provisions of this Convention, that organization and those of its members which are States Parties to this Convention shall be jointly and severally liable; provided, however, that:

(a) any claim for compensation in respect of such damage shall be first presented to the organization;

(b) only where the organization has not paid, within a period of six months, any sum agreed or determined to be due as compensation for such damage, may the claimant State invoke the liability of the members which are States Parties to this Convention for the payment of that sum.

4. Any claim, pursuant to the provisions of this Convention, for compensation in respect of damage caused to an organization which has made a declaration in accordance with paragraph 1 of this Article shall be presented by a State member of the organization which is a State Party to this Convention.

Article XXIII

1. The provisions of this Convention shall not affect other international agreements in force in so far as relations between the States Parties to such agreements are concerned.

2. No provision of this Convention shall prevent States from concluding international agreements reaffirming, supplementing or extending its provisions.

Article XXIV

1. This Convention shall be open to all States for signature. Any State which does not sign this Convention before its entry into force in accordance with paragraph 3 of this article may accede to it at any time.

2. This Convention shall be subject to ratification by signatory States. Instruments of ratification and instruments of accession shall be deposited with the Governments of the United Kingdom of Great Britain and Northern Ireland, the Union of Soviet Socialist Republics and the United States of America, which are hereby designated the Depositary Governments.

3. This Convention shall enter into force on the deposit of the fifth instrument of ratification.

4. For States whose instruments of ratification or accession are deposited subsequent to the entry into force of this Convention, it shall enter into force on the date of the deposit of their instruments of ratification or accession.

5. The Depositary Governments shall promptly inform all signatory and acceding States of the date of each signature, the date of deposit of each instrument of ratification of and accession to this Convention, the date of its entry into force and other notices.

6. This Convention shall be registered by the Depositary Governments pursuant to Article 102 of the Charter of the United Nations.

Article XXV

Any State Party to this Convention may propose amendments to this Convention. Amendments shall enter into force for each State Party to the Convention accepting the amendments upon their acceptance by a majority of the States Parties to the Convention and thereafter for each remaining State Party to the Convention on the date of acceptance by it.

Article XXVI

Ten years after the entry into force of this Convention, the question of the review of this Convention shall be included in the provisional agenda of the United Nations General Assembly in order to consider, in the light of past application of the Convention, whether it requires revision. However, at any time after the Convention has been in force for five years, and at the request of one third of the States Parties to the Convention, and with the concurrence of the majority of the States Parties, a conference of the States Parties shall be convened to review this Convention.

Article XXVII

Any State Party to this Convention may give notice of its withdrawal from the Convention one year after its entry into force by written notification to the Depositary Governments. Such withdrawal shall take effect one year from the date of receipt of this notification.

Article XXVIII

This Convention, of which the English, Russian, French, Spanish and Chinese texts are equally authentic, shall be deposited in the archives of the Depositary Governments. Duly certified copies of this Convention shall be transmitted by the Depositary Governments to the Governments of the signatory and acceding States.

IN WITNESS WHEREOF the undersigned, duly authorized thereto, have signed this Convention.

DONE in triplicate, at the cities of London, Moscow and Washington, this twenty-ninth day of March, one thousand nine hundred and seventy-two.

NOTES ON the Convention on International Liability for Damage Caused by Space Objects

Cosmos 954 was an ocean surveillance satellite[39] that had been placed in orbit by the Soviet Union on September 18, 1977. On January 6, 1978, the satellite was sharply depressurized for unknown reasons and began to fall. The Soviet satellite was equipped with a nuclear reactor[40] which caused great concern about the possibility of serious nuclear contamination in Canada.

The Cosmos-954 satellite released an enormous amount of radioactivity across the frozen barren lands of Canada's Northwest Territories in 1978. It did not result in a major catastrophe for two reasons. The first is the obvious one that the region is sparsely populated, and the second one was that almost fifty percent of the area is covered by lakes and rivers, which eventually absorbed most of the radioactive debris with minimal harm to the environment. What was probably not appreciated was that had the re-entry happened a little less than three orbits earlier, the impact trajectory would have strewn radioactive debris over a footprint extending from the Gulf of Mexico and passing close to the major population centres of Detroit and Toronto. Two and-a-bit orbits later and it would have re-entered over Hudsons Bay, putting Quebec City directly on the impact trajectory. In either case there would have been absolute mayhem.

The Canadian claim against the Soviet Union was resolved through diplomatic channels.

After three rounds of negotiations in which the Canadian claim was discussed "with full consideration given to its legal and factual implications," a settlement was reached

The Cosmos 954 incident focused international attention on the Liability Convention,[19] but failed to provide any guidelines regarding what damages are compensable under the Convention.

[39] According to United States officials, the satellite was used to conduct surveillance of United States Navy surface ships
[40] According to Soviet correspondence with Canada following the fall, the satellite carried on board a nuclear reactor powered by uranium enriched with isotope of uranium-235

As a result, a victim of space object damage is no more certain to recover "full compensation" under the Liability Convention today than it was before the Cosmos 954 incident.

CONVENTION ON REGISTRATION OF OBJECTS LAUNCHED INTO OUTER SPACE (REGISTRATION CONVENTION)

Adopted by the General Assembly in its resolution 3235 (XXIX) of 12 November 1974[41]

The States Parties to this Convention,

Recognizing the common interest of all mankind in furthering the exploration and use of outer space for peaceful purposes,

Recalling that the Treaty on Principles Governing the Activities of States in the Exploration and Use of Outer Space, including the Moon and Other Celestial Bodies,[1] of 27 January 1967 affirms that States shall bear international responsibility for their national activities in outer space and refers to the State on whose registry an object launched into outer space is carried,

Recalling also that the Agreement on the Rescue of Astronauts, the Return of Astronauts and the Return of Objects Launched into Outer Space[42] of 22 April 1968 provides that a launching authority shall, upon request, furnish identifying data prior to the return of an object it has launched into outer space found beyond the territorial limits of the launching authority,

Recalling further that the Convention on International Liability for Damage Caused by Space Objects[43] of 29 March 1972 establishes international rules and procedures concerning the liability of launching States for damage caused by their space objects,

Desiring, in the light of the Treaty on Principles Governing the Activities of States in the Exploration and Use of Outer Space,

[41] Sources: 28 UST 695; TIAS 8480; 1023 UNTS 15; Adoption by the United Nations General Assembly: 12 November 1974; Entry into force: 15 September 1976

including the Moon and Other Celestial Bodies, to make provision for the national registration by launching States of space objects launched into outer space,

Desiring further that a central register of objects launched into outer space be established and maintained, on a mandatory basis, by the Secretary-General of the United Nations,

Desiring also to provide for States Parties additional means and procedures to assist in the identification of space objects,

Believing that a mandatory system of registering objects launched into outer space would, in particular, assist in their identification and would contribute to the application and development of international law governing the exploration and use of outer space,

Have agreed on the following:

Article I

For the purposes of this Convention:

(a) The term "launching State" means:

   (i) A State which launches or procures the launching of a space object;
   (ii) A State from whose territory or facility a space object is launched;

(b) The term "space object" includes component parts[44] of a space object as well as its launch vehicle and parts thereof;

(c) The term "State of registry" means a launching State on whose registry a space object is carried in accordance with article II.

Article II

1. When a space object is launched into Earth orbit or beyond, the launching State shall register the space object by means of an entry in an appropriate registry which it shall maintain. Each launching State shall inform the Secretary-General of the United Nations of the establishment of such a registry.

---

[44] It specifically excludes small pieces and fragments that are not capable of surviving a re-entry into the atmosphere of the Earth (see William B. Wirin, Space Debris and Space Objects (1991) 34 PROC. COLL. L. OUTER SPACE 45)

2. Where there are two or more launching States in respect of any such space object, they shall jointly determine which one of them shall register the object in accordance with paragraph 1 of this article, bearing in mind the provisions of article VIII of the Treaty on Principles Governing the Activities of States in the Exploration and Use of Outer Space, including the Moon and Other Celestial Bodies, and without prejudice to appropriate agreements concluded or to be concluded among the launching States on jurisdiction and control over the space object and over any personnel thereof.

3. The contents of each registry and the conditions under which it is maintained shall be determined by the State of registry concerned.

Article III

1. The Secretary-General of the United Nations shall maintain a Register in which the information furnished in accordance with article IV shall be recorded.

2. There shall be full and open access to the information in this Register.

Article IV

1. Each State of registry shall furnish to the Secretary-General of the United Nations, as soon as practicable, the following information concerning each space object carried on its registry:

(a) Name of launching State or States;

(b) An appropriate designator of the space object or its registration number;

(c) Date and territory or location of launch;

(d) Basic orbital parameters, including:

(i) Nodal period;
(ii) Inclination;
(iii) Apogee;
(iv) Perigee;

(e) General function of the space object.

2. Each State of registry may, from time to time, provide the Secretary- General of the United Nations with additional

information concerning a space object carried on its registry.
3. Each State of registry shall notify the Secretary-General of the United Nations, to the greatest extent feasible and as soon as practicable, of space objects concerning which it has previously transmitted information, and which have been but no longer are in Earth orbit.

Article V

Whenever a space object launched into Earth orbit or beyond is marked with the designator or registration number referred to in article IV, paragraph 1 *(b)*, or both, the State of registry shall notify the Secretary-General of this fact when submitting the information regarding the space object in accordance with article IV. In such case, the Secretary-General of the United Nations shall record this notification in the Register.

Article VI

Where the application of the provisions of this Convention has not enabled a State Party to identify a space object which has caused damage to it or to any of its natural or juridical persons, or which may be of a hazardous or deleterious nature, other States Parties, including in particular States possessing space monitoring and tracking facilities, shall respond to the greatest extent feasible to a request by that State Party, or transmitted through the Secretary-General on its behalf, for assistance under equitable and reasonable conditions in the identification of the object. A State Party making such a request shall, to the greatest extent feasible, submit information as to the time, nature and circumstances of the events giving rise to the request. Arrangements under which such assistance shall be rendered shall be the subject of agreement between the parties concerned.

Article VII

1. In this Convention, with the exception of articles VIII to XII inclusive, references to States shall be deemed to apply to any international intergovernmental organization which conducts space activities if the organization declares its acceptance of the rights and obligations provided for in this Convention and if a majority of the States members of the organization are States Parties to this Convention and to the Treaty on Principles Governing the Activities of States

in the Exploration and Use of Outer Space, including the Moon and Other Celestial Bodies.

2. States members of any such organization which are States Parties to this Convention shall take all appropriate steps to ensure that the organization makes a declaration in accordance with paragraph 1 of this article.

Article VIII

1. This Convention shall be open for signature by all States at United Nations Headquarters in New York. Any State which does not sign this Convention before its entry into force in accordance with paragraph 3 of this article may accede to it at any time.
2. This Convention shall be subject to ratification by signatory States. Instruments of ratification and instruments of accession shall be deposited with the Secretary-General of the United Nations.
3. This Convention shall enter into force among the States which have deposited instruments of ratification on the deposit of the fifth such instrument with the Secretary-General of the United Nations.
4. For States whose instruments of ratification or accession are deposited subsequent to the entry into force of this Convention, it shall enter into force on the date of the deposit of their instruments of ratification or accession.
5. The Secretary-General shall promptly inform all signatory and acceding States of the date of each signature, the date of deposit of each instrument of ratification of and accession to this Convention, the date of its entry into force and other notices.

Article IX

Any State Party to this Convention may propose amendments to the Convention. Amendments shall enter into force for each State Party to the Convention accepting the amendments upon their acceptance by a majority of the States Parties to the Convention and thereafter for each remaining State Party to the Convention on the date of acceptance by it.

Article X

Ten years after the entry into force of this Convention, the question of the review of the Convention shall be included in the provisional agenda of the United Nations General Assembly in order to consider, in the light of past application of the

Convention, whether it requires revision. However, at any time after the Convention has been in force for five years, at the request of one third of the States Parties to the Convention and with the concurrence of the majority of the States Parties, a conference of the States Parties shall be convened to review this Convention. Such review shall take into account in particular any relevant technological developments, including those relating to the identification of space objects.

Article XI

Any State Party to this Convention may give notice of its withdrawal from the Convention one year after its entry into force by written notification to the Secretary- General of the United Nations. Such withdrawal shall take effect one year from the date of receipt of this notification.

Article XII

The original of this Convention, of which the Arabic, Chinese, English, French, Russian and Spanish texts are equally authentic, shall be deposited with the Secretary-General of the United Nations, who shall send certified copies thereof to all signatory and acceding States.

IN WITNESS WHEREOF the undersigned, being duly authorized thereto by their respective Governments, have signed this Convention, opened for signature at New York on the fourteenth day of January, one thousand nine hundred and seventy-five.

NOTES on the Convention on Registration of Objects Launched into Outer Space (Registration Convention)

Member States conducting space launches have been requested by the Committee to provide the United Nations with information on their launchings. A registry of launchings has been maintained by the Secretariat since 1962, in accordance with General Assembly resolution 1721 B (XVI), and information from Member States has been issued in United Nations documents in the A/AC.105/INF series. Since the Convention on Registration of Objects Launched into Outer Space entered into force in 1976, another register of launchings has been established for information received from Member States and intergovernmental organizations that are parties to the Convention.

As of 1 January 2011, 56 States have acceded/ratified, 4 have signed and two international intergovernmental organizations (European Space Agency and European Organization for the Exploitation of Meteorological Satellites) have declared their acceptance of the rights and obligations provided for in the Registration Convention. The information received in accordance with the Convention has been issued in United Nations documents in the ST/SG/SER.E series. The A/AC.105/INF series continues with information provided by States who are not party to the treaty. Approximately 93.5% of all functional space objects (satellites, probes/landers, manned spacecraft, space station components, etc) have been registered with the Secretary-General.

The Registration Convention provides that the launching State should furnish to the United Nations, as soon as practicable, the following information concerning each space object:

- Name of launching State;
- An appropriate designator of the space object or its registration number;

- Date and territory or location of launch;
- Basic orbital parameters, including:
- Nodal period (the time between two successive northbound crossings of the equator - usually in minutes);
- Inclination (inclination of the orbit - polar orbit is 90 degrees and equatorial orbit is 0 degrees);
- Apogee (highest altitude above the Earths surface - in kilometers);
- Perigee; (lowest altitude above the Earths surface - in kilometers);
- General function of the space object.

Under these arrangements information has been received from Algeria, Argentina, Australia, Brazil, Canada, China, Chile, Czech Republic, Democratic People's Republic of Korea, Denmark, Egypt, France, Germany, Greece, Hungary, India, Indonesia, Israel, Italy, Japan, Kazakhstan, Luxembourg, Malaysia, Mexico, Nigeria, Pakistan, Poland, Republic of Korea, Russian Federation, Spain, Sweden, Thailand, Turkey, Ukraine, United Arab Emirates, United Kingdom of Great Britain and Northern Ireland, United States of America and Venezuela as well as from the European Space Agency (ESA) and the European Organization for the Exploitation of Meteorological Satellites (EUMETSAT).

AGREEMENT GOVERNING THE ACTIVITIES OF STATES ON THE MOON AND OTHER CELESTIAL BODIES (MOON AGREEMENT)

Adopted by the General Assembly in its resolution 34/68 of 5 December 1979[45]

The States Parties to this Agreement,

Noting the achievements of States in the exploration and use of the moon and other celestial bodies,

Recognizing that the moon, as a natural satellite of the earth, has an important role to play in the exploration of outer space,

Determined to promote on the basis of equality the further development of co-operation among States in the exploration and use of the moon and other celestial bodies,

Desiring to prevent the moon from becoming an area of international conflict,

Bearing in mind the benefits which may be derived from the exploitation of the natural resources of the moon and other celestial bodies,

Recalling the Treaty on Principles Governing the Activities of States in the Exploration and Use of Outer Space, including the Moon and Other Celestial Bodies, the Agreement on the Rescue of Astronauts, the Return of Astronauts and the Return of Objects Launched into

5 December 1979; Entry into force: 11 July 1984

Outer Space, the Convention on International Liability for Damage Caused by Space Objects, and the Convention on Registration of Objects Launched into Outer Space,

Taking into account the need to define and develop the provisions of these international instruments in relation to the moon and other celestial bodies, having regard to further progress in the exploration and use of outer space,

Have agreed on the following:

Article 1

1. The provisions of this Agreement relating to the moon shall also apply to other celestial bodies within the solar system, other than the earth, except in so far as specific legal norms enter into force with respect to any of these celestial bodies.

2. For the purposes of this Agreement reference to the moon shall include orbits around or other trajectories to or around it.

3. This Agreement does not apply to extraterrestrial materials which reach the surface of the earth by natural means.

Article 2

All activities on the moon, including its exploration and use, shall be carried out in accordance with international law, in particular the Charter of the United Nations, and taking into account the Declaration on Principles of International Law concerning Friendly Relations and Co-operation among States in accordance with the Charter of the United Nations, adopted by the General Assembly on 24 October 1970, in the interest of maintaining international peace and security and promoting international co-operation and mutual understanding, and with due regard to the corresponding interests of all other States Parties.

Article 3

1. The moon shall be used by all States Parties exclusively for peaceful purposes.

2. Any threat or use of force or any other hostile act or threat of hostile act on the moon is prohibited. It is likewise prohibited to use the moon in order to commit any such act or to engage in any such threat in relation to the earth, the moon, spacecraft, the personnel of spacecraft or man- made space objects.

3. States Parties shall not place in orbit around or other trajectory to or around the moon objects carrying nuclear weapons or any other kinds of weapons of mass destruction or place or use such weapons on or in the moon.

4. The establishment of military bases, installations and fortifications, the testing of any type of weapons and the conduct of military maneuvers on the moon shall be forbidden. The use of military personnel for scientific research or for any other peaceful purposes shall not be prohibited. The use of any equipment or facility necessary for peaceful exploration and use of the moon shall also not be prohibited.

Article 4

1. The exploration and use of the moon shall be the province of all mankind and shall be carried out for the benefit and in the interests of all countries, irrespective of their degree of economic or scientific development. Due regard shall be paid to the interests of present and future generations as well as to the need to promote higher standards of living and conditions of economic and social progress and development in accordance with the Charter of the United Nations.

2. States Parties shall be guided by the principle of co-operation and mutual assistance in all their activities concerning the exploration and use of the moon. International co-operation in pursuance of this

Agreement should be as wide as possible and may take place on a multilateral basis, on a bilateral basis or through international intergovernmental organizations.

Article 5

1. States Parties shall inform the Secretary-General of the United Nations as well as the public and the international scientific community, to the greatest extent feasible and practicable, of their activities concerned with the exploration and use of the moon. Information on the time, purposes, locations, orbital parameters and duration shall be given in respect of each mission to the moon as soon as possible after launching, while information on the results of each mission, including scientific results, shall be furnished upon completion of the mission. In the case of a mission lasting more than sixty days, information on conduct of the mission, including any scientific results, shall be given periodically, at thirty-day intervals. For missions lasting more than six months, only significant additions to such information need be reported thereafter.

2. If a State Party becomes aware that another State Party plans to operate simultaneously in the same area of or in the same orbit around or trajectory to or around the moon, it shall promptly inform the other State of the timing of and plans for its own operations.

3. In carrying out activities under this Agreement, States Parties shall promptly inform the Secretary-General, as well as the public and the international scientific community, of any phenomena they discover in outer space, including the moon, which could endanger human life or health, as well as of any indication of organic life.

Article 6

1. There shall be freedom of scientific investigation on the moon by all States Parties without discrimination of any kind, on the basis of equality and in accordance with international law.

2. In carrying out scientific investigations and in furtherance of the provisions of this Agreement, the States Parties shall have the right to collect on and remove from the moon samples of its mineral and other substances. Such samples shall remain at the disposal of those States Parties which caused them to be collected and may be used by them for scientific purposes. States Parties shall have regard to the desirability of making a portion of such samples available to other interested States Parties and the international scientific community for scientific investigation. States Parties may in the course of scientific investigations also use mineral and other substances of the moon in quantities appropriate for the support of their missions.

3. States Parties agree on the desirability of exchanging scientific and other personnel on expeditions to or installations on the moon to the greatest extent feasible and practicable.

Article 7

1. In exploring and using the moon, States Parties shall take measures to prevent the disruption of the existing balance of its environment, whether by introducing adverse changes in that environment, by its harmful contamination through the introduction of extra-environmental matter or otherwise. States Parties shall also take measures to avoid harmfully affecting the environment of the earth through the introduction of extraterrestrial matter or otherwise.

2. States Parties shall inform the Secretary-General of the United Nations of the measures being adopted by them in accordance with paragraph 1 of this article and shall also, to the maximum extent feasible, notify him in advance of all placements by them of radio-active materials on the moon and of the purposes of such placements.

3. States Parties shall report to other States Parties and to the Secretary-General concerning areas of the moon having special scientific interest in order that, without prejudice to the rights of other States Parties, consideration may be given to the designation of such areas as international scientific preserves for which special

protective arrangements are to be agreed upon in consultation with the competent bodies of the United Nations.

Article 8

1. States Parties may pursue their activities in the exploration and use of the moon anywhere on or below its surface, subject to the provisions of this Agreement.

2. For these purposes States Parties may, in particular:

(a) Land their space objects on the moon and launch them from the moon;

(b) Place their personnel, space vehicles, equipment, facilities, stations and installations anywhere on or below the surface of the moon.

Personnel, space vehicles, equipment, facilities, stations and installations may move or be moved freely over or below the surface of the moon.

3. Activities of States Parties in accordance with paragraphs 1 and 2 of this article shall not interfere with the activities of other States Parties on the moon. Where such interference may occur, the States Parties concerned shall undertake consultations in accordance with article 15, paragraphs 2 and 3, of this Agreement.

Article 9

1. States Parties may establish manned and unmanned stations on the moon. A State Party establishing a station shall use only that area which is required for the needs of the station and shall immediately inform the Secretary-General of the United Nations of the location and purposes of that station. Subsequently, at annual intervals that State shall likewise inform the Secretary-General whether the station continues in use and whether its purposes have changed.

2. Stations shall be installed in such a manner that they do not impede the free access to all areas of the moon of personnel, vehicles and equipment of other States Parties conducting activities on the moon in accordance with the provisions of this Agreement or of article I of the Treaty on Principles Governing the Activities of States in the Exploration and Use of Outer Space, including the Moon and Other Celestial Bodies.

Article 10

1. States Parties shall adopt all practicable measures to safeguard the life and health of persons on the moon. For this purpose they shall regard any person on the moon as an astronaut within the meaning of article V of the Treaty on Principles Governing the Activities of States in the Exploration and Use of Outer Space, including the Moon and Other Celestial Bodies and as part of the personnel of a spacecraft within the meaning of the Agreement on the Rescue of Astronauts, the Return of Astronauts and the Return of Objects Launched into Outer Space.

2. States Parties shall offer shelter in their stations, installations, vehicles and other facilities to persons in distress on the moon.

Article 11

1. The moon and its natural resources are the common heritage of mankind, which finds its expression in the provisions of this Agreement, in particular in paragraph 5 of this article.

2. The moon is not subject to national appropriation by any claim of sovereignty, by means of use or occupation, or by any other means.

3. Neither the surface nor the subsurface of the moon, nor any part thereof or natural resources in place, shall become property of any State, international intergovernmental or non- governmental organization, national organization or non-governmental entity or of any natural person. The placement of personnel, space vehicles, equipment, facilities, stations and installations on or below the

surface of the moon, including structures connected with its surface or subsurface, shall not create a right of ownership over the surface or the subsurface of the moon or any areas thereof. The foregoing provisions are without prejudice to the international regime referred to in paragraph 5 of this article.

4. States Parties have the right to exploration and use of the moon without discrimination of any kind, on the basis of equality and in accordance with international law and the terms of this Agreement.

5. States Parties to this Agreement hereby undertake to establish an international regime, including appropriate procedures, to govern the exploitation of the natural resources of the moon as such exploitation is about to become feasible. This provision shall be implemented in accordance with article 18 of this Agreement.

6. In order to facilitate the establishment of the international regime referred to in paragraph 5 of this article, States Parties shall inform the Secretary-General of the United Nations as well as the public and the international scientific community, to the greatest extent feasible and practicable, of any natural resources they may discover on the moon.

7. The main purposes of the international regime to be established shall include:

(a) The orderly and safe development of the natural resources of the moon;

(b) The rational management of those resources;

(c) The expansion of opportunities in the use of those resources;

(d) An equitable sharing by all States Parties in the benefits derived from those resources, whereby the interests and needs of the developing countries, as well as the efforts of those countries which have contributed either directly or indirectly to the exploration of the moon, shall be given special consideration.

8. All the activities with respect to the natural resources of the moon shall be carried out in a manner compatible with the purposes

specified in paragraph 7 of this article and the provisions of article 6, paragraph 2, of this Agreement.

Article 12

1. States Parties shall retain jurisdiction and control over their personnel, vehicles, equipment, facilities, stations and installations on the moon. The ownership of space vehicles, equipment, facilities, stations and installations shall not be affected by their presence on the moon.

2. Vehicles, installations and equipment or their component parts found in places other than their intended location shall be dealt with in accordance with article 5 of the Agreement on the Rescue of Astronauts, the Return of Astronauts and the Return of Objects Launched into Outer Space.

3. In the event of an emergency involving a threat to human life, States Parties may use the equipment, vehicles, installations, facilities or supplies of other States Parties on the moon. Prompt notification of such use shall be made to the Secretary-General of the United Nations or the State Party concerned.

Article 13

A State Party which learns of the crash landing, forced landing or other unintended landing on the moon of a space object, or its component parts, that were not launched by it, shall promptly inform the launching State Party and the Secretary-General of the United Nations.

Article 14

1. States Parties to this Agreement shall bear international responsibility for national activities on the moon, whether such activities are carried on by governmental agencies or by non-

governmental entities, and for assuring that national activities are carried out in conformity with the provisions set forth in this Agreement. States Parties shall ensure that non-governmental entities under their jurisdiction shall engage in activities on the moon only under the authority and continuing supervision of the appropriate State Party.

2. States Parties recognize that detailed arrangements concerning liability for damage caused on the moon, in addition to the provisions of the Treaty on Principles Governing the Activities of States in the Exploration and Use of Outer Space, including the Moon and Other Celestial Bodies and the Convention on International Liability for Damage Caused by Space Objects, may become necessary as a result of more extensive activities on the moon. Any such arrangements shall be elaborated in accordance with the procedure provided for in article 18 of this Agreement.

Article 15

1. Each State Party may assure itself that the activities of other States Parties in the exploration and use of the moon are compatible with the provisions of this Agreement. To this end, all space vehicles, equipment, facilities, stations and installations on the moon shall be open to other States Parties. Such States Parties shall give reasonable advance notice of a projected visit, in order that appropriate consultations may be held and that maximum precautions may be taken to assure safety and to avoid interference with normal operations in the facility to be visited. In pursuance of this article, any State Party may act on its own behalf or with the full or partial assistance of any other State Party or through appropriate international procedures within the framework of the United Nations and in accordance with the Charter.

2. A State Party which has reason to believe that another State Party is not fulfilling the obligations incumbent upon it pursuant to this Agreement or that another State Party is interfering with the rights which the former State has under this Agreement may request consultations with that State Party. A State Party receiving such a request shall enter into such consultations without delay. Any other State Party which requests to do so shall be entitled to take part in

the consultations. Each State Party participating in such consultations shall seek a mutually acceptable resolution of any controversy and shall bear in mind the rights and interests of all States Parties. The Secretary-General of the United Nations shall be informed of the results of the consultations and shall transmit the information received to all States Parties concerned.

3. If the consultations do not lead to a mutually acceptable settlement which has due regard for the rights and interests of all States Parties, the parties concerned shall take all measures to settle the dispute by other peaceful means of their choice appropriate to the circumstances and the nature of the dispute. If difficulties arise in connection with the opening of consultations or if consultations do not lead to a mutually acceptable settlement, any State Party may seek the assistance of the Secretary-General, without seeking the consent of any other State Party concerned, in order to resolve the controversy. A State Party which does not maintain diplomatic relations with another State Party concerned shall participate in such consultations, at its choice, either itself or through another State Party or the Secretary-General as intermediary.

Article 16

With the exception of articles 17 to 21, references in this Agreement to States shall be deemed to apply to any international intergovernmental organization which conducts space activities if the organization declares its acceptance of the rights and obligations provided for in this Agreement and if a majority of the States members of the organization are States Parties to this Agreement and to the Treaty on Principles Governing the Activities of States in the Exploration and Use of Outer Space, including the Moon and Other Celestial Bodies. States members of any such organization which are States Parties to this Agreement shall take all appropriate steps to ensure that the organization makes a declaration in accordance with the foregoing.

Article 17

Any State Party to this Agreement may propose amendments to the Agreement. Amendments shall enter into force for each State Party to the Agreement accepting the amendments upon their acceptance by a majority of the States Parties to the Agreement and thereafter for each remaining State Party to the Agreement on the date of acceptance by it.

Article 18

Ten years after the entry into force of this Agreement, the question of the review of the Agreement shall be included in the provisional agenda of the General Assembly of the United Nations in order to consider, in the light of past application of the Agreement, whether it requires revision. However, at any time after the Agreement has been in force for five years, the Secretary-General of the United Nations, as depository, shall, at the request of one third of the States Parties to the Agreement and with the concurrence of the majority of the States Parties, convene a conference of the States Parties to review this Agreement. A review conference shall also consider the question of the implementation of the provisions of article 11, paragraph 5, on the basis of the principle referred to in paragraph 1 of that article and taking into account in particular any relevant technological developments.

Article 19

1. This Agreement shall be open for signature by all States at United Nations Headquarters in New York.

2. This Agreement shall be subject to ratification by signatory States. Any State which does not sign this Agreement before its entry into force in accordance with paragraph 3 of this article may accede to it at any time. Instruments of ratification or accession shall be deposited with the Secretary-General of the United Nations.

3. This Agreement shall enter into force on the thirtieth day following the date of deposit of the fifth instrument of ratification.

4. For each State depositing its instrument of ratification or accession after the entry into force of this Agreement, it shall enter

into force on the thirtieth day following the date of deposit of any such instrument.

5. The Secretary-General shall promptly inform all signatory and acceding States of the date of each signature, the date of deposit of each instrument of ratification or accession to this Agreement, the date of its entry into force and other notices.

Article 20

Any State Party to this Agreement may give notice of its withdrawal from the Agreement one year after its entry into force by written notification to the Secretary-General of the United Nations. Such withdrawal shall take effect one year from the date of receipt of this notification.

Article 21

The original of this Agreement, of which the Arabic, Chinese, English, French, Russian and Spanish texts are equally authentic, shall be deposited with the Secretary-General of the United Nations, who shall send certified copies thereof to all signatory and acceding States.

IN WITNESS WHEREOF the undersigned, being duly authorized thereto by their respective Governments, have signed this Agreement, opened for signature at New York on 18 December 1979.

NOTES on the Moon Agreement

The Moon Agreement was considered and elaborated by the Legal Subcommittee from 1972 to 1979. The Agreement was adopted by the General Assembly in 1979 in resolution 34/68.

It was not until June 1984, however, that the fifth country, Austria, ratified the Agreement, allowing it to enter into force in July 1984.

The Agreement reaffirms and elaborates on many of the provisions of the Outer Space Treaty as applied to the Moon and other celestial bodies, providing that those bodies should be used exclusively for peaceful purposes, that their environments should not be disrupted, that the United Nations should be informed of the location and purpose of any station established on those bodies. In addition, the Agreement provides that the Moon and its natural resources are the common heritage of mankind and that an international regime should be established to govern the exploitation of such resources when such exploitation is about to become feasible.

PART II: PRINCIPLES ADOPTED BY THE GENERAL ASSEMBLY

DECLARATION OF LEGAL PRINCIPLES GOVERNING THE ACTIVITIES OF STATES IN THE EXPLORATION AND USE OF OUTER SPACE[46]

The General Assembly,

Inspired by the great prospects opening up before mankind as a result of man's entry into outer space,

Recognizing the common interest of all mankind in the progress of the exploration and use of outer space for peaceful purposes,

Believing that the exploration and use of outer space should be carried on for the betterment of mankind and for the benefit of States irrespective of their degree of economic or scientific development,

Desiring to contribute to broad international co-operation in the scientific as well as in the legal aspects of exploration and use of outer space for peaceful purposes,

Believing that such co-operation will contribute to the development of mutual understanding and to the strengthening of friendly relations between nations and peoples,

Recalling its resolution 110 (II) of 3 November 1947, which condemned propaganda designed or likely to provoke or encourage any threat to the peace, breach of the peace, or act of aggression, and considering that the aforementioned resolution is applicable to outer space,

Taking into consideration its resolutions 1721 (XVI) of 20 December 1961 and 1802 (XVII) of 14 December 1962, adopted unanimously by the States Members of the United Nations,

Solemnly declares that in the exploration and use of outer space States should be guided by the following principles:

1. The exploration and use of outer space shall be carried on for the benefit and in the interests of all mankind.

2. Outer space and celestial bodies are free for exploration and use by all States on a basis of equality and in accordance with international law.

3. Outer space and celestial bodies are not subject to national appropriation by claim of sovereignty, by means of use or occupation, or by any other means.

4. The activities of States in the exploration and use of outer space shall be carried on in accordance with international law, including the Charter of the United Nations, in the interest of maintaining international peace and security and promoting international co-operation and understanding.

5. States bear international responsibility for national activities in outer space, whether carried on by governmental agencies or by non-governmental entities, and for assuring that national activities are carried on in conformity with the principles set forth in the present Declaration. The activities of non-governmental entities in outer space shall require authorization and continuing supervision by the State concerned. When activities are carried on in outer space by an international organization, responsibility for compliance with the principles set forth in this Declaration shall be borne by the international organization and by the States participating in it.

6. In the exploration and use of outer space, States shall be guided by the principle of co- operation and mutual assistance and shall conduct all their activities in outer space with due regard for

the corresponding interests of other States. If a State has reason to believe that an outer space activity or experiment planned by it or its nationals would cause potentially harmful interference with activities of other States in the peaceful exploration and use of outer space, it shall undertake appropriate international consultations before proceeding with any such activity or experiment. A State which has reason to believe that an outer space activity or experiment planned by another State would cause potentially harmful interference with activities in the peaceful exploration and use of outer space may request consultation concerning the activity or experiment.

7. The State on whose registry an object launched into outer space is carried shall retain jurisdiction and control over such object, and any personnel thereon, while in outer space. Ownership of objects launched into outer space, and of their component parts, is not affected by their passage through outer space or by their return to the earth. Such objects or component parts found beyond the limits of the State of registry shall be returned to that State, which shall furnish identifying data upon request prior to return.

8. Each State which launches or procures the launching of an object into outer space, and each State from whose territory or facility an object is launched, is internationally liable for damage to a foreign State or to its natural or juridical persons by such object or its component parts on the earth, in air space, or in outer space.

9. States shall regard astronauts as envoys of mankind in outer space, and shall render to them all possible assistance in the event of accident, distress, or emergency landing on the territory of a foreign State or on the high seas. Astronauts who make such a landing shall be safely and promptly returned to the State of registry of their space vehicle.

PRINCIPLES GOVERNING THE USE BY STATES OF ARTIFICIAL EARTH SATELLITES FOR INTERNATIONAL DIRECT TELEVISION BROADCASTING

The General Assembly,

Recalling its resolution 2916 (XXVII) of 9 November 1972, in which it stressed the necessity of elaborating principles governing the use by States of artificial Earth satellites for international direct television broadcasting, and mindful of the importance of concluding an international agreement or agreements,

Recalling further its resolutions 3182 (XXVIII) of 18 December 1973, 3234 (XXIX) of 12 November 1974, 3388 (XXX) of 18 November 1975, 31/8 of 8 November 1976, 32/196 of 20 December 1977, 33/16 of 10 November 1978, 34/66 of 5 December 1979 and 35/14 of 3 November 1980, and its resolution 36/35 of 18 November 1981 in which it decided to consider at its thirty-seventh session the adoption of a draft set of principles governing the use by States of artificial Earth satellites for international direct television broadcasting,

Noting with appreciation the efforts made in the Committee on the Peaceful Uses of Outer Space and its Legal Subcommittee to comply with the directives issued in the above-mentioned resolutions,

Considering that several experiments of direct broadcasting by satellite have been carried out and that a number of direct broadcasting satellite systems are operational in some countries and may be commercialized in the very near future,

Taking into consideration that the operation of international direct broadcasting satellites will have significant international political, economic, social and cultural implications,

Believing that the establishment of principles for international direct television broadcasting will contribute to the strengthening of international cooperation in this field and further the purposes and principles of the Charter of the United Nations,

Adopts the Principles Governing the Use by States of Artificial Earth Satellites for International Direct Television Broadcasting set forth in the annex to the present resolution.

Annex

Principles Governing the Use by States of Artificial Earth Satellites for International Direct Television Broadcasting

A. Purposes and objectives

1. Activities in the field of international direct television broadcasting by satellite should be carried out in a manner compatible with the sovereign rights of States, including the principle of non-intervention, as well as with the right of everyone to seek, receive and impart information and ideas as enshrined in the relevant United Nations instruments.

2. Such activities should promote the free dissemination and mutual exchange of information and knowledge in cultural and scientific fields, assist in educational, social and economic development, particularly in the developing countries, enhance the qualities of life of all peoples and provide recreation with due respect to the political and cultural integrity of States.

3. These activities should accordingly be carried out in a manner compatible with the development of mutual understanding and the strengthening of friendly relations and cooperation among all States and peoples in the interest of maintaining international peace and security.

B. Applicability of international law

4. Activities in the field of international direct television broadcasting by satellite should be conducted in accordance with international law, including the Charter of the United Nations, the Treaty on Principles Governing the Activities of States in the Exploration and Use of Outer Space, including the Moon and Other Celestial Bodies, of 27 January 1967, the relevant provisions of the International 1 Telecommunication Convention and its Radio Regulations and of international instruments relating to friendly relations and cooperation among States and to human rights.

C. Rights and benefits

5. Every State has an equal right to conduct activities in the field of international direct television broadcasting by satellite and to authorize such activities by persons and entities under its jurisdiction. All States and peoples are entitled to and should enjoy the benefits from such activities. Access to the technology in this field should be available to all States without discrimination on terms mutually agreed by all concerned.

D. International cooperation

6. Activities in the field of international direct television broadcasting by satellite should be based upon and encourage international cooperation. Such cooperation should be the subject of appropriate arrangements. Special consideration should be given to the needs of the developing countries in the use of international direct television broadcasting by satellite for the purpose of accelerating their national development.

E. Peaceful settlement of disputes

7. Any international dispute that may arise from activities covered by these principles should be settled through established procedures for the peaceful settlement of disputes agreed upon by the parties to the dispute in accordance with the provisions of the Charter of the United Nations.

F. State responsibility

8. States should bear international responsibility for activities in the field of international direct television broadcasting by satellite carried out by them or under their jurisdiction and for the conformity of any such activities with the principles set forth in this document.

9. When international direct television broadcasting by satellite is carried out by an international intergovernmental organization, the responsibility referred to in paragraph 8 above should be borne both by that organization and by the States participating in it.

G. Duty and right to consult

10. Any broadcasting or receiving State within an international direct television broadcasting satellite service established between them requested to do so by any other broadcasting or receiving State within the same service should promptly enter into consultations with the requesting State regarding its activities in the field of international direct television broadcasting by satellite, without prejudice to other consultations which these States may undertake with any other State on that subject.

H. Copyright and neighbouring rights

11. Without prejudice to the relevant provisions of international law, States should cooperate on a bilateral and multilateral basis for protection of copyright and neighbouring rights by means of appropriate agreements between the interested States or the

competent legal entities acting under their jurisdiction. In such cooperation they should give special consideration to the interests of developing countries in the use of direct television broadcasting for the purpose of accelerating their national development.

I. Notification to the United Nations

12. In order to promote international cooperation in the peaceful exploration and use of outer space, States conducting or authorizing activities in the field of international direct television broadcasting by satellite should inform the Secretary-General of the United Nations, to the greatest extent possible, of the nature of such activities. On receiving this information, the Secretary-General should disseminate it immediately and effectively to the relevant specialized agencies, as well as to the public and the international scientific community.

J. Consultations and agreements between States

13. A State which intends to establish or authorize the establishment of an international direct television broadcasting satellite service shall without delay notify the proposed receiving State or States of such intention and shall promptly enter into consultation with any of those States which so requests.

14. An international direct television broadcasting satellite service shall only be established after the conditions set forth in paragraph 13 above have been met and on the basis of agreements and/or arrangements in conformity with the relevant instruments of the International Telecommunication Union and in accordance with these principles.

15. With respect to the unavoidable overspill of the radiation of the satellite signal, the relevant instruments of the International Telecommunication Union shall be exclusively applicable.

PRINCIPLES RELATING TO REMOTE SENSING OF THE EARTH FROM OUTER SPACE

The General Assembly,

Recalling its resolution 3234 (XXIX) of 12 November 1974, in which it recommended that the Legal Subcommittee of the Committee on the Peaceful Uses of Outer Space should consider the question of the legal implications of remote sensing of the Earth from space, as well as its resolutions 3388 (XXX) of 18 November 1975, 31/8 of 8 November 1976, 32/196 A of 20 December 1977, 33/16 of 10 November 1978, 34/66 of 5 December 1979, 35/14 of 3 November 1980, 36/35 of 18 November 1981, 37/89 of 10 December 1982, 38/80 of 15 December 1983, 39/96 of 14 December 1984 and 40/162 of 16 December 1985, in which it called for a detailed consideration of the legal implications of remote sensing of the Earth from space, with the aim of formulating draft principles relating to remote sensing,

Having considered the report of the Committee on the Peaceful Uses of Outer Space on the work of its twenty-ninth session (A/41/20) and the text of the draft principles relating to remote sensing of the Earth from space, annexed thereto,

Noting with satisfaction that the Committee on the Peaceful Uses of Outer Space, on the basis of the deliberations of its Legal Subcommittee, has endorsed the text of the draft principles relating to remote sensing of the Earth from space,

Believing that the adoption of the principles relating to remote sensing of the Earth from space will contribute to the strengthening of international cooperation in this field,

Adopts the principles relating to remote sensing of the Earth from space set forth in the annex to the present resolution.

Annex

Principles Relating to Remote Sensing of the Earth from Outer Space

Principle I

For the purposes of these principles with respect to remote sensing activities:

(a) The term "remote sensing" means the sensing of the Earth's surface from space by making use of the properties of electromagnetic waves emitted, reflected or diffracted by the sensed objects, for the purpose of improving natural resources management, land use and the protection of the environment;

(b) The term "primary data" means those raw data that are acquired by remote sensors borne by a space object and that are transmitted or delivered to the ground from space by telemetry in the form of electromagnetic signals, by photographic film, magnetic tape or any other means;

(c) The term "processed data" means the products resulting from the processing of the primary data, needed to make such data usable;

(d) The term "analysed information" means the information resulting from the interpretation of processed data, inputs of data and knowledge from other sources;

(e) The term "remote sensing activities" means the operation of remote sensing space systems, primary data collection and storage stations, and activities in processing, interpreting and disseminating the processed data.

Principle II

Remote sensing activities shall be carried out for the benefit and in the interests of all countries, irrespective of their degree of economic, social or scientific and technological development, and taking into particular consideration the needs of the developing countries.

Principle III

Remote sensing activities shall be conducted in accordance with international law, including the Charter of the United Nations, the Treaty on Principles Governing the Activities of States in the Exploration and Use of Outer Space, including the Moon and Other Celestial Bodies, and the relevant instruments of the International Telecommunication Union.

Principle IV

Remote sensing activities shall be conducted in accordance with the principles contained in article I of the Treaty on Principles Governing the Activities of States in the Exploration and Use of Outer Space, including the Moon and Other Celestial Bodies, which, in particular, provides that the exploration and use of outer space shall be carried out for the benefit and in the interests of all countries, irrespective of their degree of economic or scientific development, and stipulates the principle of freedom of exploration and use of outer space on the basis of equality. These activities shall be conducted on the basis of respect for the principle of full and permanent sovereignty of all States and peoples over their own wealth and natural resources, with due regard to the rights and interests, in accordance with international law, of other States and entities under their jurisdiction. Such activities shall not be conducted in a manner detrimental to the legitimate rights and interests of the sensed State.

Principle V

States carrying out remote sensing activities shall promote international cooperation in these activities. To this end, they shall make available to other States opportunities for participation therein. Such participation shall be based in each case on equitable and mutually acceptable terms.

Principle VI

In order to maximize the availability of benefits from remote sensing activities, States are encouraged, through agreements or other arrangements, to provide for the establishment and operation of data collecting and storage stations and processing and interpretation facilities, in particular within the framework of regional agreements or arrangements wherever feasible.

Principle VII

States participating in remote sensing activities shall make available technical assistance to other interested States on mutually agreed terms.

Principle VIII

The United Nations and the relevant agencies within the United Nations system shall promote international cooperation, including technical assistance and coordination in the area of remote sensing.

Principle IX

In accordance with article IV of the Convention on Registration of Objects Launched into Outer Space and article XI of the Treaty on Principles Governing the Activities of States in the Exploration and Use of Outer Space, including the Moon and Other Celestial Bodies, a State carrying out a programme of remote sensing shall inform the Secretary-General of the United Nations. It shall, moreover, make available any other relevant information to the greatest extent feasible and practicable to any other State, particularly any developing country that is affected by the programme, at its request.

Principle X

Remote sensing shall promote the protection of the Earth's natural environment.

To this end, States participating in remote sensing activities that have identified information in their possession that is capable of averting any phenomenon harmful to the Earth's natural environment shall disclose such information to States concerned.

Principle XI

Remote sensing shall promote the protection of mankind from natural disasters.

To this end, States participating in remote sensing activities that have identified processed data and analysed information in their possession that may be useful to States affected by natural disasters, or likely to be affected by impending natural disasters, shall transmit such data and information to States concerned as promptly as possible.

Principle XII

As soon as the primary data and the processed data concerning the territory under its jurisdiction are produced, the sensed State shall have access to them on a non-discriminatory basis and on reasonable cost terms. The sensed State shall also have access to the available analysed information concerning the territory under its jurisdiction in the possession of any State participating in remote sensing activities on the same basis and terms, taking particularly into account the needs and interests of the developing countries.

Principle XIII

To promote and intensify international cooperation, especially with regard to the needs of developing countries, a State carrying out remote sensing of the Earth from space shall, upon request, enter into consultations with a State whose territory is sensed in order to make available opportunities for participation and enhance the mutual benefits to be derived therefrom.

Principle XIV

In compliance with article VI of the Treaty on Principles Governing the Activities of States in the Exploration and Use of Outer Space, including the Moon and Other Celestial Bodies, States operating remote sensing satellites shall bear international responsibility for their activities and assure that such activities are conducted in accordance with these principles and the norms of international law, irrespective of whether such activities are carried out by governmental or non-governmental entities or through international organizations to which such States are parties. This principle is without prejudice to the applicability of the norms of international law on State responsibility for remote sensing activities.

Principle XV

Any dispute resulting from the application of these principles shall be resolved through the established procedures for the peaceful settlement of disputes.

PRINCIPLES RELEVANT TO THE USE OF NUCLEAR POWER SOURCES IN OUTER SPACE

The General Assembly,

Having considered the report of the Committee on the Peaceful Uses of Outer Space on the work of its thirty-fifth session and the text of the Principles Relevant to the Use of Nuclear Power Sources in Outer Space as approved by the Committee and annexed to its report,

Recognizing that for some missions in outer space nuclear power sources are particularly suited or even essential owing to their compactness, long life and other attributes,

Recognizing also that the use of nuclear power sources in outer space should focus on those applications which take advantage of the particular properties of nuclear power sources,

Recognizing further that the use of nuclear power sources in outer space should be based on a thorough safety assessment, including probabilistic risk analysis, with particular emphasis on reducing the risk of accidental exposure of the public to harmful radiation or radioactive material,

Recognizing the need, in this respect, for a set of principles containing goals and guidelines to ensure the safe use of nuclear power sources in outer space,

Affirming that this set of Principles applies to nuclear power sources in outer space devoted to the generation of electric power on board space objects for non-propulsive purposes, which have characteristics generally comparable to those of systems used and missions performed at the time of the adoption of the Principles,

Recognizing that this set of Principles will require future revision in view of emerging nuclear power applications and of evolving international recommendations on radiological protection,

Adopts the Principles Relevant to the Use of Nuclear Power Sources in Outer Space as set forth below.

Principle 1. Applicability of international law

Activities involving the use of nuclear power sources in outer space shall be carried out in accordance with international law, including in particular the Charter of the United Nations and the Treaty on Principles Governing the Activities of States in the Exploration and Use of Outer Space, including the Moon and Other Celestial Bodies.

Principle 2. Use of terms

1. For the purpose of these Principles, the terms "launching State" and "State launching" mean the State which exercises jurisdiction and control over a space object with nuclear power sources on board at a given point in time relevant to the principle concerned.

2. For the purpose of principle 9, the definition of the term "launching State" as contained in that principle is applicable.

3. For the purposes of principle 3, the terms "foreseeable" and "all possible" describe a class of events or circumstances whose overall probability of occurrence is such that it is considered to encompass only credible possibilities for purposes of safety analysis. The term "general concept of defence-in-depth" when applied to nuclear power sources in outer space refers to the use of design

features and mission operations in place of or in addition to active systems, to prevent or mitigate the consequences of system malfunctions. Redundant safety systems are not necessarily required for each individual component to achieve this purpose. Given the special requirements of space use and of varied missions, no particular set of systems or features can be specified as essential to achieve this objective. For the purposes of paragraph 2 (d) of principle 3, the term "made critical" does not include actions such as zero-power testing which are fundamental to ensuring system safety.

Principle 3. Guidelines and criteria for safe use

In order to minimize the quantity of radioactive material in space and the risks involved, the use of nuclear power sources in outer space shall be restricted to those space missions which cannot be operated by non-nuclear energy sources in a reasonable way.

1. General goals for radiation protection and nuclear safety

(a) States launching space objects with nuclear power sources on board shall endeavour to protect individuals, populations and the biosphere against radiological hazards. The design and use of space objects with nuclear power sources on board shall ensure, with a high degree of confidence, that the hazards, in foreseeable operational or accidental circumstances, are kept below acceptable levels as defined in paragraphs 1 (b) and (c).

Such design and use shall also ensure with high reliability that radioactive material does not cause a significant contamination of outer space.

(b) During the normal operation of space objects with nuclear power sources on board, including re-entry from the sufficiently high orbit as defined in paragraph 2 (b), the appropriate radiation protection objective for the public recommended by the International Commission on Radiological Protection shall be observed. During such normal operation there shall be no significant radiation exposure.

(c) To limit exposure in accidents, the design and construction of the nuclear power source systems shall take into account relevant and generally accepted international radiological protection guidelines.

Except in cases of low-probability accidents with potentially serious radiological consequences, the design for the nuclear power source systems shall, with a high degree of confidence, restrict radiation exposure to a limited geographical region and to individuals to the principal limit of 1 mSv in a year. It is permissible to use a subsidiary dose limit of 5 mSv in a year for some years, provided that the average annual effective dose equivalent over a lifetime does not exceed the principal limit of 1 mSv in a year.

The probability of accidents with potentially serious radiological consequences referred to above shall be kept extremely small by virtue of the design of the system.

Future modifications of the guidelines referred to in this paragraph shall be applied as soon as practicable.

(d) Systems important for safety shall be designed, constructed and operated in accordance with the general concept of defence-in-depth. Pursuant to this concept, foreseeable safety-related failures or malfunctions must be capable of being corrected or counteracted by an action or a procedure, possibly automatic.

The reliability of systems important for safety shall be ensured, *inter alia*, by redundancy, physical separation, functional isolation and adequate independence of their components.

Other measures shall also be taken to raise the level of safety.

2. Nuclear reactors

(a) Nuclear reactors may be operate

(i) On interplanetary missions;

(ii) In sufficiently high orbits as defined in paragraph 2 (b);

(iii) In low-Earth orbits if they are stored in sufficiently high orbits after the operational part of their mission.

(b) The sufficiently high orbit is one in which the orbital lifetime is long enough to allow for a sufficient decay of the fission products to approximately the activity of the actinides. The sufficiently high orbit must be such that the risks to existing and future outer space missions and of collision with other space objects are kept to a minimum. The necessity for the parts of a destroyed reactor also to attain the required decay time before re-entering the Earth's atmosphere shall be considered in determining the sufficiently high orbit altitude.

(c) Nuclear reactors shall use only highly enriched uranium 235 as fuel. The design shall take into account the radioactive decay of the fission and activation products.

(d) Nuclear reactors shall not be made critical before they have reached their operating orbit or interplanetary trajectory.

(e) The design and construction of the nuclear reactor shall ensure that it cannot become critical before reaching the operating orbit during all possible events, including rocket explosion, re-entry, impact on ground or water, submersion in water or water intruding into the core.

(f) In order to reduce significantly the possibility of failures in satellites with nuclear reactors on board during operations in an orbit with a lifetime less than in the sufficiently high orbit (including operations for transfer into the sufficiently high orbit), there shall be a highly reliable operational system to ensure an effective and controlled disposal of the reactor.

3. Radioisotope generators

(a) Radioisotope generators may be used for interplanetary missions and other missions leaving the gravity field of the Earth. They may also be used in Earth orbit if, after conclusion of the operational part of their mission, they are stored in a high orbit. In any case ultimate disposal is necessary.

(b) Radioisotope generators shall be protected by a containment system that is designed and constructed to withstand the heat and aerodynamic forces of re-entry in the upper atmosphere under foreseeable orbital conditions, including highly elliptical or hyperbolic orbits where relevant. Upon impact, the containment system and the physical form of the isotope shall ensure that no radioactive material is scattered into the environment so that the impact area can be completely cleared of radioactivity by a recovery operation.

Principle 4. Safety assessment

1. A launching State as defined in principle 2, paragraph 1, at the time of launch shall, prior to the launch, through cooperative arrangements, where relevant, with those which have designed, constructed or manufactured the nuclear power sources, or will operate the space object, or from whose territory or facility such an object will be launched, ensure that a thorough and comprehensive safety assessment is conducted. This assessment shall cover as well all relevant phases of the mission and shall deal with all systems involved, including the means of launching, the space platform, the nuclear power source and its equipment and the means of control and communication between ground and space.

2. This assessment shall respect the guidelines and criteria for safe use contained in principle 3.

3. Pursuant to article XI of the Treaty on Principles Governing the Activities of States in the Exploration and Use of Outer Space, including the Moon and Other Celestial Bodies, the results of this safety assessment, together with, to the extent feasible, an indication of the approximate intended time-frame of the launch, shall be made publicly available prior to each launch, and the Secretary-General of the United Nations shall be informed on how States may

obtain such results of the safety assessment as soon as possible prior to each launch.

Principle 5. Notification of re-entry

1. Any State launching a space object with nuclear power sources on board shall in a timely fashion inform States concerned in the event this space object is malfunctioning with a risk of re-entry of radioactive materials to the Earth. The information shall be in accordance with the following format:

(a) System parameters:

(i) Name of launching State or States, including the address of the authority which may be contacted for additional information or assistance in case of accident;

(ii) International designation;

(iii) Date and territory or location of launch;

(iv) Information required for best prediction of orbit lifetime, trajectory and impact region;

(v) General function of spacecraft;

(b) Information on the radiological risk of nuclear power source(s):

(i) Type of nuclear power source: radioisotopic/reactor;

(ii) The probable physical form, amount and general radiological characteristics of the fuel and contaminated and/or activated components likely to reach the ground. The term "fuel" refers to the nuclear material used as the source of heat or power.

2. The information, in accordance with the format above, shall be provided by the launching State as soon as the malfunction has become known. It shall be updated as frequently as practicable and the frequency of dissemination of the updated information shall increase as the anticipated time of re-entry into the dense layers of the Earth's atmosphere approaches so that the international community will be informed of the situation and will have sufficient time to plan for any national response activities deemed necessary.

3. The updated information shall also be transmitted to the Secretary-General of the United Nations with the same frequency.

Principle 6. Consultations

States providing information in accordance with principle 5 shall, as far as reasonably practicable, respond promptly to requests for further information or consultations sought by other States.

Principle 7. Assistance to States

1. Upon the notification of an expected re-entry into the Earth's atmosphere of a space object containing a nuclear power source on board and its components, all States possessing space monitoring and tracking facilities, in the spirit of international cooperation, shall communicate the relevant information that they may have available on the malfunctioning space object with a nuclear power source on board to the Secretary-General of the United Nations and the State concerned as promptly as possible to allow States that might be affected to assess the situation and take any precautionary measures deemed necessary.

2. After re-entry into the Earth's atmosphere of a space object containing a nuclear power source on board and its components:

(a) The launching State shall promptly offer and, if requested by the affected State, provide promptly the necessary assistance to eliminate actual and possible harmful effects, including assistance to identify the location of the area of impact of the nuclear power source on the Earth's surface, to detect the re-entered material and to carry out retrieval or clean-up operations;

(b) All States, other than the launching State, with relevant technical capabilities and international organizations with such technical capabilities shall, to the extent possible, provide necessary assistance upon request by an affected State.

In providing the assistance in accordance with subparagraphs (a) and (b) above, the special needs of developing countries shall be taken into account.

Principle 8. Responsibility

In accordance with article VI of the Treaty on Principles Governing the Activities of States in the Exploration and Use of Outer Space, including the Moon and Other Celestial Bodies, States shall bear international responsibility for national activities involving the use of nuclear power sources in outer space, whether such activities are carried on by governmental agencies or by non-governmental entities, and for assuring that such national activities are carried out in conformity with that Treaty and the recommendations contained in these Principles. When activities in outer space involving the use of nuclear power sources are carried on by an international organization, responsibility for compliance with the aforesaid Treaty and the recommendations contained in these Principles shall be borne both by the international organization and by the States participating in it.

Principle 9. Liability and compensation

1. In accordance with article VII of the Treaty on Principles Governing the Activities of States in the Exploration and Use of Outer Space, including the Moon and Other Celestial Bodies, and the provisions of the Convention on International Liability for Damage Caused by Space Objects, each State which launches or procures the launching of a space object and each State from whose

territory or facility a space object is launched shall be internationally liable for damage caused by such space objects or their component parts. This fully applies to the case of such a space object carrying a nuclear power source on board. Whenever two or more States jointly launch such a space object, they shall be jointly and severally liable for any damage caused, in accordance with article V of the above-mentioned Convention.

2. The compensation that such States shall be liable to pay under the aforesaid Convention for damage shall be determined in accordance with international law and the principles of justice and equity, in order to provide such reparation in respect of the damage as will restore the person, natural or juridical, State or international organization on whose behalf a claim is presented to the condition which would have existed if the damage had not occurred.

3. For the purposes of this principle, compensation shall include reimbursement of the duly substantiated expenses for search, recovery and clean-up operations, including expenses for assistance received from third parties.

Principle 10. Settlement of disputes

Any dispute resulting from the application of these Principles shall be resolved through negotiations or other established procedures for the peaceful settlement of disputes, in accordance with the Charter of the United Nations.

Principle 11. Review and revision

These Principles shall be reopened for revision by the Committee on the Peaceful Uses of Outer Space no later than two years after their adoption.

DECLARATION ON INTERNATIONAL COOPERATION IN THE EXPLORATION AND USE OF OUTER SPACE FOR THE BENEFIT AND IN THE INTEREST OF ALL STATES, TAKING INTO PARTICULAR ACCOUNT THE NEEDS OF DEVELOPING COUNTRIES

The General Assembly,

Having considered the report of the Committee on the Peaceful Uses of Outer Space on the work of its thirty-ninth session [1] and the text of the Declaration on International Cooperation in the Exploration and Use of Outer Space for the Benefit and in the Interest of All States, Taking into Particular Account the Needs of Developing Countries, as approved by the Committee and annexed to its report,

Bearing in mind the relevant provisions of the Charter of the United Nations,

Recalling notably the provisions of the Treaty on the Principles Governing the Activities of States in the Exploration and Use of Outer Space, including the Moon and Other Celestial Bodies, [3]

Recalling also its relevant resolutions relating to activities in outer space,

Bearing in mind the recommendations of the Second United Nations Conference on the Exploration and Peaceful Uses of Outer Space, [4] and of other international conferences relevant in this field,

Recognizing the growing scope and significance of international cooperation among States and between States and international organizations in the exploration and use of outer space for peaceful purposes,

Considering experiences gained in international cooperative ventures,

Convinced of the necessity and the significance of further strengthening international cooperation in order to reach a broad and efficient collaboration in this field for the mutual benefit and in the interest of all parties involved,

Desirous of facilitating the application of the principle that the exploration and use of outer space, including the Moon and other celestial bodies, shall be carried out for the benefit and in the interest of all countries, irrespective of their degree of economic or scientific development, and shall be the province of all mankind,

Adopts the Declaration on International Cooperation in the Exploration and Use of Outer Space for the Benefit and in the Interest of All States, Taking into Particular Account the Needs of Developing Countries, set forth in the annex to the present resolution.

Annex

Declaration on International Cooperation in the Exploration and Use of Outer Space for the Benefit and in the Interest of all States, Taking into Particular Account the Needs of Developing Countries

1. International cooperation in the exploration and use of outer space for peaceful purposes (hereafter "international cooperation") shall be conducted in accordance with the provisions of international law, including the Charter of the United Nations and the Treaty on the Principles Governing the Activities of States in the Exploration and Use of Outer Space, including the Moon and Other Celestial Bodies. It shall be carried out for the benefit and in the interest of all States, irrespective of their degree of economic, social or scientific and technological development, and shall be the province of all mankind. Particular account should be taken of the needs of developing countries.

2. States are free to determine all aspects of their participation in international cooperation in the exploration and use of outer space on an equitable and mutually acceptable basis. Contractual terms in such cooperative ventures should be fair and reasonable and they should be in full compliance with the legitimate rights and interests of the parties concerned as, for example, with intellectual property rights.

3. All States, particularly those with relevant space capabilities and with programmes for the exploration and use of outer space, should contribute to promoting and fostering international cooperation on an equitable and mutually acceptable basis. In this context, particular attention should be given to the benefit for and the interests of developing countries and countries with incipient space programmes stemming from such international cooperation conducted with countries with more advanced space capabilities.

4. International cooperation should be conducted in the modes that are considered most effective and appropriate by the countries concerned, including, inter alia, governmental and non-governmental; commercial and non-commercial; global, multilateral, regional or bilateral; and international cooperation among countries in all levels of development.

5. International cooperation, while taking into particular account the needs of developing countries, should aim, *inter alia*, at the following goals, considering their need for technical assistance and rational and efficient allocation of financial and technical resources:

(a) Promoting the development of space science and technology and of its applications;

(b) Fostering the development of relevant and appropriate space capabilities in interested States;

(c) Facilitating the exchange of expertise and technology among States on a mutually acceptable basis.

6. National and international agencies, research institutions, organizations for development aid, and developed and developing countries alike should consider the appropriate use of space

applications and the potential of international cooperation for reaching their development goals.

7. The Committee on the Peaceful Uses of Outer Space should be strengthened in its role, among others, as a forum for the exchange of information on national and international activities in the field of international cooperation in the exploration and use of outer space.

8. All States should be encouraged to contribute to the United Nations Programme on Space Applications and to other initiatives in the field of international cooperation in accordance with their space capabilities and their participation in the exploration and use of outer space.

PART III: NATIONAL LEGISLATION

FRANCE

Low no. 2008-518 of 3rd June 2008 regarding the space operations

TITLE I

DEFINITIONS

Article 1
For the purposes of this Act :
1° The term "damage" means damage to persons or property, and in particular to public health or to the environment,
directly caused by a space object as part of a space operation, to the exclusion of the consequences arising from the use of the signal transmitted by this object for users;
2° The term "space operator", thereafter referred to as "the operator": means any natural or juridical person carrying out a space operation under its responsibility and independently;
3° The term "space operation" means any activity consisting in launching or attempting to launch an object into outer space, or of ensuring the commanding of a space object during its journey in outer space, including the Moon and other celestial bodies, and, if necessary, during its return to Earth;
4° The term "launching phase" means the period of time which, as part of a space operation, starts at the moment when the launching operations become irreversible and which, without prejudice to provisions contained, if necessary, in the authorization granted pursuant to the present act, ends when the object to be put in outer space is separated from its launch vehicle.
5° The term "phase of command" means the period of time starting as part of a space operation at the moment when the object to be put in outer space is separated from its launch vehicle and ending when the first of the following events occurs:
- when the final manoeuvres for de-orbiting and the passivation activities have been completed;
- when the operator has lost control over the space object;
- the return to Earth or the full disintegration of the
space object into the atmosphere;

6° The term "third party to a space operation" means any natural or juridical person other than those taking part in the space operation or in the production of the space object(s) the launch or command of which is part of the operation. In particular, the space operator, its contractors, its subcontractors and its customers, as the contractors and subcontractors of its customers, are not regarded as third parties.

7° The term "space-based data primary operator" means any natural or juridical person ensuring the programming of an Earth observation satellite system or the reception of Earth observation data from outer space.

TITLE II
AUTHORIZATION OF SPACE OPERATIONS
CHAPTER 1
OPERATIONS SUBJECT TO AUTHORIZATION

Article 2

The following shall obtain an authorization from the administrative authority:

1° Any operator, whatever its nationality, intending to proceed with the launching of a space object from the national territory or from means or facilities falling under French jurisdiction, or intending to proceed with the return of such an object onto the national territory or onto facilities falling under French jurisdiction;

2° Any French operator intending to proceed with the launching of a space object from the territory of a foreign State or from means or facilities falling under the jurisdiction of a foreign State or from an area that is not subject to the sovereignty of a State, or intending to proceed with the return of such an object onto the territory of a foreign State or onto means and facilities falling under the jurisdiction of a foreign State or onto an area that is not subject to the sovereignty of a State;

3° Any natural person having French nationality or juridical person whose headquarters are located in France, whether it is an operator or not, intending to procure the launching of a space object or any French operator intending to command such an object during its journey in outer space.

Article 3

The transfer to a third party of the commanding of a space object which has been authorized pursuant to the terms of the present act is subject to prior authorization from the administrative authority.

Pursuant to the provisions of paragraph 3 of Article 2, any French operator intending to take the control of a space object whose launching or control has not been authorized under the present act shall obtain to this end a prior authorization from the administrative authority.

The terms of application of the present article are set forth by decree passed at the Council of State.

CHAPTER 2
CONDITIONS FOR GRANTING AUTHORIZATIONS

Article 4

Authorizations to launch, to command or to transfer the commanding of a space object launched and to proceed with its return to Earth are granted once the administrative authority has checked the moral, financial and professional guarantees of the applicant, and if necessary of its shareholders, and has ascertained that the systems and procedures that it intends to implement are compliant with the technical regulations set forth, in particular for the safety of persons and property, the protection of public health and the environment.

Authorizations cannot be granted when the operations for which they were requested, regarding in particular the systems intended to be implemented, are likely to jeopardize national defence interests or the respect by France of its international commitments.

Licenses certifying for a determined time period that a space operator satisfies moral, financial and professional guarantees may be granted by the administrative authority competent for issuing authorizations. These licenses may also attest the compliance of the systems and procedures referred to in the first paragraph with the technical regulations set forth. Lastly, these licenses may be equivalent to authorizations for certain operations.

A decree passed at the Council of State shall set forth the terms of application of the present article. It shall specify in particular:

1° The information and documents to be provided to support applications for authorizations, as well as the granting procedure for these authorizations;

2° The administrative authority competent for granting authorizations and for setting forth the technical regulations referred to in the first paragraph;

3° The conditions in which the licenses mentioned in the third paragraph can be granted, and the modes in which the beneficiary of such a license informs the administrative authority of the space operations he undertakes;

4° When an authorization is solicited for an operation which is to be carried out from the territory of a foreign State or from means or facilities falling under the jurisdiction of a foreign State, the conditions in which the administrative authority may exempt the applicant from all or any part of the compliance checking mentioned in the first paragraph, when the national and international commitments made by that State as well as its legislation and practices include sufficient guarantees regarding the safety of persons and property and the protection of public health and the environment, and liability matters.

CHAPTER III
OBLIGATIONS OF AUTHORIZATIONS HOLDERS

Article 5
The authorizations granted pursuant to the present act may include requirements set forth for the safety of persons and property, protection of public health and the environment, in particular in order to limit risks related to space debris[47].

These requirements may also be set forth in order to protect the national defence interests or to ensure the respect by France of its international commitments.

Article 6
I. – Any operator subject to authorization pursuant to the present act shall have and maintain, as long as it can be held liable pursuant to Article 13 and for the amount set out in Articles 16 and 17 a difficult situation arises when the space object cannot be identified, and as result, claims for damages can be very difficult to substantiate. the Convention failed to foresee this situation.

insurance or another financial guarantee approved by the competent authority.

A decree passed at the Council of State shall set forth the terms of insurance, the nature of the financial guarantees that may be accepted by the competent authority and the conditions in which the fulfilment of the requirements referred to in the previous paragraph is proved to the authority having granted the authorization. It also specifies conditions in which the administrative authority may exempt the operator from the requirements set out in the previous paragraph.

II. – The insurance or financial guarantee must cover the risk of having to compensate for the damages that could be caused to third parties to the space operation up to the amount mentioned in the first paragraph.

III. – The insurance or financial guarantee must cover the following persons to the extent of their liability for the damage caused by a space object:

1° The Government and its public bodies;
2° The European Space Agency and its Member States;
3° The operator and the persons having taken part in the production of the space object or in the space operation.

Article 7

I. – The following are empowered to proceed with the necessary controls in order to ascertain that the obligations set out in the present chapter are fulfilled:

1° The agents commissioned by the administrative authority mentioned in Article 2 in the conditions set forth in a decree passed at the Council of State, and belonging to the Government departments in charge of Space, Defence, Research, Environment or to its public bodies carrying out their missions in the same fields;

2° The agents empowered to perform technical checkings aboard aircrafts;

3° The members of the Insurance Control Body mentioned in Article L. 310-13 of the Insurance Code;

4° The agents mentioned in Article L. 1421-1 of the Public Health Code;

5° The administrators and inspectors of maritime affairs, the officers from the technical and administrative body of maritime affairs, the maritime affairs controller, the commandants of the State ships and aircrafts in charge of maritime surveillance.

The agents mentioned above are bound by professional confidentiality under the conditions and penalties set out by Article 226-13 and 226-14 of the Penal Code.

II. – Agents mentioned in part I. above shall have access at any time to the buildings, premises and facilities where space operations are conducted and to the space object itself. These provisions are not applicable to the part of the premises being used as a residence, except between 6 a.m. and 9 p.m. upon authorization from the President of the tribunal de grande in- stance (court of first instance of general jurisdiction) or by the judge it empowered to do so.

The operator is informed at the latest when the controlling operations begin that he may attend the operations and be assisted by any person of his choice, or that he can be represented for that purpose.

III. – As part of their controlling assignment, the agents mentioned in part I. above can ask for any document or useful item, irrespective of their medium. They can make copies and gather any necessary information and justification, in situ or upon notification.

The agents can take documents away only after having established a list countersigned by the operator. This list specifies the nature and quantity of the documents.

The operator shall be informed by the administrative authority mentioned in Article 2 of the control follow up and may transmit its observations.

If the operator or the person empowered to grant access to the building, premise or facility can not be contacted or if he denies access, the agents mentioned in part I. above may seek permission from the President of the Tribunal de grande instance, or from the judge empowered to do so.

Article 8

Concerning the launching or the control of the space object, the administrative authority, or the agents acting on its authority and empowered by it to this end, may at any moment give instructions and require any measures they consider necessary for the safety of persons and property, the protection of public health and the environment.

The administrative authority and the agents acting on its authority shall consult the operator beforehand, unless there is an immediate danger.

A decree passed at the Council of State shall specify the terms of delegation and capacitation of the agents in charge of the enforcement of the present article.

CHAPTER IV
ADMINISTRATIVE AND PENAL SANCTIONS

Article 9
The authorizations granted according to the terms of the present Act can be revoked or suspended in case the holder contravenes to its obligations, or when the operations for which they were sought are likely to jeopardise the national defence interests or the respect by France of its international commitments.

In case of suspension or withdrawal of the authorization to command a launched space object, the administrative authority may enjoin the operator to take, at its own expenses, the appropriate measures regarding the commonly admitted good rules of conduct to limit the risks of damage due to that object.

Article 10
In addition to the judicial police officers and agents acting following the prescriptions of the Code of Criminal Procedure, the sworn agents mentioned in the first paragraph of Article 7 are authorized to investigate and record breaches to the prescriptions of the present Chapter and of the texts issued for its enforcement. To this end, they exercise the powers set out in paragraphs II. and IV. of the same article.

They record these breaches in reports which are considered authentic unless the contrary is proved. They are sent to the Procureur de la République (Head of the Prosecution Department at courts of first instance of general jurisdiction) within five days after their issuing.
A decree adopted passed at the Council of State shall set forth the terms of application of the present article.

Article 11
I. – The following shall give rise to a fine of € 200 000:
1° Any operator, whatever its nationality, proceeding without authorization to the launching of a space object from the national territory or from means or facilities falling under French

jurisdiction, or to the return of such an object onto the national territory or onto means or facilities falling under French jurisdiction;

2° Any French operator proceeding without authorization to the launching of a space object from the territory of a foreign State, from means or facilities falling under the jurisdiction of a foreign State, or from an area not subject to a State's sovereignty or to the return of such an object onto the territory of a foreign State, onto means or facilities falling under the jurisdiction of a foreign State or onto an area not subject to a State's sovereignty.

3° Any natural person having French nationality or juridical person having its headquarters in France procuring the launching of a space object without authorization, or commanding it without authorization during its journey into outer space.

II. – The following shall give rise to a fine of € 200 000:

1° Transferring to a third party without authorization the commanding of a space object which launching or commanding has been authorized according to the terms of the present act;

2° Any French operator undertaking without authorization the commanding of a space object which launching has not been authorized according to the present law.

III. – An operator shall be fined € 200 000 in the case of:

1° pursuing the space operation in breach of an administrative measure or court decision ordering its ceasing or suspension;

2° pursuing the space operation without complying with an administrative summon to comply with a prescription.

IV. – Is fined € 200 000 the fact for operators or individuals to prevent controls undertaken pursuant to Article 7.

TITLE III
REGISTRATION OF LAUNCHED SPACE OBJECTS

Article 12

In the event France has a registration obligation according to Article II of the Convention dated 14 September 1975 relating to

Registration of objects launched into outer space, and, if necessary, of other international agreements, the launched space objects are registered in a registry hold by the Centre National d'Etudes Spatiales on behalf of the State, following the prescriptions set out in a decree passed at the Council of State.

TITLE IV
LIABILITY
CHAPTER 1
LIABILITY TOWARDS THIRD PARTIES

Article 13
The operator shall be solely liable for damages caused to third parties by the space operations which it conducts in the following conditions:

1° He shall be absolutely liable for damages caused on the ground or in airspace;

2° He shall be liable only due to his fault for damages caused elsewhere than on the ground or in airspace. This liability may only be reduced or set aside in case the fault of the victim is proven.

Except in case of wilful misconduct, the liability set forth in 1° and 2° ends when all the obligations set out in the authorization or the license are fulfilled, or at the latest one year after the date on which these obligations should have been fulfilled. The Government shall be liable in the operator's place for damages occurring after this period.

Article 14
When the Government has paid compensation for damage according to the stipulations of the Treaty dated 27 January 1967 relating to Principles Governing the Activities of States in the Exploration and Use of outer Space, including the Moon and other Celestial Bodies, or of the Convention dated 19 march 1972 relating to International Liability for Damage caused by Space Objects, it may present a claim for indemnification against the operator having caused the damage for which France was held internationally liable, to the extent that the Government has not already benefited from the insurance or financial guarantees of the operator up to the amount of the compensation.

If the damage was caused by a space object used as a part of an operation authorized according to the terms of the present Act, the claim for indemnification may be brought:

1° within the limit of the amount set out pursuant to the conditions mentioned in article 16 in the case of damage caused during the launching phase;

2° within the limit of the amount set out pursuant to the conditions mentioned in Article 17 in the case of damage caused after the launching phase, including when the space object returns to Earth.

In case of a willful misconduct of the operator, the limitations set out in 1° and 2° shall not apply.

The Government shall not present a claim for indemnification if the damage was caused by a space object used as a part of an operation authorized according to the terms of the present
Act and resulting from acts targeting governmental interests.

Article 15

When an operator has been condemned to compensate a third party for a damage caused by a space object used as a part of an operation authorized according to the terms of the present Act, and if that operation has been undertaken from the French territory or from the territory of another Member State of the European Union or from the territory of a State party to the European Economic Area Agreement, or from means or facilities falling under the jurisdiction of France or another Member State of the European Union or of a State party to the European Economic Area Agreement, that operator shall benefit, except in case of a willful misconduct, from the governmental guarantee, according to the terms of the Finance Act:

1° For the part of the compensation exceeding the amount set out in the conditions mentioned in Article 16, in the case of a damage caused during the launching phase;

2° For the part of the compensation exceeding the amount set out in the conditions mentioned in Article 17, in the case of a damage caused on the ground or in airspace after the launching phase, including when the space object returns to Earth.

In the case of damage caused during the launching phase, the governmental guarantee shall benefit, if necessary and in the conditions set out in the paragraphs above, to the persons who are not third parties to a space operation pursuant to the present Act.

Article 16

Within the framework set forth in the Finance Act, the authorization granted pursuant to the present Act shall set out, given the risks incurred and regarding in particular the characteristics of the launching site, the amount respectively below and beyond which the claim for indemnification is exercised and the governmental guarantee is granted, in the case of a damage caused during the launching phase.

Article 17
Within the framework set forth in the Finance Act, the authorization granted pursuant to the present Act shall set out, given the risks incurred, the amount respectively below and beyond which the claim for indemnification is exercised and the governmental guarantee is granted, in the case of a damage caused after the launching phase.

Article 18
Any person questioned before a court because of a damage for which he could benefit from the governmental guarantee shall inform the competent administrative authority, which may exercise all the defense rights in the proceedings on behalf of the Government. If he fails to do so, the questioned person shall be deemed to having waived to the governmental guarantee.

CHAPTER II
LIABILITY TOWARDS PERSONS TAKING PART IN THE SPACE OPERATION

Article 19
When the insurance or financial guarantee mentioned in Article 6 as well as, if necessary, the governmental guarantee have been laid out to indemnify a third party, one of the persons having taken part in the space operation or in the production of the space object which caused the damage cannot be held liable by another of these persons, except in case of a willful misconduct.

Article 20
In the case of a damage caused by a space operation or the production of a space object to a person taking part in this operation or in that production, any other person taking part in the space operation or in the production of the space object having caused the damage and bound to the previous one by a contract cannot be held liable because of that damage, unless otherwise expressly stipulated regarding the damage caused during the production phase of a space object which is to be commanded in outer space or during its commanding in orbit, or in case of a willful misconduct.

TITLE V
PROVISIONS RELATING TO THE RESEARCH CODE

Article 21

The Research Code is amended as follows:

1° Article L. 331-6 is drafted as follows:

"Art. L. 331-6. – I. – The President of the Centre National d'Etudes Spatiales shall exercise on behalf of the State the special Police for the exploitation of the facilities of the Guiana Space Centre, within a perimeter defined by the competent administrative authority. As such, it shall be in charge of a general mission of safeguard consisting in controlling the technical risks related to the preparation and carrying out of the launches from the Guiana Space Centre in order to ensure the protection of persons, property, public health and the environment, on the ground and during the flight, and it shall set out to this end the specific regulations applicable within the limits of the perimeter defined above.

"II. Under the authority of the Government representative in the Département of Guiana, the President of the Centre National d'Etudes Spatiales shall coordinate the implementation by companies and other entities settled in the perimeter defined in part I. above of measures taken in order to ensure the security of the facilities and of the activities undertaken therein, and shall verify that those companies and agencies fulfill their obligations in this respect.

"III. To the extent strictly necessary for the accomplishment of the missions set out in parts I. and II., the agents empowered by the President of the Centre National d'Etudes Spatiales have access to the land and premises used exclusively for professional purposes and occupied by the companies and agencies settled at the Guiana Space Centre in the perimeter defined in part I. above."

2°Articles L. 331-7 and L. 331-8 are inserted after Article L. 331-6 and are drafted as follows: "Art. L. 331-7. – The President of the Centre National d'Etudes Spatiales may take for any space operation, by delegation of the administrative authority mentioned in Article 8 of the Act n° 2008-518 dated June 3rd relating to space operations, the necessary measures provided for in the same article to ensure the safety of persons and property, as well as the protection of public health and the environment."

"Art. L. 331-8. – A decree passed at the Council of State shall set forth the terms of application of the present chapter, particularly the conditions in which the President of the Centre National d'Etudes Spatiales may delegate its competence mentioned in Article L. 331-6."

TITLE VI
INTELLECTUAL PROPERTY

Article 22
I. – Article L. 611-1 of the Intellectual Property Code is completed by a paragraph drafted as follows:
"Unless otherwise provided in an international agreement to which France is a party, the provisions of the present article apply to the inventions made or used in outer space, including onto celestial bodies and into or onto space objects placed under national jurisdiction according to article VIII of the Treaty dated 27 January 1967 relating to Principles Governing the Activities of States in the Exploration and Use of Outer Space, including the Moon and other celestial bodies."

II. – Article L. 613-5 of the same Code is completed by an
e) drafted as follows:
"e) To the objects intended to be launched in outer space brought onto the French territory."

TITLE VII
SPACE-BASED DATA

Article 23
Any primary space-based data operator undertaking in France an activity having certain technical characteristics defined in a decree passed at the Council of State must preliminarily declare it to the competent administrative authority.

These technical characteristics are related in particular to the resolution, location accuracy, observation frequency band and quality of the Earth observation data which are received or for which a satellite system is programmed.

Article 24
The competent administrative authority ascertains that the activity undertaken by the primary operators of space-based data

does not harm fundamental interests of the Nation, particularly defence matters, foreign policy and international commitments of France.

To this end, it may at any time prescribe measures restraining the activity of the primary space-based data operators, which are necessary to safeguard these interests.

Article 25

Any primary space-based data operator undertaking an activity showing the technical characteristics mentioned in Article 23 shall be fined € 200 000 in the case:

1° it fails to proceed with the declaration mentioned in Article 23;

2° it fails to comply with the restriction measures taken pursuant to Article 24.

TITLE VIII
TRANSITORY AND FINAL PROVISIONS

Article 26

The present Act does not apply to the launching and guiding, for the needs of national defence, of vehicles which trajectory passes through outer space, in particular ballistic missiles.

The activities of the Ministry of Defence acting as primary space-based data operator are not subject to the provisions of Title VII.

Article 27

As they fall under the scope of a public mission assigned to the Centre National d'Etudes Spatiales after approval by the administrative authority pursuant to paragraph 4 of Article L. 331-2 of the Research Code, the operations of launching, returning to Earth, commanding or transfer of commanding of a space object are not subject to the provisions of Titles II and IV, and the Earth observation satellite activities and the reception of Earth observation data are not subject to the provisions of Title VII

Article 28

Article L. 331-2 of the Research Code is completed by an f), a g) and an h) drafted as follows:

"f) To assist the Government in the definition of the technical regulations relating to space operations;

"g) To verify, by delegation of the minister in charge of space, that the systems and procedures implemented by the space operators comply with the technical regulation mentioned in paragraph f);

"h) To hold the register of the space objects on behalf of the Government."

Article 29

Articles 16 and 17 of the present Act shall enter into force at the date of publication of the Finance Act setting out the minimum and the maximum amounts between which is included the amount beyond which the governmental guarantee is granted.

Article 30

The provisions of the present Act are applicable in New Caledonia, in French Polynesia, in the Islands of Wallis and Futuna and in the French southern and Antarctic lands.

This Act shall be implemented as a State Act.
Paris, 3rd of June 2008

REPUBLIC OF KOREA

Law No.8852 of 8852 of Dec. 21, 2007 - Space Liability Act[48]

Article 1 (Purpose)
The purpose of this act is to protect the aggrieved party and to contribute to the sound development of space activities by deciding the extent of damages and the limit of liability in case the damage occurs by the space activities.

Article 2 (Definitions)
The terms in this act are defined as follows:
2.1. "Space objects" means the space objects defined at Article 2.3 of the space development promotion act.
2.2. "launching party" means a person who makes a preliminary registration or formal registration in accordance with Article 8, or a person who obtains a launch permit in accordance with Article 11 of the space development promotion act.
2.3. "launching" means the launching of a space object by the person who obtains a launch permit under Article 11.1 of the space development promotion act and includes preparation of launching, test launching and failed launching.
2.4. "space damage" means physical damage such as death, bodily injury or other impairment of health of the 3rd party and property loss such as destruction of, damage to or loss of property according to launching and operation of space objects.

Article 3 (Relation to International Treaties)
3.1. In the event the Korean government has paid compensation for damage to a foreign state according to the "Convention on International Liability for Damage caused by Space Objects", the Korean government may present a claim for indemnification to the launching party.

[48] Unofficial English Translation

3.2. The application of this act can be prevented or limited to the natural, legal person, organization or the government of the state which prevents or limits compensation for damage caused by space objects to the natural, legal person, organization or the government of Korea.

Article 4 (Absolute liability and waiver of liability)

4.1. In case space damage occurs, the launching party shall have responsibility to pay compensation. However, in case of space damage caused by armed conflict, hostile activity, civil war or rebellion or caused in outer space, the launching party shall be liable only if the damage is due to his wilful misconduct or negligence.

4.2. The launching party who paid compensation for damage caused by the 3rd party's wilful misconduct or negligence may present a claim for indemnification to that 3rd party. However, if the damage was due to the supply of components, materials or service (including, labor service), the launching party may present a claim for indemnification to the supplier only if the damage is due to wilful misconduct or gross negligence of the supplier or his employees.

4.3. "Product Liability Act" is not applied for space damage.

Article 5 (limit on compensation)

The amount of compensation to be paid by the launching party is limited to two hundred billion (200,000,000,000) won.

Article 6 (Third-party liability insurance)

6.1. Any person seeking to obtain a launch permit for space launch vehicles according to Article 11 of "Space Development Promotion Act" shall insure against the 3rd party liability.

6.2. The minimum amount of the 3rd party liability insurance in accordance with Article 6.1 of this Act is, within the compensation limit under Article 5, set by ordinance of the Ministry of Education, Science and Technology with consideration of the characteristics of space objects, the difficulties of technology, circumstances around the launch site and the domestic and foreign insurance markets.

Article 7 (governmental measures)

7.1. The government shall take necessary actions to rescue the victims and to prevent further damage when space damage occurs.

7.2. The government may provide the launching party with the financial support, when it thinks appropriate in order to achieve the purpose of this Act in case the amount of the compensation under Article 4.1 would exceed the insured amount under Article 6.2.

7.3 The support from the government under Article 7.2 shall be limited to the extent allowed by the National Congress resolution.

Article 8 (Lapse of right)

8.1. The right of claim for compensation under this Act will lapse unless the aggrieved party or his legal representative would not make a claim within one year after the day on which the person became aware of the damage and the responsible party under Article 4.1 of this Act.

8.2. The right of claim for compensation under this Act will lapse after three years after the day on which the space damage occurs.

Additional Clauses

1. (Enforcement Date) This Act takes effect six(6) months from the date of promulgation.

2. (Amendment of other Act) The Space Development Promotion Act will be amended as follows:
Article 15 is deleted.

Space Development Promotion Act
Law Number 7538 of May 31, 2005

Article 1 (Purpose)

The purpose of this act is to promote the peaceful use and scientific exploration of outer space, to ensure national security, to further develop the national economy, and to raise the national standard of living through the systematic promotion of space development and the effective use and management of space objects.

Article 2 (Definitions)

The terms in this act are defined as follows:
1. "Space development" means any one of the following items:
(a) Research activities and technology development activities relevant to the design, manufacturing, launch, and/or operation of space objects and
(b) The use and exploration of outer space as well as activities that promote such activities.
2. "Space development project" means projects that promote space development and projects that promote the development of the relevant sectors in education, technology, information, and industry, etc.
3. "Space objects" are objects designed and manufactured for use in outer space including space launch vehicles, artificial satellites, and spaceships and their components.
4. "Space accident" means an accident causing loss of life, personal injury or damage to property due to the fall, collision, or explosion of space objects and/or similar situations.
5. "Satellite information" means imagery, voice, sound, data or any information resulting from the combination of the above (including its processing and use) gained from artificial satellites.

Article 3 (Government Responsibilities)

(1) The Korean government shall carry out space development in conformity with space treaties concluded with other countries and international organizations, and shall use outer space peacefully.
(2) The Korean government shall plan and implement overall policies for space development.

Article 4 (Relation to Other Acts)

Subject to provisions in other Acts, this Act shall apply to the promotion of space development and to the use and management of space objects.

Article 5 (Establishing Basic Plan for Promoting Space Development)

(1) The Korean government shall establish a basic plan (hereinafter referred to as "Basic Plan") for promoting space development and for using and managing space objects. The Basic Plan shall include the following items:
1. Purpose and scope of space development policies;
2. Organizational structure and strategy for space development;
3. Implementation plan for space development;
4. Plans for expanding the foundation and infrastructure necessary for space development;
5. Investment planning for obtaining the financial resources necessary for space development;
6. Plans for training specialists necessary for space development;
7. Outlines for international cooperation to promote space development;
8. Guidelines for promoting space development projects;
9. Matters related to the use and management of space objects;
10. Practical applications using the results of space development, such as satellite information, etc; and
11. Other provisions designated by Presidential Decree for the promotion of space development and the use and management of space objects.

(2) The Korean government shall develop a Basic Plan every five(5) years and it shall be confirmed by the National Space Committee in accordance with Article 6.1. When amending the Basic Plan, the same procedure shall apply, except for minor changes set by the Presidential Decree.

(3) The Minister of Science and Technology shall release the confirmed Basic Plan and develop an execution plan in accordance with the Basic Plan every year. This execution plan shall be deliberated on by the heads of related central administrative agencies(the "head of the National Intelligence Service" is included hereinafter); Information concerning national security may not be released.

Article 6 (National Space Committee) (1) The National Space Committee (hereinafter referred to as "Committee") is established and placed under the control of the President to deliberate provisions regarding space development including establishing the Basic Plan, etc.

(2) The Committee deliberates on the issues listed below. In the case of Subsection 6, the deliberation may be omitted if deemed necessary for reasons of national security, etc:

1. The Basic Plan;
2. Primary government policies relevant to the Basic Plan; and the role of related central administrative agencies (the "National Intelligence Service" is included hereinafter);
3. Designation and management of Space Development Institutes in accordance with Article 7;
4. Assessment of the use and management of space development projects;
5. Generation of the financial resources necessary for space development projects and an investment plan;
6. Launch permits for space objects;
7. Modification of space development activities pursuant to Article 19.2; and
8. Other provisions the Chair submits to the Committee.

(3) The Committee is composed of no more than fifteen (15) members including the Chair.

(4) The Minister of Science and Technology shall be Chair of the Committee. other members of the committee shall be:

1. Heads and public servants of related central administrative agencies designated by Presidential Decree; and
2. Civilian experts having extensive knowledge and experience in the area of space development who are appointed by the President.

(5) The Committee shall have a Practical Affairs Subcommittee for the Promotion of Space Development to carry out its affairs effectively; the Vice-Minister of Science and Technology assumes the chair of this subcommittee.

(6) Details relevant to the implementation and operation of the Committee and the Practical Affairs Subcommittee for the Promotion of Space Development are determined by Presidential Decree.

Article 7 (Designation as a Space Development Institute)

(1) The Minister of Science and Technology may designate and support an expert body (hereinafter referred to as "Space Development Institute") to systematically and effectively implement space development projects.

(2) The Space Development Institute carries out the following projects:
1. Execution of space development projects in accordance with the Basic Plan;
2. Integrated development, launch, and operation of space objects; and
3. Other affairs relevant to space development projects set by Presidential Decree.
(3) The details regarding the designation criteria, and support, etc for the Space Development Institute are set by Presidential Decree.

Article 8 (Domestic Registration of Space Objects)

(1) If Korean citizens (legal or natural. The same shall apply hereinafter) desire to launch a space object (excluding space launch vehicles, the same applies in8, 9 and 10) inside or outside of the country, a preliminary registration shall be made to the Minister of Science and Technology in accordance with Presidential Decree one hundred and eighty (180) days before the scheduled launch date. (2) The conditions under which foreigners shall make a preliminary registration to the Minister of Science and Technology in accordance with Article 8.1 are following items:
1. Launching in an area or facility within Korean territory or its jurisdiction; or
2. Launching in a foreign country, utilizing a space launch vehicle owned by the Korean government or Korean citizens.
(3) Any person wanting to make a preliminary registration of space objects in accordance with Articles 8.1 and 8.2 shall provide a launch plan which includes all of the following provisions:
1. Use and purpose of the space object;
2. Ownership or user of the space object;
3. Estimated lifetime and operation period of the space object;
4. Launch site and scheduled launch date of the space object;
5. Basic orbital parameters of the space object;
6. Launch vehicle provider and launch vehicle performance and specifications;
7. Liability for damage arising out of a space accident;
8. Manufacturer, manufacturing number and manufacturing date of the space object; and
9. Other provisions relevant to the launch, use, and management of space objects set by Presidential Decree.
(4) If the Minister of Science and Technology reviews the launch plan under Article 8.3 and concludes that the plan does not

demonstrate adequate liability for damage in accordance with Article 14, the Minister may demand further revisions.

(5) Any person, who makes a preliminary registration of space objects according to Articles 8.1 and 8.2, shall then formally register the space objects with the Minister of Science and Technology in accordance with Presidential Decree within ninety (90) days after the space object reaches its planned orbit, except for space objects registered in foreign countries under agreement with the government of the launching country in accordance with the "Convention on Registration of Objects Launched into Outer Space."

(6) If there are changes to any item of Article 8.3, parties having filed the preliminary registration of space objects under Articles 8.1 and 8.2 or formally registered space objects under Article 8.5 shall report the change(s) to the Minister of Science and Technology within fifteen (15) days from the date of the change(s).

Article 9 (International Registration of Space Objects)

(1) If space objects are registered according to Article 8.5, the Minister of Science and Technology shall register the objects with the United Nations by way of the Minister of Foreign Affairs and Trade in accordance with "Convention on Registration of Objects Launched into Outer Space," with the exception of satellites to be registered with the United Nations in accordance with "Radio Wave Act" Article 44.1.

(2) If there are any changes in the contents registered to the United Nations in accordance with Article 9.1 due to the termination, etc. of space objects, the Minister of Science and Technology shall inform the United Nations via the Minister of Foreign Affairs and Trade.

Article 10 (Management of Space Objects Registry)

The Minister of Science and Technology shall maintain and manage the preliminary registry and the formal registry of space objects in accordance with Ministerial Decree of the Ministry of Science and Technology.

Article 11 (A Launch permit of a Space Launch Vehicle)

(1) If a person who wants to launch a space launch vehicle falls under any of the following subsections, the person shall obtain a permit from the Minister of Science and Technology. Changes to the permitted item shall also be permitted by the Minister of Science and Technology except for minor changes set by Presidential

Decree, of which the person seeking a launch permit shall report the changes within thirty (30) days after the changes are made:
1. Launching in an area or facility within Korean territory or its jurisdiction; or
2. Launching in a foreign country, utilizing a space launch vehicle owned by the Korean government or Korean citizens.
(2) Any person who wants to obtain a launch permit in accordance with Article 11.1 shall, according to Presidential Decree, submit to the Minister of Science and Technology a launch plan including a safety analysis report, a payloads operation plan, and the damage liability coverage.
(3) The Minister of Science and Technology shall consider the following subsections when granting a launch permit according to Article 11.1:
1. Use and purpose of the space launch vehicle;
2. Safety management of the space launch vehicle;
3. Financial capability including liability insurance for damages occurring from a space accident; and
4. Other items, which are set by Ministerial Decree from the Ministry of Science and Technology, necessary for launch and launch preparations, including the transportation of space launch vehicles.
(4) The Minister of Science and Technology may make any necessary stipulations when granting a permit according to Article 11.1.

Article 12 (Disqualification)

Any person who falls under any of the following sections shall not obtain a launch permit for space launch vehicles in accordance with Article 11.:
1. Any person deemed incompetent or quasi-incompetent;
2. Any person who is bankrupt at the time of registration;
3. Any person who is within two years after the date of completion (including deemed completion) or commutation of a prison sentence for violating this Act;
4. Any person on probation for violating this Act; and
5. Any corporation represented by a person who falls under Articles 12.1 to 12.4.

Article 13 (Cancellation of Launch Permit and the Hearing)

(1) The Minister of Science and Technology may revoke a launch permit for any reason which falls under the following subsections:
1. Delay of the launch for more than one (1) year from the permitted launch date without due cause;
2. Obtaining a launch permit by false means;
3. A request by the head of a related central administrative agency in anticipation of a serious threat to security;
4. Abnormalities in the safety management of the space launch vehicle before launch including fuel leakage, and communication system defects, etc;
5. Violation of Article 11.1 due to a failure to obtain a permit for changes; or
6. The person who obtained the launch permit for the space launch vehicle falls under any part of Article 12. However, in the case of Article 12.5, an exception is made when the representative has been replaced within three (3) months from the date of disqualification.
(2) If the Minister of Science and Technology intends to cancel the launch permit of a space launch vehicle under Article 13.1, a hearing shall be held. In cases that fall under Article 13.1.3 and 13.1.4, the Minister may forgo the hearing process.

Article 14 (Liability for Damages due to Space Accidents)

A person who launches space objects according to Articles 8 and 11 shall assume the liability for damages owing to space accidents caused by the space objects. The scope of liability for damages and the limit of responsibility are specified by other laws.

Article 15 (Third-Party Liability Insurance)

(1) Any person seeking to obtain a launch permit for space launch vehicles according to Article 11 shall insure against any liability. The third-party liability insurance shall be of an amount capable of compensating for damage possibly occurring due to space accidents.
(2) The minimum amount of third-party liability insurance in accordance with 15.1 is set by Ministerial decree of the Ministry of Science and Technology with consideration of the domestic and foreign insurance markets.

Article 16 (Formation of a Space Accident Inquiry Committee)

(1) The Minister of Science and Technology may form a Space Accident Inquiry Committee under the supervision of the Minister

of Science and Technology to investigate space accidents which are defined by Presidential Decree.
(2) The Space Accident Inquiry Committee will consist of five (5) to eleven (11) members including the chair. Committee members shall be nominated from specialists in related fields by the Minister of Science and Technology. The Chair shall be appointed from among the committee members by the Minister of Science and Technology. In case the space accident is involved in national security which is determined by Presidential Decree, a separate Space Accident Inquiry Committee may be formed by Presidential Decree.
(3) The Space Accident Inquiry Committee may investigate a person falling under any one of following items. In this case, the person to be investigated shall, unless the person has a valid reason not to, comply with the investigation:
1. Any person who has submitted a preliminary registration or formal registration of space objects in accordance with Article 8;
2. Any person who has obtained a launch permit for a space launch vehicle in accordance with Article 11 ; and
3. Any other person related to the space object such as the manufacturer, and performance tester, etc.
(4) The Space Accident Inquiry Committee may request cooperation from the heads of the related administrative agencies in connection with access control to the area of a space accident and other investigations of relevance. The head of the related administrative agency receiving the request shall comply with the request, unless the agency has a valid reason not to.
(5) Details relevant to the formation date, member qualifications and management, etc. of the Space Accident Inquiry Committee shall be set by Presidential Decree.

Article 17 (Utilization of Satellite Information)

(1) The Minister of Science and Technology may take action, such as designating or establishing an agency responsible for promoting the distribution and use of satellite information gained by artificial satellites developed in accordance with the Basic Plan. In this case, geographical information relevant to the "Act on the Establishment and Utilization of National Geographic Information System" shall be discussed with the Minister of Construction and Transportation.
(2) The Minister of Science and Technology may provide funding for promoting the distribution and use of satellite information within the budgetary limits.
(3) The government shall make every effort not to invade the privacy of individuals when using satellite information.

Article 18 (Support of Civil Space Development Activities)

(1) The Minister of Science and Technology shall adopt policies to promote private space development activities and R&D investment by providing space development man power, tax benefits and financial support, and procurement, etc.
(2) The Minister of Science and Technology may request cooperation from the heads of related central administrative agencies for support of policies in accordance with Article 18.1.

Article 19 (Suspension and Modification of Space Development Activities)

(1) If the Minister of Defense requests the Minister of Science and Technology the suspension of space development activities by Korean citizens for the carrying out of military operations during a time of war, national emergency or situations of similar proportion, the Minister of Science and Technology shall order the suspension of such space development activities to the Korean citizens.
(2) If the head of a related central administrative agency requests the Minister of Science and Technology the modification of space development activities by Korean citizens for reasons of public order or national security, the Minister of Science and Technology may order the modification of such space development activities to the Korean citizens after deliberation by the National Space Committee.

Article 20 (Requesting and Cooperation for Space Development)

(1) The Minister of Science and Technology may request support and cooperation on the following from the heads of related central administrative agencies or the heads of local self-governing bodies if deemed necessary for the implementation of space development activities. In this case, the heads of the related central administrative agencies or local self-governing bodies shall comply unless the agency or body has a valid reason not to:
1. Access control to the surrounding area (including territorial waters and air space) used for the domestic launch of space objects; and
2. Matters related to communications, fire control, emergency salvage and rescue, and safety management, etc.
(2) When the Minister of Science and Technology requests support and cooperation in accordance with Article 20.1, the request shall be

limited to the minimum level required for the implementation of the space development activities.

Article 21 (Implementation of Space Development Activities Relevant to National Security)

(1) The Minister of Science and Technology shall discuss with the head of the related central administrative agencies in advance when implementing space development activities relevant to national security.
(2) Necessary provisions on the establishment and execution of security measures for the space development project falling under Article 21.1 shall be set by Presidential Decree.

Article 22 (Rescue of Astronauts)

When astronauts from a foreign space object makes an emergency landing, is lost, or is involved in an accident in Korean territory or neighboring international waters, the Korean government will render them necessary assistance and return them to the country of launch, country of registration or international organization responsible for the launch of the said space object.

Article 23 (Return of Space Objects)

In the case of foreign space objects falling to or making an emergency landing on Korean territory, the Korean government will return the foreign space objects to the country of launch, country of registration or international organization responsible for the launch of the space objects.

Article 24 (Collection of information and fact-finding surveys on Space Development Activities)

(1) The Minister of Science and Technology may collect information and conduct fact-finding surveys on space development activities and space industry for the systematic promotion and effective implementation of space development activities.
(2) The Minister of Science and Technology may request the related central administrative agencies, research centers, educational organizations, or related companies to submit relevant data or statements if deemed necessary for conducting domestic fact-finding surveys in accordance with Article 24.1.
(3) Details concerning the scope, period, and procedure for the collection of information or fact-finding surveys in accordance with Article 24.1 shall be set by Presidential Decree.

Article 25 (Confidentiality)

Any person currently engaged or previously engaged in any work under this Act shall not disclose any information they encounter during their duty, or not use that information except for the purpose of this Act.

Article 26 (Consignment of Power)

By Presidential Decree, the Minister of Science and Technology may consign the following activities to government-funded research institutes in the area of science and technology established in accordance with "the Law on the Establishment, Operation and Promotion of Government-Funded Research Institutes in the Area of Science and Technology" or other related expert institutes:
1. Safety review relevant to the permits or permits for changes in accordance with Article 11.1; and
2. Collection of information and fact-finding surveys on space development activities and space industry in accordance with Article 24.

Article 27 (Penalty Clauses)

(1) Any person not obtaining a permit (including a permit for changes) in accordance with Article 11.1 who launches a space launch vehicle shall be sentenced to imprisonment for up to five (5) years, or face fines not exceeding fifty million (50,000,000) Won.
(2) Any person who falls under any of the following items shall be sentenced to imprisonment for up to three (3) years, or face fines not exceeding thirty million (30,000,000) Won.:
1. Any person who does not comply with a suspension or modification order in accordance with Article 19; and
2. Any person who violates Article 25.

Article 28 (Dual Penalization)

If a representative, agent, servant or other employee of a legal entity or an agent, servant or other employee of an individual violates Article 27, the offender shall face punishment. In addition, the legal entity itself and the individual himself shall be fined in accordance with Article 27.Article 29 (Penalty) (1) Any person falling under any of the following sections shall be sentenced to a fine not exceeding ten million (10,000,000) won.:
1. Any person who violates Article 8.1 or 8.2 by failing to make a preliminary registration of space objects;

2. Any person who violates Article 8.5 by failing to make a formal registration of space objects; or
3. Any person who violates the proviso of Article 11.1 by failing to report changes.
(2) Any person falling under any of the following sections shall be sentenced to a fine not exceeding five million (5,000,000) won:
1. Any person who violates Article 8.6 by failing to inform or falsely informing about any changes within fifteen (15) days of the change; and
2. Any person who denies, interferes, or evades the investigation of an accident in accordance with Article 16.3.
(3) The Minister of Science and Technology shall impose and collect the fines stated in Article 29.1 and 29.2 according to Presidential Decree.
(4) Any person who does not agree with the fine imposed in accordance with Article 29.3 may make an objection to the Minister of Science and Technology within thirty (30) days of notice of the fine.
(5) If the person who was fined based on Article 29.3 raises an objection in accordance with Article 29.4, the Minister of Science and Technology shall inform this fact to the governing court without delay. The informed court shall hold a trial on the imposed fine in accordance with "the Voluntary Matters Proceedings Act."
(6) If the person does not raise an objection within the period stated in Article 29.4 nor pay the fine, the fine shall be paid in accordance with the procedure of disposition for failure of tax payment.

Additional Clauses

1. (Enforcement Date) This Act takes effect six (6) months from the date of promulgation.
2. (Intermediate Measures for the Basic Plan) Until the Basic Plan for Promoting Space Development stated in Article 5 is established, the Mid-to-Long Term Space Development Basic Plan, which was reviewed by the Committee of National Science and Technology in accordance with Article 9 of "Basic Law of Science and Technology", shall be regarded as the Basic Plan for Promoting Space Development.
3. (Intermediate Measures for the Registration of Space Objects) Space objects registered with the United Nations by the Republic of Korea prior to this Act are regarded as registered space objects in accordance with Article 8.

ITALY

Law 23, 25 January 1983 49 - Norms for the implementation for the Convention on International Liability for Damage caused by Space Objects, signed in London, Moscow and Washington
March 29, 1972.

Art.1.
The present law applies in cases of damage caused by space objects launched by foreign States which are party to the Convention on International Liability for Damage caused by Space Objects, signed in London, Moscow and Washington 29 March 1972, and which will be referred to as the Convention in the following provisions.

For the purposes of the present law the definitions contained in Article 1 of the Convention apply.

Art.2.
Italian persons, natural and juridical, can obtain compensation from the Italian State for the damage indicated in Article 1 to the extent which the Italian State has requested and obtained, in accordance with Article VIII, n. 1 of the Convention, compensation from the launching State for damage caused to them.

In the case that the Italian State has not presented a request under Article VIII, n.1, of the Convention, it has an obligation to compensate those persons indicated in the first clause for damage suffered, as long as the State on whose territory the damage occurred or the State in which the aforementioned persons are permanent residents have not requested and obtained compensation for the same damage from the launching State in accordance with respectively Article VIII, n. 2 or n. 3 of the Convention.

Natural and juridical persons can obtain from the Italian State compensation for damage stated in Article 1 when and in the measure which the Italian State requested and obtained the compensation for said damage from the launching State following Article VIII, n. 2 or n. 3, of the Convention.

Art.3.
The Italian State has the obligation to compensate natural and juridical Italians for the damage indicated in Article 1 even when it has formulated a request under Article VIII, n. 1 of the Convention but that request remains unsatisfied.

Art.4.
Persons may, under Article 2, request compensation for damage from the Italian State within five years following the date on which the damage occurred or of the date on which the effects of that damage are exhausted.

Art.5.
The responsibility of the Italian State towards those persons indicated in Articles 2 and 3 for the damage indicated in Article 1 is absolute in nature and does not admit exoneration.
In the cases provided in Article 2, clause 2 and in Article 3 the level of compensation is established in accordance with Articles 2056, 1223, and 1226 of the Civil Code and the victim may request restitution under the terms of Article 2058 of the Civil Code.

Art.6.
The provisions of the preceding Articles are not applicable in the case that the persons damaged by a space object have made direct representation to the courts or administrative bodies of a launching State seeking compensation for damage caused by a space object.

NETHERLANDS

Rules Concerning Space Activities and the Establishment of a Registry of Space Objects (Space Activities Act)[50]

BILL
(13.06.06)

We Beatrix, by the grace of God Queen, Princess of Orange-Nassau, etc., etc., etc.

Greetings to all who shall see or hear these presents! Be it known: Whereas We have considered that it is necessary to lay down rules with regard to space activities and the establishment and management of a registry of space objects; We, therefore, having heard the Council of State, and in consultation with the States General, have approved and decreed as We hereby approve and decree:

CHAPTER 1. GENERAL PROVISIONS

Section 1

The following definitions shall apply in this Act and its constituent provisions:
a. Our Minister: Our Minister of Economic Affairs;
b. space activities: the launch, the flight operation or the guidance of space objects in outer space;
c. space object: any object launched or destined to be launched into outer space;
d. Dutch ship: a ship as referred to in Section 1, paragraph b, of the Netherlands Seafarers Manning Act;
e. Dutch aircraft: an aircraft registered in the Netherlands under

Section 3.3 of the Aviation Act;
f. Outer Space Treaty: the Treaty on Principles Governing the Activities of States in the Exploration and Use of Outer Space, including the Moon and Other Celestial Bodies (Bulletin of Treaties 1967, 31), concluded on 27 January 1967 in London/Moscow/Washington;
g. Liability Convention: the Convention on International Liability for Damage Caused by Space Objects (Bulletin of Treaties 1981, 37), concluded on 29 March 1972 in London/Moscow/Washington.

Section 2

1. This Act applies to space activities that are performed in or from within the Netherlands or else on or from a Dutch ship or Dutch aircraft.
2. By Order in Council this Act can also be declared wholly or partly applicable to:
a. designated space activities that are performed by a Dutch natural or juridical person on or from the territory of a State that is not party to the Outer Space Treaty or on or from a ship or aircraft that falls under the jurisdiction of a State that is not party to the Outer Space Treaty;
b. the organization of outer-space activities by a natural or juridical person from within the Netherlands.

CHAPTER 2. LICENCES

§ 1. Licence for space activities

Section 3

1. It is prohibited to perform space activities as referred to in Section 2 without a licence issued for this purpose by Our Minister.
2. Subsection 1 is not applicable to space activities that are performed under the responsibility of one or more of Our Ministers.
3. Regulations and restrictions can be attached to the licence for the following purposes:
a. the safety of persons and goods;
b. protection of the environment in outer space;
c. financial security;
d. protection of public order;
e. security of the State;

f. fulfilment of the international obligations of the State.
4. The licence is issued on the condition that the prospective holder shall have and maintain what Our Minister considers to be the maximum possible cover for the liability arising from the space activities for which a licence is requested. Account is taken here of what can reasonably be covered by insurance.
5. A time limit can be attached to the licence within which the licence-holder must begin the space activities.
6. The licence is issued for the duration of the space activities.
7. Further rules can be imposed by Ministerial Order in order to implement the provisions of subsection 4.

§ 2. Licence application

Section 4

1. The licence application shall be submitted to Our Minister.
2. Further rules can be imposed by Ministerial Order with regard to the way in which the application takes place and the information and documents that are furnished by the applicant.
3. In addition, requirements can be imposed by Ministerial Order which the applicant must fulfil in order to be eligible for a licence. These requirements may relate to:
a. the applicant's knowledge and experience;
b. authorization for the use of frequency space.

Section 5

Our Minister will decide on a licence application within six months after having received it.

Section 6

1. A licence will be refused if:
a. this is necessary in order to comply with a treaty or a binding decision of an international institution;
b. in the view of Our Minister, facts or circumstances suggest that the safety of persons and goods, environmental protection in outer space, the maintenance of public order or national security might be jeopardized by issuing the licence;
c. its issuance would contravene rules laid down by or pursuant to this Act.

2. A licence can be refused by Our Minister if:
a. a previously issued licence has been revoked owing to infringement of rules laid down by or pursuant to this Act or of the regulations attached to the licence;
b. the applicant has not discharged his obligations under a previously issued licence;
c. the application or the applicant does not comply with the rules laid down by or pursuant to this Act;
d. there is good reason to fear that that the applicant will not act in accordance with the rules laid down by or pursuant to this Act;
e. this is necessary in order to protect the interests referred to in Section 3, subsection 3.

Section 7

1. The licence will be revoked if:
a. this is requested by the licence-holder;
b. this is necessary in order to comply with a treaty or a binding decision of an international institution;
c. there is good reason to fear that the maintenance of the licence will jeopardize the safety of persons and goods, environmental protection in outer space, the maintenance of public order or national security.
2. A licence can be revoked by Our Minister if:
a. the rules laid down by or pursuant to this Act or the regulations pertaining to the licence have been, or are being, infringed;
b. the space activities have not been commenced within the stipulated time limit;
c. the purpose of the space activities for which the licence was issued has changed substantially;
d. this is justified by a change in the technical or financial capabilities of the licence-holder;
e. the information or documents furnished with the application prove to be so incorrect or incomplete that a different decision would have been made on the application if the true circumstances had been known at the time of its assessment;
f. this is necessary in order to protect the interests referred to in Section 3, subsection 3.
3. Before the licence is revoked, Our Minister will take any steps necessary to ensure the safety of persons and goods, environmental protection in outer space, the maintenance of public order or national security. Our Minister will provide the necessary

instructions to the party whose licence will be revoked. This party is obliged to follow the instructions.
4. Our Minister can also amend the licence on the grounds referred to in subsection 2 instead of revoking it.

Section 8

1. The licence is not transferable.
2. On request, Our Minister can adjust the name entered in the registry if the licence is held by a juridical person that is merged, divided or changes its name.

Section 9

1. It can be decreed by Order in Council that, in order to cover the costs of work or services designed to implement the provisions by or pursuant to this Act, compensation is payable by the party for whom work or services have been performed in accordance with rules laid down by or pursuant to Order in Council.
2. If a sum payable under subsection 1 has not been paid within the appointed period, the statutory interest will be added to the sum in question, calculated from the day on which that time limit elapsed.
3. If payment is not made within the period referred to in subsection 2, the offending party will be ordered in writing to pay the sum it owes within two weeks, plus the statutory interest and the costs of the demand for payment.

§ 3. Disasters

Section 10

1. If an incident occurs or has occurred that may jeopardize the safety of persons and goods, environmental protection in outer space, the maintenance of public order or national security, or otherwise cause damage, the licence-holder shall, without delay, take the steps that can reasonably be expected of it in order to prevent the consequences of that event or, where those consequences cannot be prevented, to limit and rectify them as far as possible.
2. The licence-holder shall, without delay, notify Our Minister of an incident as referred to in subsection 1 and shall also, as soon as practicable, furnish information with regard to:
a. the causes of the incident and the circumstances under which the

incident occurred;
b. the relevant information that is needed in order to assess the nature and the seriousness of the consequences of the incident;
c. the steps that have been taken or are being contemplated in order to prevent, limit or rectify the consequences of the incident;
d. the steps that have been taken or are being contemplated in order to prevent such an incident recurring during a space activity.

CHAPTER 3. REGISTRY OF SPACE OBJECTS

Section 11

1. Our Minister shall maintain a registry with information concerning space objects that are being used in connection with space activities as referred to in Section 2.
2. The licence-holder shall, at times to be determined by Order in Council, furnish the information required for the registry.
3. Our Minister will be responsible for registering space objects that are being used in connection with space activities that are performed under the responsibility of one or more of Our Ministers.
4. Rules will be laid down by or pursuant to an Order in Council with a view to implementing this Section.

CHAPTER 4. REDRESS

Section 12

1. If the State is obliged to pay compensation under Article VII of the Outer Space Treaty or the Liability Convention, the State is entitled to recover this sum, in full or in part, from the party whose space activity has caused the damage.
2. For each event or series of events with the same cause, the licence-holder is liable for damage caused by its space activities, up to the value of the sum insured, as specified in Section 3, subsection 4.
3. Should the occasion arise, the State will exercise the right of redress, as specified in subsection 1, against the licence-holder up to the value of the sum insured, as specified in Section 3, subsection 4.
4. Should the occasion arise, the State can likewise exercise the right of redress, as specified in subsection 3, against the licence-holder's insurer.

CHAPTER 5. ENFORCEMENT

Section 13

1. The officials designated by order of Our Minister have been charged with the supervision of compliance with the provisions by or under Section 3, Section 7, subsection 3, third sentence, Section 10 and Section 11, subsection 2.
2. An order such as that referred to in the subsection 1 will be announced by placement in the Government Gazette.

Section 14

1. Our Minister is empowered to use administrative orders to enforce Section 3, Section 7, subsection 3, Section 10 and Section 11, subsections 2 and 4, of this Act and Section 5:20 of the General Administrative Law Act.

2. For the application of subsection 1, the requirement of speed as referred to in Section 5:24, subsection 5, of the General Administrative Law Act is, in any case, present if the non-fulfilment of the obligations referred to in subsection 1 poses a serious and direct threat to the safety of persons and goods, national security or public order.

Section 15

1. If the provisions by or pursuant to Section 3, subsections 1, 3 and 4, Section 7, subsection 3, third sentence, Section 10, or Section 5:20 of the General Administrative Law Act are contravened, Our Minister can impose an administrative penalty of up to ☐ 450,000 or 10 per cent of the relevant annual sales of the company in the Netherlands, whichever is the greater.
2. If the provisions by or pursuant to Section 11, subsections 2 and 4, are contravened, Our Minister can impose an administrative penalty of up to ☐ 100,000.
3. The size of the administrative penalty shall in any event be commensurate with the seriousness and duration of the

infringement, and also with the extent to which the perpetrator is at fault.

Section 16

1. Our Minister shall not impose an administrative penalty if the infringement cannot be imputed to the perpetrator.
2. Our Minister shall not impose an administrative penalty if:
a. the perpetrator is deceased;
b. an administrative penalty has already been imposed on the perpetrator previously for the same infringement;
c. notice has been published, as referred to in Section 20, subsection 3, paragraph a;
d. criminal proceedings have been instituted and the hearing has begun, or
e. the right to institute criminal proceedings under Section 74 or 74c of the Netherlands Criminal Code or under Section 37 of the Economic Offences Act has lapsed.
3. An administrative penalty will expire if it is not irrevocable at the time of the death of the perpetrator. An irrevocable administrative penalty will expire if it has not yet been paid at that time.

Section 17

1. The power to impose an administrative penalty will lapse five years after the infringement is committed.
2. If objections are raised to the administrative penalty or an appeal is brought, the expiry date will be deferred until a final and conclusive decision has been made on the objection or appeal.

Section 18

1. If an official as referred to in Section 13 determines that an infringement as referred to in Section 15 has been committed, he shall prepare a report.
2. The report is dated and states:
a. the name of the perpetrator;
b. the infringement and also the statutory provision that has been contravened;
c. the facts and circumstances on the basis of which it has been determined that an infringement has been committed;

d. where and when the facts and circumstances referred to under c occurred.
3. A copy of the report will be sent to the party that has committed the infringement.
4. If so requested by an interested party who does not adequately understand the report owing to his poor knowledge of the Dutch language, Our Minister shall, as far as possible, ensure that the party concerned is notified of the content of the report in a language that he understands.

Section 19

1. A person with regard to whom an act is performed by Our Minister from which he can reasonably deduce that an administrative penalty will be imposed on him on account of an infringement shall not be obliged to make any statement regarding the matter.
2. The perpetrator shall be notified thereof before he is requested to furnish information.

Section 20

1. Notwithstanding Chapter 4.1.2 of the General Administrative Law Act, the person concerned will be summoned in writing to express his views with regard to the report, either in writing or verbally, as he chooses.
2. If the person concerned expresses his views verbally, Our Minister shall, if so requested by the person concerned who does not adequately understand the Dutch language, ensure that an interpreter is appointed who can assist the person concerned at the hearing, unless it can reasonably be assumed that this is not necessary.
3. The perpetrator shall be notified in writing if, after the perpetrator has put forward his views, Our Minister should decide that:
a. no administrative penalty will be imposed for the infringement, or
b. the infringement will still be brought before the public prosecutor.
.

Section 21

1. The decision to impose an order with conditional penalty payments or an administrative penalty will, in any event, state:
a. the infringement for which it has been imposed, and also the statutory regulation that has been infringed;
b. if an order with conditional penalty payments is imposed, the name of the perpetrator, the content of the order and the period to which it applies;
c. if an administrative penalty is imposed, the name of the perpetrator, the sum of money to be paid and also an explanation concerning the amount of the penalty.
2. If so requested by the perpetrator who does not adequately understand the decision owing to his poor knowledge of the Dutch language, Our Minister shall, as far as possible, ensure that the information given in that decision is communicated to the perpetrator in a language that he understands.
3. Our Minister shall, within 13 weeks after the date of the report, make a decision with regard to the imposition of an administrative penalty.

Section 22

1. An administrative penalty shall be paid within six weeks after the decision imposing the penalty has come into force.
2. Statutory interest will be added to the penalty, counting from six weeks from the day on which the decision referred to in subsection 1 was published.
3. If payment is not made within the period specified in subsection 1, the party concerned will be ordered in writing to pay the amount of the administrative penalty within two weeks, plus the interest payable under subsection 2 and the costs of the demand for payment.
4. The effect of a decision as referred to in subsection 1 will be suspended until the period for lodging an appeal has expired or, if an appeal has been lodged, until a decision has been given on the appeal.

Section 23

1. Where payment has not been made within the two-week period

specified in Section 22, subsection 3, Our Minister can issue a notice demanding payment of the penalty owed by the perpetrator, plus the interest payable under Section 22, subsection 2, and the costs relating to the demand for payment and collection.

2. The notice demanding payment will be served by bailiff's writ, at the expense of the perpetrator, and shall be enforceable within the meaning of the Second Book of the Netherlands Code of Civil Procedure.

3. For six weeks following the day on which the writ is served, objections to the notice demanding payment may be made by a writ against the State.

4. The objection has the effect of suspending execution. At the request of the State, the courts may cancel the suspension of execution.

CHAPTER 6. AMENDMENTS TO OTHER LEGISLATION

Section 24

1. The following has been inserted, in alphabetical order, in Section 1(1) of the Economic Offences Act: the Space Activities Act, Section 3, subsections 1 and 3, Section 7, subsection 3, and Section 10.

2. The following has been inserted, in alphabetical order, in Section 1(4) of the Economic Offences Act: the Space Activities Act, Section 11, subsections 2 and 4.

CHAPTER 7. CONCLUDING PROVISIONS

Section 25

1. Activities in outer space as referred to in Section 2 which are taking place on the date this Act comes into force can be continued without a licence for a period of 12 months from that date.

2. Anyone shall, within six months after the date this Act comes into force, notify Our Minister of the space activities that he is performing that may fall under this Act.

Section 26

If the Bill containing supplementary provisions to the General Administrative Law Act (Fourth tranche of the General Administrative Law Act, Parliamentary Papers II 2003/04, 29 702,

No. 2), as submitted by Royal Message of 22 July 2004, is enacted and comes into force then Section 15, subsection 3, and Sections 16 to 23 of this Act shall cease to apply.

Section 27

This Act shall enter into force on a date to be determined by Royal Decree.

Section 28

This Act may be cited as: the Space Activities Act.
We order and command that this Act shall be placed in the Bulletin of Acts and Decrees and that all ministries, authorities, bodies and officials whom it may concern shall diligently implement it.

Done

The Minister of Economic Affairs

AUSTRALIA

Space Activities Act - 1998

Act No. 123 of 1998 as amended

This compilation was prepared on 3 March 2010 taking into account amendments up to Act No. 8 of 2010

An Act about space activities, and for related purposes

Part 1—Introduction

1 Short title [*see* Note 1]

This Act may be cited as the *Space Activities Act 1998*.

2 Commencement [*see* Note 1]

This Act commences on the day on which it receives the Royal Assent.

3 Objects of Act

The objects of this Act are:
(a) to establish a system for the regulation of space activities carried on either from Australia or by Australian nationals outside Australia; and
(b) to provide for the payment of adequate compensation for damage caused to persons or property as a result of space activities regulated by this Act; and
(c) to implement certain of Australia's obligations under the UN Space Treaties; and
(d) to implement certain of Australia's obligations under specified space cooperation agreements.

Note: This Act does not limit the operation of other laws of the Commonwealth (except so far as the other laws are inconsistent with this Act): see section 105.

4 Simplified outline of Act

The following is a simplified outline of this Act:

- Certain space activities carried on in Australia must be covered by an approval under Part 3.

- An Australian national who carries on certain space activities outside Australia must also be covered by such an approval.

- Part 4 has rules about liability for damage that space activities cause.

- A Register of Space Objects is established under Part 5.

- Part 5A provides a framework for implementation of specified space cooperation agreements.

- Part 6 deals with civil penalties.

- Part 7 provides for investigating accidents and incidents.

5 Act binds the Crown

(1) This Act binds the Crown in each of its capacities.

Note: Division 1 of Part 3 does not bind the Commonwealth: see section 16.

(2) However, this Act does not make the Crown liable to be prosecuted for an offence.

6 External Territories

This Act extends to the external Territories.

7 Application of *Criminal Code*

The *Criminal Code* applies to all offences against this Act.

Part 2—Definitions

8 Definitions

In this Act, unless the contrary intention appears:

accident has the meaning given by section 85.

accident site has the meaning given by section 98.

accident site premises has the meaning given by section 98.

approved scientific or educational organisation means an educational institution, a scientific organisation or a non-profit body, in respect of which a declaration under section 8A is in force.

Australia, when used in a geographical sense, includes the external Territories.

Australian national means:
(a) an Australian citizen; or
(b) a body incorporated by or under a law of the Commonwealth, of a State or of a Territory; or
(c) the Commonwealth, a State or a Territory.

civil penalty provision has the meaning given by section 80.

damage has the same meaning as in the Liability Convention.

exemption certificate means a certificate issued under section 46.

fault has the same meaning as in the Liability Convention.

gross negligence has the meaning given by the regulations. But if the regulations do not give the term a meaning, it has the same meaning as in the Liability Convention.

incident has the meaning given by section 86.

insured amount, for a launch permit, overseas launch certificate or section 43 authorisation, means the amount for which the holder of the permit, certificate or authorisation is required to be insured under Division 7 of Part 3 in respect of the launch or launches, and any return, covered by the permit, certificate or authorisation. In determining this amount, disregard paragraph 47(2)(b) (which deals with direct financial responsibility).

intergovernmental agreement with Russia means the Agreement between the Government of Australia and the Government of the Russian Federation on Cooperation in the Field of the Exploration and Use Of Outer Space for Peaceful Purposes done at Canberra on 23 May 2001 the English text of which is set out in Schedule 6, and includes that Agreement as amended from time to time in relation to Australia.

Investigator means a person appointed under section 88.

launch a space object means launch the object into an area beyond the distance of 100 km above mean sea level, or attempt to do so.

launch facility means a facility (whether fixed or mobile) or place specifically designed or constructed as a facility or place from which space objects can be launched, and includes all other facilities at the facility or place that are necessary to conduct a launch.

launching State has the same meaning as in the Liability Convention.

launch permit means a permit granted under section 26.

Launch Safety Officer, for a licensed launch facility, means the person appointed by the Minister under section 50 for the facility.

launch vehicle means a vehicle that can carry a payload into or back from an area beyond the distance of 100 km above mean sea level.

Liability Convention means the Convention on International Liability for Damage Caused by Space

Objects done at London, Moscow and Washington on 29 March 1972 and whose English text is set out in Schedule 1.

liability period means:
(a) for the launch of a space object—the period of 30 days beginning when the launch takes place, or such other period as is specified in the regulations; and
(b) for the return of a space object—the period beginning when the relevant re-entry manoeuvre is begun and ending when the object has come to rest on Earth, or such other period as is specified in the regulations.

licensed launch facility means a launch facility for which a person holds a space licence: see section 18.

occupier of premises includes a person present at the premises who apparently represents the occupier.

overseas launch certificate means a certificate granted under section 35.

payload includes a load to be carried for testing purposes or otherwise on a non-profit basis.

premises includes a place and a conveyance.

Register means the Register of Space Objects kept under section 76.

Registration Convention means the Convention on Registration of Objects Launched into Outer Space done at New York on 14 January 1975 and whose English text is set out in Schedule 2.

related party has the meaning given by section 9.

responsible party, for the launch or return of a space object, means:
(a) in the case of a launch or return authorised by a launch permit—the holder of the permit; or

(b) in the case of a return authorised by a permission under subsection 43(1)—the holder of the permission; or
(c) in the case of a return authorised by an agreement between the Minister and another person under subsection 43(2)—that other person; or
(d) in the case of a launch or return that:
  (i) is not authorised as mentioned in paragraph (a), (b) or (c); but
  (ii) is covered by an exemption certificate (see section 46);
  the holder of the exemption certificate; or
(e) in the case of a launch authorised by an overseas launch certificate—the holder of the certificate; or
(f) in any other case—each of the following persons:
  (i) the person or persons who carried out the launch or return of the space object;
  (ii) any person who, at any time during the liability period for the launch or return, owned all or some of any payload forming part of the space object concerned;
  (iii) any other person specified in regulations made for the purposes of this definition.

But, in relation to a launch to which paragraph (f) applies, if the space object was launched from a launch facility outside Australia, a person is only a *responsible party* if the person is also an Australian national.

return a space object means return the space object from an area beyond the distance of 100 km above mean sea level to Earth, or attempt to do so.

space licence means a licence granted under section 18.

space object means a thing consisting of:
(a) a launch vehicle; and
(b) a payload (if any) that the launch vehicle is to carry into or back from an area beyond the distance of 100 km above mean sea level;

or any part of such a thing, even if:
(c) the part is to go only some of the way towards or back from an area beyond the distance of 100 km above mean sea level; or
(d) the part results from the separation of a payload or payloads from a launch vehicle after launch.

standard launch permit condition means a condition to which a launch permit is subject because of section 29.

third party, for the launch or return of a space object, means a person who is not a responsible party for the launch or return and who is not a related party (see section 9) of any responsible party for the launch or return.

UN space treaties means the following:
(a) the Liability Convention;
(b) the Registration Convention;
(c) the Treaty on Principles Governing the Activities of States in the Exploration and Use of Outer Space, Including the Moon and Other Celestial Bodies done at London, Moscow and Washington on 27 January 1967 and whose English text is set out in Schedule 3;
(d) the Agreement Governing the Activities of States on the Moon and Other Celestial Bodies done at New York on 18 December 1979 and whose English text is set out in Schedule 4;
(e) the Agreement on the Rescue of Astronauts, the Return of Astronauts and the Return of Objects Launched into Outer Space done at London, Moscow and Washington on 22 April 1968 and whose English text is set out in Schedule 5.

8A Approved scientific or educational organisations

The Minister may, by writing, declare an educational institution, a scientific organisation or a non-profit body to be an approved scientific or educational organisation for the purposes of this Act.

Note: Under subsection 33(3) of the *Acts Interpretation Act 1901*, the Minister may vary or revoke such a declaration.

8B Guidelines for making a declaration

(1) The Minister must develop written guidelines that he or she must have regard to when deciding whether or not to make a declaration under section 8A.

(2) The guidelines are to be made available for inspection on the internet.

(3) The guidelines are a disallowable instrument for the purposes of section 46A of the *Acts Interpretation Act 1901*.

8C Applying for a declaration

An application for a declaration under section 8A must be made in accordance with the regulations.

9 Related party

(1) A person (the ***first person***) is a ***related party*** of a responsible party for the launch or return of a space object if:
  (a) the first person has a financial or ownership interest in all or part of the space object; or
  (b) the first person was involved in preparing all or part of the space object for the launch or return; or
  (c) the first person is a contractor, subcontractor or supplier involved in the launch or return or the preparation of all or part of the space object for the launch or return; or
  (d) the first person is a director, officer, employee or agent of the responsible party.

(2) However, the regulations may provide that specified persons are, or are not, ***related parties*** of a responsible party.

Part 3—Regulation of space activities

10 Simplified outline

The following is a simplified outline of this Part:

- Under Division 1, certain space activities are prohibited unless appropriate approvals are obtained.

- The various approvals are dealt with in Division 2 (space licences), Division 3 (launch permits), Division 4 (overseas launch certificates), Division 5 (return of overseas-launched space objects) and Division 6 (exemption certificates).

- Some of those approvals have insurance/financial requirements, which are set out in Division 7.

- The Minister is to appoint a Launch Safety Officer for each licensed launch facility: see Division 8.

- Division 9 has some rules about administration etc.

Division 1—Certain space activities require approvals etc.

11 Launch in Australia requires a launch permit or exemption certificate

If:

(a) a person launches a space object from a launch facility located in Australia; and

(b) the launch is not authorised by a launch permit held by any person; and

(c) no exemption certificate (see section 46) covering the launch is held by any person; and

(d) the launch is not conducted in accordance with any agreement of the kind mentioned in subsection 109(1);

the first-mentioned person is guilty of an offence punishable on conviction by:

(e) in the case of a body corporate—a fine not exceeding 100,000 penalty units; or

(f) in the case of an individual—imprisonment for a term not exceeding 10 years, or a fine not exceeding 600 penalty units, or both.

Note 1: Chapter 2 of the *Criminal Code* sets out the general principles of criminal responsibility.

Note 2: See section 4AA of the *Crimes Act 1914* for the current value of a penalty unit.

12 Overseas launch requires an overseas launch certificate

If:

(a) a space object is launched from a launch facility located outside Australia; and

(b) the launch is not authorised by an overseas launch certificate held by any person; and

(c) an Australian national is a responsible party for the launch;

the Australian national is guilty of an offence punishable on conviction by:

(d) in the case of a body corporate—a fine not exceeding 100,000 penalty units; or
(e) in the case of an individual—imprisonment for a term not exceeding 10 years, or a fine not exceeding 600 penalty units, or both.

Note 1: Chapter 2 of the *Criminal Code* sets out the general principles of criminal responsibility.

Note 2: See section 4AA of the *Crimes Act 1914* for the current value of a penalty unit.

13 Return to Australia of Australian-launched space object requires a launch permit or exemption certificate

If:
(a) a person returns a space object to a place anywhere in Australia; and
(b) the object, or any part of it, was launched from a launch facility located in Australia; and
(c) the return is not authorised by a launch permit held by any person; and
(d) no exemption certificate (see section 46) covering the return is held by any person; and
(e) the return is not conducted in accordance with any agreement of the kind mentioned in subsection 109(1);

the first-mentioned person is guilty of an offence punishable on conviction by:
(f) in the case of a body corporate—a fine not exceeding 100,000 penalty units; or
(g) in the case of an individual—imprisonment for a term not exceeding 10 years, or a fine not exceeding 600 penalty units, or both.

Note 1: Chapter 2 of the *Criminal Code* sets out the general principles of criminal responsibility.

Note 2: See section 4AA of the *Crimes Act 1914* for the current value of a penalty unit.

14 Return to Australia of overseas-launched space object requires authorisation

If:

(a) a person returns a space object to a place anywhere in Australia; and

(b) neither the object, nor any part of it, was launched from a launch facility located within Australia; and

(c) the return of the object to that place is not authorised under section 43;

the person is guilty of an offence punishable on conviction by:

(d) in the case of a body corporate—a fine not exceeding 100,000 penalty units; or

(e) in the case of an individual—imprisonment for a term not exceeding 10 years, or a fine not exceeding 600 penalty units, or both.

Note 1: Chapter 2 of the *Criminal Code* sets out the general principles of criminal responsibility.

Note 2: See section 4AA of the *Crimes Act 1914* for the current value of a penalty unit.

15 Space licence required to operate a launch facility in Australia

A person must not operate a launch facility in Australia, or do anything directly connected with operating a launch facility in Australia, using a particular kind of launch vehicle, unless:

(a) the person holds a space licence (see Division 2) for the facility and the kind of launch vehicle; or

(b) the person is a related party (see section 9), for any launches conducted from the facility, of a person who holds such a licence; or

(c) the person is acting as an employee, contractor or agent of a person who holds such a licence; or

(d) an exemption certificate (see section 46) covering:

　(i) the operation of the facility, or the things connected with the operation; and

　(ii) the kind of launch vehicle;

is held by any person; or

(e) the operation of the facility, or the things connected with the operation, are done in accordance with an agreement of the kind mentioned in subsection 109(1).

Note: Contravening this section is not an offence. However, a person who contravenes this section is liable to a civil penalty under Part 6.

16 Commonwealth not bound

This Division does not apply to:

(a) the Commonwealth; or

(b) a person acting as an employee or agent of the Commonwealth or as a member of the Defence Force.

Example: The Commonwealth and a private company are to carry out a launch as joint venturers. The Commonwealth would not need a space licence or launch permit etc. to do so, but the private company would (unless the company were acting as an agent of the Commonwealth, in which case it too would be exempt from this Division).

17 Activities of international space organisations

(1) If an agreement between Australia and another country or countries provides for the establishment of an international organisation whose sole or principal function is to carry on activities in outer space, this Division does not apply in relation to anything done in accordance with the agreement.

(2) This section applies whether the agreement was made before or after the commencement of this Act.

Division 2—Space licences
18 Granting a space licence

The Minister may grant to a person a space licence covering a particular launch facility in Australia, a particular kind of launch vehicle and particular flight paths, if:

(a) the Minister is satisfied that the person is competent to operate the launch facility and launch vehicles of that kind; and

(aa) the person is a corporation to which paragraph 51(xx) of the Constitution applies; and

(b) the Minister is satisfied that all necessary environmental approvals under Australian law have been obtained, and that an adequate environmental plan has been made, for the construction and operation of the launch facility; and

(c) the Minister is satisfied that the person has sufficient funding to construct and operate the launch facility; and

(d) the Minister is satisfied that the probability of the construction and operation of the launch facility causing substantial harm to public health or public safety or causing substantial damage to property is as low as is reasonably practicable; and

(e) the Minister does not consider that, for reasons relevant to Australia's national security, foreign policy or international obligations, the space licence should not be granted; and

(f) the criteria (if any) prescribed by the regulations are satisfied in relation to the launch facility; and

(g) the criteria (if any) prescribed by the regulations are satisfied in relation to that kind of launch vehicle; and

(h) the criteria (if any) prescribed by the regulations are satisfied in relation to each flight path specified in the application for the licence.

Example: For the purposes of paragraph (g), the regulations could prescribe criteria dealing with matters such as the design of the launch vehicle and technical aspects of the way in which such vehicles are to be operated.

Note: Under subsection 33(3) of the *Acts Interpretation Act 1901*, the Minister may vary or revoke a space licence.

19 Terms of space licence

A space licence:
(a) must specify the day on which it comes into force; and
(b) remains in force for the period specified in the licence, which must be no longer than 20 years; and
(c) is granted subject to the standard space licence conditions in section 20 and any other conditions specified in the licence.

20 Standard space licence conditions

The following are conditions of each space licence granted to a person, except to the extent that the licence otherwise specifies:
(a) the holder of the licence must give the Minister any information that the Minister asks for under section 60 about the licence;
(b) the holder must:
  (i) allow the Launch Safety Officer for the facility (see Division 8) reasonable access to the facility and to any space object at the facility; and
  (ii) ensure that the Launch Safety Officer is given any information or assistance that the Launch Safety Officer reasonably requests for the proper performance of a function;
(c) any other condition specified in the regulations.

21 Breaching a space licence condition

The holder of a space licence must not contravene a condition of the licence.

Note: Contravening this section is not an offence. However, a person who contravenes this section is liable to a civil penalty under Part 6.

22 Transfer of space licence

(1) The Minister may, by written notice, transfer a space licence to another person if the Minister could grant the space licence to the other person under section 18.

(2) The transfer takes effect at the time specified in the notice.

(3) The licence continues to cover the same launch facility and the same kind of launch vehicle.

(4) The licence has effect subject to the same conditions as the original licence (unless the Minister varies the conditions).

(5) The period for which the licence remains in force continues to run despite the transfer.

23 Applying for the grant, variation or transfer of a space licence

An application for the grant, variation or transfer of a space licence must be made in accordance with the regulations.

24 Procedure etc.

(1) If the Minister considers that there may be grounds to vary, revoke or transfer a space licence (other than at the licensee's request), the Minister must:
 (a) give the licensee written notice of the Minister's opinion specifying the reasons for that opinion; and
 (b) invite the licensee to make a written submission to the Minister about the matter within a reasonable period specified in the notice.

(2) In deciding whether to vary, revoke or transfer a space licence, the Minister must consider the matters raised in any submission received within the period specified in the notice.

(3) A space licence must not be varied in a way that changes the location of the licensed launch facility.

(4) The regulations may prescribe other ways in which a space licence must not be varied.

25 Suspending a space licence

(1) The Minister may, by written notice, suspend a space licence if:
  (a) the holder of the licence contravenes a condition of the licence; or
  (b) the Minister considers that, for reasons relevant to Australia's national security, foreign policy or international obligations, the licence should be suspended.

Note: Under subsection 33(3) of the *Acts Interpretation Act 1901*, the Minister may revoke a suspension.

(2) A space licence has no effect while suspended, but the period for which it remains in force continues to run despite the suspension.

(3) A space licence may be revoked or varied even while it is suspended.

25A Annual review of space licence

The Minister may conduct an annual review of a space licence:
  (a) for the purpose of monitoring compliance by the licence holder with this Act and with the conditions of the licence; or
  (b) for any other reason that the Minister considers appropriate.

Division 3—Launch permits

26 Granting a launch permit

(1) The Minister may grant a launch permit to a person authorising:
  (a) the launch of a particular space object; or
  (b) a particular series of launches of space objects that, in the Minister's opinion, having regard to the

nature of any payloads to be carried, may appropriately be authorised by a single launch permit;

from a specified launch facility in Australia using a specified kind of launch vehicle.

> Note: Under subsection 33(3) of the *Acts Interpretation Act 1901*, the Minister may vary or revoke a launch permit granted under this section.

(2) The launch permit may also authorise particular space objects to be returned, in connection with the launch or launches, to a specified place or area in Australia.

> Note: A returning space object need not be the same as the space object launched. For example, a launch vehicle could carry a payload into an area beyond the distance of 100 km above mean sea level and return without it, or even collect a different payload from an area beyond the distance of 100 km above mean sea level and return that to Earth.

(3) The Minister may grant the launch permit to the person only if all of the following criteria are satisfied:
   (a) the person holds a space licence (see Division 2) covering the launch facility and the kind of launch vehicle concerned;
   (b) the person is a corporation to which paragraph 51(xx) of the Constitution applies;
   (c) the Minister is satisfied that the person who is to carry out the launch or launches, and any connected return, is competent to do so;
   (d) the Minister is satisfied that the insurance/financial requirements in Division 7 will be satisfied for the launch or launches, and any connected return;

(e) the Minister is satisfied that the probability of the launch or launches, or any connected return, causing substantial harm to public health or public safety or causing substantial damage to property is as low as is reasonably practicable;

(f) the space object or objects concerned are not and do not contain a nuclear weapon or a weapon of mass destruction of any other kind;

(g) the Minister does not consider that, for reasons relevant to Australia's national security, foreign policy or international obligations, the launch permit should not be granted;

(h) any other criteria prescribed by the regulations.

(4) If a country other than Australia is also a launching State for the space object or any of the space objects, the Minister may, in deciding whether to grant the launch permit, have regard to:

(a) whether there is an agreement between Australia and that other country under which that country assumes any liability, and indemnifies Australia, for any damage that the space object or objects may cause; and

(b) the terms of that agreement.

Note: This subsection does not, by implication, limit the matters to which the Minister may have regard.

27 Australian launches: continuing requirement for space licence

If the launch facility specified in a launch permit is in Australia, the permit has no effect during any period when the holder of the permit does not also hold a space licence (see Division 2) covering the facility and the kind of launch vehicle concerned.

28 Terms of launch permit

(1) A launch permit authorising the launch of a space object or objects, and any connected return:

(a) must specify the day on which it comes into force and the period for which it remains in force; and

(b) is granted subject to the standard launch permit conditions in section 29 and any other conditions specified in the regulations or in the launch permit.

(2) A launch permit may specify that the period during which it remains in force ends on the occurrence of a particular event (rather than at a specified time). For this purpose, the regulations may set out how to determine when events of a particular kind occur.

Example: A launch permit might specify that it expires when the relevant launch has been (successfully or unsuccessfully) completed. The regulations could set out how to determine when this is.

(3) At any time when a launch permit is in force, the Minister may, by written notice, extend or further extend the period for which the permit remains in force.

29 Standard launch permit conditions

The following are conditions of each launch permit (called **standard launch permit conditions**), except to the extent that the permit otherwise specifies:

(a) the launch or launches, and any connected return, must not be conducted in a way that is likely to cause substantial harm to public health or public safety or to cause substantial damage to property;

(b) the space object or objects must not be or contain a nuclear weapon or a weapon of mass destruction of any other kind;

(c) the space object or objects must not contain any fissionable material unless the Minister's written approval has first been obtained;

(d) the holder of the permit must satisfy the insurance/financial requirements in Division 7 for each launch, and each return, conducted under the permit.

30 Breaching a launch permit condition

(1) The holder of a launch permit must not contravene a condition of the launch permit (whether or not the condition is a standard launch permit condition).

Note: Contravening this subsection is not an offence. However, a person who contravenes this subsection is liable to a civil penalty under Part 6.

(2) If the holder of a launch permit:
  (a) by any intentional act or omission, contravenes a standard launch permit condition (see section 29) of the permit; and
  (b) is reckless as to whether the act or omission contravenes the condition;
  the holder is guilty of an offence punishable on conviction by:
  (c) in the case of a body corporate—a fine not exceeding 100,000 penalty units; or
  (d) in the case of an individual—imprisonment for a term not exceeding 10 years, or a fine not exceeding 600 penalty units, or both.

Note 1: Chapter 2 of the *Criminal Code* sets out the general principles of criminal responsibility.

Note 2: See section 4AA of the *Crimes Act 1914* for the current value of a penalty unit.

(3) The Minister may take civil proceedings under Part 6 against a person who is alleged to have breached a standard launch permit condition of a launch permit, as an alternative to prosecution for an offence against subsection (2).

31 Transfer of launch permit

(1) The Minister may, by written notice, transfer a launch permit to another person if the Minister could grant the launch permit to the other person under section 26.

(2) The transfer takes effect at the time specified in the notice.

(3) The permit continues to cover the same launch facility, the same kind of launch vehicle and the same space object or objects.

(4) The permit has effect subject to the same conditions as the original permit (unless the Minister varies the conditions).

(5) The period for which the permit remains in force continues to run despite the transfer.

32 Applying for the grant, variation or transfer of a launch permit

An application for the grant, variation or transfer of a launch permit must be made in accordance with the regulations.

33 Procedure etc.

(1) If the Minister considers that there may be grounds to vary, revoke or transfer a launch permit (other than at the permit holder's request), the Minister must:
  (a) give the holder of the permit written notice of the Minister's opinion specifying the reasons for that opinion; and
  (b) invite the holder to make a written submission to the Minister about the matter within a reasonable period specified in the notice.

(2) In deciding whether to vary, revoke or transfer the permit, the Minister must consider the matters raised in any submission received within the period specified in the notice.

(3) A launch permit must not be varied in a way that changes the location of the relevant launch facility.

(4) The regulations may prescribe other ways in which a launch permit must not be varied.

34 Suspending a launch permit

(1) The Minister may, by written notice, suspend a launch permit if:
  (a) the holder of the permit contravenes a condition of the permit; or
  (b) the Minister considers that, for reasons relevant to Australia's national security, foreign policy or international obligations, the permit should be suspended; or

(c) an incident involving a space object covered by the permit occurs during the liability period for the launch or return of the object.

Note: Under subsection 33(3) of the *Acts Interpretation Act 1901*, the Minister may revoke a suspension.

(2) A launch permit has no effect while suspended, but the period for which it remains in force continues to run despite the suspension.

(3) A launch permit may be revoked or varied even while it is suspended.

Division 4—Overseas launch certificates
35 Granting an overseas launch certificate

(1) The Minister may grant an overseas launch certificate to a person authorising:
   (a) the launch of a particular space object; or
   (b) a particular series of launches of space objects that, in the Minister's opinion, having regard to the nature of any payloads to be carried, may appropriately be authorised by a single overseas launch certificate;
from a specified launch facility outside Australia using a specified kind of launch vehicle.

Note 1: Overseas launch certificates are only required if an Australian national would be a responsible party for the launch—see section 12.

Note 2: Under subsection 33(3) of the *Acts Interpretation Act 1901*, the Minister may vary or revoke an overseas launch certificate granted under this section.

(2) The Minister may grant the overseas launch certificate to the person only if all of the following criteria are satisfied:
   (a) the Minister is satisfied either:

(i) that the insurance/financial requirements in Division 7 will be satisfied for each launch to be conducted under the certificate; or

(ii) that, having regard to the nature and purpose of the space object or space objects concerned, it is not necessary to insist that those insurance/financial requirements be satisfied;

(b) the Minister is satisfied that the probability of the launch or launches causing substantial harm to public health or public safety or causing substantial damage to property is sufficiently low;

(c) the Minister does not consider that, for reasons relevant to Australia's national security, foreign policy or international obligations, the overseas launch certificate should not be granted;

(d) any other criteria prescribed by the regulations.

(3) The Minister may, in deciding whether to grant the overseas launch certificate, have regard to:

(a) whether there is an agreement or arrangement between Australia and the other launching State, or any of the other launching States, under which that State or those States assume liability, and indemnify Australia, for any damage that the space object or objects may cause; and

(b) the terms of that agreement or arrangement.

Note: This subsection does not, by implication, limit the matters to which the Minister may have regard.

36 Terms of overseas launch certificate

(1) An overseas launch certificate authorising the launch of a space object or objects:

(a) must specify the day on which it comes into force and the period for which it remains in force; and

(b) is granted subject to any conditions specified in the certificate.

(2) An overseas launch certificate may specify that the period during which it remains in force ends on the occurrence of a particular event (rather than at a

specified time). For this purpose, the regulations may set out how to determine when events of a particular kind occur.

> Example: An overseas launch certificate might specify that its period expires when the relevant launch has been (successfully or unsuccessfully) completed. The regulations could set out how to determine when this is.

(3) At any time when an overseas launch certificate is in force, the Minister may, by written notice, extend or further extend the period for which the certificate remains in force.

37 Breaching a condition

The holder of an overseas launch certificate must not contravene a condition of the certificate.

> Note: Contravening this section is not an offence. However, a person who contravenes this section is liable to a civil penalty under Part 6.

38 Transfer of overseas launch certificate

(1) The Minister may, by written notice, transfer an overseas launch certificate to another person if the Minister would have power to grant the overseas launch certificate to the other person under section 35.

(2) The transfer takes effect at the time specified in the notice.

(3) The certificate continues to cover the same launch facility, the same kind of launch vehicle and the same space object or objects.

(4) The certificate has effect subject to the same conditions as the original certificate (unless the Minister varies the conditions).

(5) The period for which the certificate remains in force continues to run despite the transfer.

39 Applying for the grant, variation or transfer of an overseas launch certificate

An application for the grant, variation or transfer of an overseas launch certificate must be made in accordance with the regulations.

40 Procedure etc.

(1) If the Minister considers that there may be grounds to vary, revoke or transfer an overseas launch certificate (other than at the certificate holder's request), the Minister must:
   (a) give the holder of the certificate written notice of the Minister's opinion specifying the reasons for that opinion; and
   (b) invite the holder to make a written submission to the Minister about the matter within a reasonable period specified in the notice.

(2) In deciding whether to vary, revoke or transfer the certificate, the Minister must consider the matters raised in any submission received within the period specified in the notice.

(3) An overseas launch certificate must not be varied in a way that changes the location of the relevant launch facility.

(4) The regulations may prescribe other ways in which an overseas launch certificate must not be varied.

41 Suspending an overseas launch certificate

(1) The Minister may, by written notice, suspend an overseas launch certificate if:
   (a) the holder of the certificate contravenes a condition of the certificate; or
   (b) in a subparagraph 35(2)(a)(i) case—the Minister is satisfied that the insurance/financial requirements in Division 7 are not satisfied for a launch to be conducted under the certificate; or
   (c) the Minister considers that, for reasons relevant to Australia's national security, foreign policy or international obligations, the certificate should be suspended.

Note: Under subsection 33(3) of the *Acts Interpretation Act 1901*, the Minister may revoke a suspension.

(2) An overseas launch certificate has no effect while suspended, but the period for which it remains in force continues to run despite the suspension.

(3) An overseas launch certificate may be revoked or varied even while it is suspended.

Division 5—Authorisation of return of overseas-launched space objects

42 Scope of Division

This Division applies if:
(a) a space object is launched, or is proposed to be launched, from a launch facility outside Australia; and
(b) in connection with that launch, a space object is proposed to be returned to an area or place within Australia.

Note: The returning space object need not be the same as the space object launched. For example, a launch vehicle could carry a payload into an area beyond the distance of 100 km above mean sea level and return without it, or even collect a different payload from an area beyond the distance of 100 km above mean sea level and return that to Earth.

43 Returns may be authorised by permission or by agreement

(1) The Minister may give a person written permission authorising:
(a) the return of the space object concerned to a specified place or area in Australia; or
(b) a particular series of such returns that, in the Minister's opinion, having regard to the nature of the space objects to be returned, may appropriately be authorised by a single permission.

Note: Under subsection 33(3) of the *Acts Interpretation Act 1901*, the Minister may vary or revoke an authorisation granted under this section.

(2) Alternatively, the Minister may, on behalf of the Commonwealth, enter into an agreement with a person under which such a return or such a series of returns is authorised.

(3) The return or returns may be authorised under this section only if all of the following criteria are satisfied:
   (a) the Minister is satisfied that the person who is to carry out the return or returns is competent to do so;
   (b) the Minister is satisfied that the insurance/financial requirements in Division 7 will be satisfied for the return or returns;
   (c) the Minister is satisfied that the probability of the return or returns causing substantial harm to public health or public safety or causing substantial damage to property is as low as is reasonably practicable;
   (d) the space object or objects concerned are not and do not contain a nuclear weapon or a weapon of mass destruction of any other kind;
   (e) the Minister does not consider that, for reasons relevant to Australia's national security, foreign policy or international obligations, the authorisation should not be given;
   (f) any other criteria prescribed by the regulations.

(4) The Minister may, in deciding whether to give an authorisation under this section, have regard to:
   (a) whether there is an agreement or arrangement between Australia and any country that is a launching State for any space object concerned under which that country assumes any liability, and indemnifies Australia, for any damage that the space object may cause; and
   (b) the terms of that agreement or arrangement.

Note: This subsection does not, by implication, limit the matters to which the Minister may have regard.

(5) An authorisation under this section may be given subject to any conditions that the Minister determines.

44 Offences relating to returns

(1) If a person returns a space object purportedly in accordance with an authorisation of the kind mentioned in section 43 and:
   (a) the return is conducted in a way that is likely to cause substantial harm to public health or public safety or to cause substantial damage to property; or
   (b) the space object is or contains a nuclear weapon or a weapon of mass destruction of any other kind; or
   (c) the space object contains any fissionable material and the Minister's written approval for this has not first been obtained; or
   (d) the insurance/financial requirements in Division 7 are not satisfied for the return;
   the person is guilty of an offence punishable on conviction by:
   (e) in the case of a body corporate—a fine not exceeding 100,000 penalty units; or
   (f) in the case of an individual—imprisonment for a term not exceeding 10 years, or a fine not exceeding 600 penalty units, or both.

   Note 1: Chapter 2 of the *Criminal Code* sets out the general principles of criminal responsibility.

   Note 2: See section 4AA of the *Crimes Act 1914* for the current value of a penalty unit.

(2) The Minister may take civil proceedings under Part 6 against a person who is alleged to have committed an offence against subsection (1), as an alternative to prosecution.

45 Breaching a condition

A person who is authorised under section 43 to return a space object must not contravene a condition of the authorisation.

Note: Contravening this section is not an offence. However, a person who contravenes this section is liable to a civil penalty under Part 6.

45A Applying for an authorisation or for the variation of an authorisation

An application for an authorisation under section 43, or for the variation of such an authorisation, must be made in accordance with the regulations.

45B Procedure etc.

(1) If the Minister considers that there may be grounds to vary or revoke an authorisation under section 43 (other than at the authorisation holder's request), the Minister must:

(a) give the holder of the authorisation written notice of the Minister's opinion specifying the reasons for that opinion; and

(b) invite the holder to make a written submission to the Minister about the matter within a reasonable period specified in the notice.

(2) In deciding whether to vary or revoke the authorisation, the Minister must consider the matters raised in any submission received within the period specified in the notice.

45C Suspending an authorisation under section 43

(1) The Minister may, by written notice, suspend an authorisation under section 43 if:

(a) the holder of the authorisation contravenes a condition of the authorisation; or

(b) the Minister considers that, for reasons relevant to Australia's national security, foreign policy or international obligations, the authorisation should be suspended; or

(c) an incident involving a space object covered by the authorisation occurs during the liability period for the return of the object.

Note: Under subsection 33(3) of the *Acts Interpretation Act 1901*, the Minister may revoke a suspension.

(2) An authorisation under section 43 has no effect while suspended.

(3) An authorisation under section 43 may be varied or revoked even while it is suspended.

Division 6—Exemption certificates
46 Exemption certificates

(1) The Minister may issue to any person an exemption certificate covering specified conduct that might otherwise be prohibited under section 11, 13 or 15.

> Note 1: Under subsection 33(3) of the *Acts Interpretation Act 1901*, the Minister may vary or revoke an exemption certificate.

> Note 2: Under subsection 33(3A) of the *Acts Interpretation Act 1901*, conduct may be specified by reference to a particular class or classes of conduct.

(2) The regulations may set out matters to which the Minister must have regard in deciding whether to issue an exemption certificate.

> Example: The regulations might set out criteria such as whether a launch would be in the national interest or would confer a significant national benefit, whether there is a risk that a launch might cause substantial harm to public health or public safety or damage to property or whether there is a risk that a launch might expose the Commonwealth to liability for damage caused.

> Note: This subsection does not, by implication, limit the matters to which the Minister may have regard.

(3) Within 7 sitting days of issuing an exemption certificate under this section, the Minister must cause a copy of the exemption certificate to be tabled in each House of the Parliament.

46A Terms of exemption certificate

(1) An exemption certificate:
　(a) comes into force on a specified day or when a specified event happens; and

(b) remains in force for a specified period (which may be a period that ends on the occurrence of a specified event).

(2) For the purposes of subsection (1), the regulations may set out how to determine when events of a particular kind occur.

(3) At any time when an exemption certificate is in force, the Minister may, by written notice, extend or further extend the period for which the certificate remains in force.

(4) An exemption certificate is granted subject to any conditions specified in the certificate.

46B Breaching a condition

The holder of an exemption certificate must not contravene a condition of the certificate.

Note: Contravening this section is not an offence. However, a person who contravenes this section is liable to a civil penalty under Part 6.

Division 7—Insurance/financial requirements

47 Satisfying the insurance/financial requirements

(1) This Division sets out the *insurance/financial requirements* mentioned in Divisions 3, 4 and 5.

(2) The holder of a launch permit, overseas launch certificate or section 43 authorisation, covering a launch or return, satisfies the *insurance/financial requirements* for the launch or return if:
  (a) throughout the liability period for the launch or return, the insurance requirements in section 48 are satisfied; or
  (b) the holder has, in accordance with the regulations, shown direct financial responsibility for the launch or return for an amount not less than the amount that would otherwise have been applicable under subsection 48(3) for the launch or return.

48 Insurance requirements

(1) The insurance requirements are satisfied for:

(a) a launch or return authorised by a launch permit; or
(b) a return authorised under section 43;
if:
(c) the holder of the permit or authorisation is insured (to the extent required by subsection (3)) against any liability that the holder might incur under this Act to pay compensation for any damage to third parties that the launch or return causes; and
(d) the Commonwealth is insured (to the extent required by subsection (3)) against any liability that the Commonwealth might incur, under the Liability Convention or otherwise under international law, to pay compensation for such damage.

Note 1: The insurance cover mentioned in paragraphs (c) and (d) may be provided by separate policies. Alternatively, the holder of the permit or authorisation could take out a single policy that insures both the holder and the Commonwealth.

Note 2: The Commonwealth is under no duty to take out any insurance cover under this subsection—the onus is on the holder of the permit or authorisation to ensure that the insurance/financial requirements are satisfied.

(2) The insurance requirements are satisfied for a launch authorised by an overseas launch certificate if the Commonwealth is insured (to the extent required by subsection (3)) against any liability of the Commonwealth, under the Liability Convention or otherwise under international law, to pay compensation for any damage to third parties that the launch causes.

Note 1: The holder of the certificate could take out a single policy that insures both the holder and the Commonwealth.

Note 2: The Commonwealth is under no duty to take out any insurance cover under this subsection—the onus is on the holder of the certificate to ensure that the insurance/financial requirements are satisfied.

(3) The total insurance, for each launch or return concerned, must be for an amount not less than the lesser of the amount of $750 million (as indexed from time to time in accordance with the regulations) and:
   (a) the amount of the maximum probable loss that may be incurred in respect of damage to third parties caused by the launch or return, as determined using the method set out in the regulations; or
   (b) if the regulations set out a different method of determining a minimum amount for the purposes of this subsection—the amount determined using that method.

49 Additional insurance not precluded

Nothing in this Act prevents any person from taking out any additional insurance.

Division 8—Launch Safety Officer

50 Launch Safety Officer

For each licensed launch facility, the Minister must, by writing, appoint a Launch Safety Officer. The same person may be Launch Safety Officer for more than one facility.

51 Functions of Launch Safety Officer

The functions of the Launch Safety Officer for a licensed launch facility are:
   (a) to ensure that notice is given, in accordance with the regulations, of launches conducted at the facility; and
   (aa) to ensure that notice is given, in accordance with the regulations, of returns of space objects that were launched from the facility; and
   (b) to ensure that no person or property is endangered by any launch conducted at the facility, until the space object is safely in Earth orbit or beyond; and
   (ba) to ensure that no person or property is endangered by any return of a space object that was launched from the facility; and

(c) to monitor the compliance by persons who hold a space licence or launch permit relating to the facility with this Act and with the conditions of the licence or permit.

52 Powers of Launch Safety Officer

(1) The Launch Safety Officer for a licensed launch facility may do all things that are reasonably necessary or convenient to be done for the performance of his or her functions.

(2) In particular, the Launch Safety Officer for a licensed launch facility may:
   (a) with the consent of the holder of the relevant space licence, or of any person authorised by the holder to give that consent:
      (i) enter and inspect the facility and any space object at the facility; and
      (ii) inspect and test any other equipment at the facility; and
   (b) ask the holder, or any employee, agent or contractor of the holder, to give him or her any information or assistance, for which he or she reasonably asks, to assist in the proper performance of his or her functions; and
   (c) give any directions about the launch of a space object carried out, or proposed to be carried out, at the facility that he or she considers necessary to avoid any danger to public health or to persons or property, including directions to stop the launch or destroy the space object (whether before or after it is launched); and
   (d) give any directions about the return of a space object that was launched from the facility that he or she considers necessary to avoid any danger to public health or to persons or property, including directions to stop the return or destroy the space object.

(3) The Launch Safety Officer's powers under this section do not entitle him or her to enter a licensed launch facility without the consent of the holder of the relevant space

licence or of a person authorised by the holder to give that consent.

(4) The Launch Safety Officer for a licensed launch facility is not entitled to exercise any powers under this section at or on the facility if:
   (a) the holder of the relevant space licence, or an employee or agent of the holder, has required the Launch Safety Officer to show identification; and
   (b) the Launch Safety Officer fails to comply with the requirement.

(5) The Launch Safety Officer's functions and powers do not entitle him or her to be involved in the normal business operations of the holder of a space licence or launch permit.

53 Offence of failing to comply with directions

A person who fails to comply with a direction that the Launch Safety Officer for a licensed launch facility gives under paragraph 52(2)(c) or (d) is guilty of an offence.

Maximum penalty: 100 penalty units.

Note 1:   Chapter 2 of the *Criminal Code* sets out the general principles of criminal responsibility.

Note 2:   See section 4AA of the *Crimes Act 1914* for the current value of a penalty unit.

54 Procedure for giving and complying with directions

(1) The regulations may prescribe the procedure to be followed by:
   (a) the Launch Safety Officer for a licensed launch facility in giving directions under paragraph 52(2)(c) or (d); and
   (b) any person to whom the Launch Safety Officer gives such a direction.

(2) The regulations may prescribe penalties not exceeding 100 penalty units for contravening regulations made for the purposes of paragraph (1)(b) of this section.

55 Launch Safety Officer to comply with Minister's instructions

(1) In performing a function or exercising a power under this Act, the Launch Safety Officer for a licensed launch facility must comply with any instructions the Minister gives the Launch Safety Officer.

(2) The Minister may give different instructions for different licensed launch facilities.

(3) Within 15 sitting days of giving an instruction to a Launch Safety Officer the Minister must cause a copy of the instruction to be tabled in each House of the Parliament.

56 Seizures in emergency situations

(1) If, while exercising powers at or on a licensed launch facility, the Launch Safety Officer for the facility suspects, on reasonable grounds, that:
  (a) a thing relevant to an offence against this Act is at or on the facility; and
  (b) because the circumstances are so serious and urgent, it is necessary to:
    (i) search the facility, and any receptacle at or on the facility, for the thing; or
    (ii) seize the thing;
  to stop the thing from being concealed, lost or destroyed;
  the Launch Safety Officer may do so.

(2) The Launch Safety Officer's functions and powers do not entitle him or her to seize anything otherwise than in accordance with this section.

57 Launch Safety Officer may obtain assistance

The Launch Safety Officer for a licensed launch facility may arrange for other persons to assist him or her in the performance of his or her functions for the facility.

58 Identity cards

(1) The Minister must issue the Launch Safety Officer for a licensed launch facility with an identity card.

(2) An identity card must include a recent photograph of the person.

(3) As soon as practicable after a person ceases to be the Launch Safety Officer for a licensed launch facility, the person must return his or her identity card to the Minister.

(4) A person who fails to do so is guilty of an offence.

> Maximum penalty: 1 penalty unit.

> Note 1:   Chapter 2 of the *Criminal Code* sets out the general principles of criminal responsibility.

> Note 2:   See section 4AA of the *Crimes Act 1914* for the current value of a penalty unit.

Division 9—Administration etc.
59 Fees

(1) The applicant for a launch permit, or for a transfer or variation of a launch permit, must pay the Commonwealth any fee the regulations set in respect of the application.

(2) The applicant for an overseas launch certificate, or for a transfer or variation of an overseas launch certificate, must pay the Commonwealth any fee the regulations set in respect of the application.

(2A) The applicant for an authorisation under section 43, or for the variation of such an authorisation, must pay the Commonwealth any fee the regulations set in respect of the application.

(3) The applicant for a space licence, or for a transfer or variation of a space licence, must pay the Commonwealth any fee the regulations set in respect of the application.

(3A) The holder of a space licence must pay the Commonwealth any annual licence fee the regulations set in respect of the licence.

(4) The applicant for an exemption certificate must pay the Commonwealth any fee the regulations set in respect of the application.

(5) A person who inspects the Register must pay the Commonwealth any fee the regulations set in respect of the inspection.

(6) The regulations may set a fee mentioned in this section by setting the amount of the fee or a way of working out the fee.

(6A) The regulations may make provision for approved scientific or educational organisations to be charged different fees under this section than other persons.

(7) A fee must not be such as to amount to taxation.

(8) The regulations may specify the time for payment of a fee.

(9) The regulations may prescribe the circumstances in which the Minister may wholly or partly waive fees that would otherwise be payable under this section.

60 Request for information

The Minister may, by written notice, ask:
  (a) an applicant for, or the holder of, a space licence; or
  (b) an applicant for, or the holder of, a launch permit; or
  (c) an applicant for, or the holder of, an overseas launch certificate; or
  (d) an applicant for, or the holder of, an authorisation under section 43;

to give the Minister, within the period specified in the notice, any information the Minister requires for the purposes of performing functions or exercising powers under this Act in relation to the licence, permit, certificate or authorisation.

61 Review of decisions

An application may be made to the Administrative Appeals Tribunal for review of any decision of the Minister:
  (a) refusing to grant, vary or transfer a space licence; or
  (b) varying, revoking, suspending or transferring a space licence; or
  (c) refusing to grant, vary or transfer a launch permit or overseas launch certificate; or
  (d) varying, revoking, suspending or transferring a launch permit or overseas launch certificate; or
  (e) refusing to extend, or further extend, the period for which a launch permit or overseas launch certificate remains in force; or
  (f) refusing to give or vary an authorisation under section 43; or
  (g) varying, revoking or suspending an authorisation under section 43; or
  (h) refusing to grant or vary an exemption certificate; or
  (i) varying or revoking an exemption certificate; or

(ia) refusing to extend, or further extend, the period for which an exemption certificate remains in force; or

(j) imposing a particular condition or conditions on a space licence, launch permit, overseas launch certificate, authorisation under section 43 or exemption certificate; or

(k) refusing to make a declaration under section 8A; or

(l) varying or revoking a declaration under section 8A.

62 Notice of decisions

If the Minister varies, revokes, suspends, reinstates or transfers a space licence, launch permit, overseas launch certificate, exemption certificate or authorisation under section 43, the Minister must publish in the *Gazette* a notice that this has happened.

Part 4—Liability for damage by space objects
Division 1—Scope of Part
63 Damage covered

(1) This Part applies to damage a space object causes if:
   (a) either:
      (i) the object is launched from a launch facility in Australia; or
      (ii) Australia is a launching State in relation to the object; and
   (b) the damage is caused during the liability period for the launch.

(2) This Part also applies to damage a space object causes if:
   (a) the object is returned to a place in Australia; and
   (b) the damage is caused during the liability period for the return.

(2A) This Part also applies to damage a space object causes if:
   (a) either:
      (i) the object is launched from a launch facility in Australia; or
      (ii) Australia is a launching State in relation to the object; and

(b) the object is returned to a place outside Australia; and

(c) the damage is caused during the liability period for the return.

(3) This Part applies to damage mentioned in subsection (1), (2) or (2A):

(a) whether the damage happens on Earth, in the air or in space; and

(b) whether the damage happens in Australia or outside it; and

(c) whether or not the launch or return was authorised under this Act; and

(d) whether or not the launch or return was covered by an exemption certificate.

64 Compensation for third party damage by space objects to be determined solely under this Part

(1) Compensation for damage to which this Part applies caused to third parties is only payable in accordance with this Part.

(2) However, this section does not prevent Australia from complying with any obligation to pay compensation under the Liability Convention, or otherwise under international law, for such damage.

> Note: This section does not affect the rights of persons who are not third parties (for example, employees of a responsible party) from seeking compensation outside of this Act for damage to which this Part applies. However, see also section 65 (which allows the regulations to make provision in relation to the waiver of such rights).

65 Regulations about waivers

The regulations may make provision in relation to the waiver of some or all of the rights of persons connected with a launch or return, and of their employees, contractors and subcontractors, to seek compensation for damage to which this Part applies.

Division 2—Liability for third party damage

Subdivision A—Rules for damage caused by launches and most returns

66 Scope of Subdivision

This Subdivision applies to all damage to which this Part applies, except for damage a space object causes in connection with the return of the space object where:

(a) neither the object, nor any part of it, was launched from a launch facility located within Australia; and

(b) the responsible party for the return is not an Australian national.

Note: Subdivision B deals with that other kind of damage.

67 Damage on Earth or in the air

(1) The responsible party for the launch or return of a space object is liable to pay compensation for any damage the space object causes to a third party:

(a) on Earth; or

(b) as a result of damage to aircraft in flight.

(2) However, the responsible party is not liable to the extent that the responsible party establishes that the damage resulted from:

(a) the gross negligence of the third party; or

(b) any conduct (whether by act or omission) that the third party engaged in with intent to cause the damage.

68 Damage to other space objects

The responsible party for the launch or return of a space object is liable to pay compensation for any damage the space object causes, otherwise than on Earth or as a result of damage to aircraft in flight:

(a) to a space object launched or operated by a third party; or

(b) to a third party, or the property of a third party, on board such a space object;

to the extent that the damage is due to the fault of the responsible party or of a related party.

69 Limit on amount of permit or certificate holder's liability

(1) This section applies if:
   (a) the launch or return of a space object that causes damage covered by this Subdivision was authorised by a launch permit; and
   (b) the damage did not result from a breach of any of the conditions of the permit or of the relevant space licence, from any conduct (whether by act or omission) that the responsible party or a related party engaged in with intent to cause the damage or from the gross negligence of the responsible party or a related party.

(2) This section also applies if:
   (a) the launch of a space object that causes damage covered by this Subdivision was authorised by an overseas launch certificate; and
   (b) the damage did not result from a breach of any of the conditions of the certificate, any conduct (whether by act or omission) that the responsible party or a related party engaged in with intent to cause the damage or from the gross negligence of the responsible party or a related party.

(3) The responsible party is not liable to pay compensation for the damage to the extent that the amount of the compensation would exceed the insured amount for the launch permit or overseas launch certificate.

(4) If:
   (a) the responsible party has paid compensation for the damage of an amount equal to the insured amount for the launch permit or overseas launch certificate; and
   (b) apart from this section, the responsible party would be liable to pay further compensation to Australian nationals for the damage of an amount (the **excess amount**) in excess of the insured amount for the launch permit or overseas launch certificate;

then the Commonwealth is liable to pay compensation to the Australian nationals for the damage of an amount equal to so much of the excess amount as does not exceed $3 billion.

(5) The Consolidated Revenue Fund is appropriated for the purposes of payments by the Commonwealth under subsection (4).

Subdivision B—Rules for certain returns conducted by overseas nationals

70 Scope of Subdivision

This Subdivision applies to damage to which this Part applies that a space object causes in connection with the return of the space object where:

(a) neither the object, nor any part of it, was launched from a launch facility located within Australia; and

(b) the responsible party for the return is not an Australian national.

Note: Subdivision A deals with the other kinds of damage to which this Part applies.

71 Liability

The responsible party for the return is liable to pay compensation for any damage the space object causes to a third party.

Division 3—Procedure etc.
72 Federal Court has jurisdiction

The Federal Court has jurisdiction to hear and determine actions for compensation for damage to which this Part applies.

73 Action for compensation

(1) An action for compensation for damage to which this Part applies may only be brought:
  (a) within one year after the day on which the damage occurred; or
  (b) if, when the damage occurred, the person bringing the action did not know that it had occurred—within one year after the day on which the person:
    (i) became aware of the damage; or
    (ii) would have become aware of the damage, if the person had exercised due diligence.

(2) If, in accordance with the Liability Convention or otherwise under international law:
  (a) a foreign country has presented a claim against Australia for compensation for damage caused by a space object to which a launch permit, overseas launch certificate, section 43 authorisation or exemption certificate relates; or
  (b) such a claim made by a foreign country has been settled;

a person who has suffered damage covered by the claim may not commence an action, against the responsible party, seeking compensation for that damage.

Division 4—Compensation claims by foreign countries
74 Responsible party's liability to the Commonwealth

(1) This section applies if, in accordance with the Liability Convention or otherwise under international law:
   (a) a foreign country has presented a claim against Australia for compensation for damage covered by this Part; and
   (b) Australia becomes liable to any extent to pay compensation for the damage.

(2) The responsible party for the relevant launch or return is liable to pay the Commonwealth an amount equal to the lesser of the following amounts:
   (a) the amount of that compensation;
   (b) if the launch or return of the space object concerned was authorised by a launch permit or overseas launch certificate, and section 69 applies—the insured amount for the permit or certificate.

Note: A foreign country could not present a claim against Australia under the Liability Convention if proceedings under this Part were already in progress in respect of the same damage: see Article XI.2 of the Convention.

75 Claims Commission

If, in accordance with the Liability Convention, it is necessary to establish a Claims Commission to settle a claim presented to the Commonwealth, the Commonwealth may do anything that it is required to do under the Convention to establish the Commission and enable it to give a decision or award as provided under the Convention.

Part 5—Register of space objects

76 Minister to keep Register

(1) The Minister must keep a Register of Space Objects.

(2) The Minister must enter in the Register the following particulars for a space object that is launched into Earth orbit or beyond under an authorisation provided under this Act:
   (a) the registration number given to the space object under section 77;
   (b) the launch facility;
   (c) the date of the launch;
   (d) the space object's basic orbital parameters, including:
      (i) the nodal period; and
      (ii) its inclination; and
      (iii) its apogee and perigee;
   (e) the space object's general functions;
   (f) if a country other than Australia is also a launching State for the space object—the name of that country;
   (g) any other prescribed particulars.

(3) In keeping the Register, the Minister must have regard to the Registration Convention and any other international agreement or arrangement relating to the registration of space objects to which Australia is a party.

(4) The Minister may vary or remove an entry on the register as needed.

77 Registration number

(1) When the Minister grants a launch permit authorising the launch of a space object from a launch facility, the Minister must allocate to the space object a registration number by which it can be identified.

(2) The Minister may allocate a registration number to a space object at any other time.

78 Register may be kept on computer

The Minister may keep the Register in whole or in part by using a computer.

79 Inspection of Register

(1) The Minister must make the Register available for any person to inspect it at the times and places published in the *Gazette*.

(2) The Minister may do so by allowing a person who wants to inspect the Register reasonable access to a computer terminal from which he or she can read on a screen, or get a printed copy of, an entry in the Register.

Part 5A—Implementation of space cooperation agreements

79A Implementation of intergovernmental agreement with Russia

(1) Regulations may be made for and in relation to giving effect to one or more provisions of the intergovernmental agreement with Russia.

(2) Regulations under subsection (1) must not come into operation on a day earlier than the day on which the agreement enters into force in Australia.

79B Regulations may amend Schedule

Regulations may be made to amend Schedule 6 for the purposes of ensuring that Schedule 6 correctly sets out the English text of the intergovernmental agreement with Russia as in force from time to time.

Part 6—Civil penalties

80 Civil penalty provisions

This Part applies to a contravention of any of the following provisions (called ***civil penalty provisions***):

(a) section 15 (space licence required to operate launch facility);

(b) section 21 (breaching a space licence condition);

(c) subsections 30(1) and (2) (breaching a launch permit condition);

(d) section 37 (breaching a condition of an overseas launch certificate);

(e) section 44 (offences relating to returns);

(f) section 45 (breaching a condition of a section 43 authorisation);

(fa) section 46B (breaching a condition of an exemption certificate);

(g) subsection 109(3) (pre-existing agreements).

81 Fines for contravening civil penalty provisions

(1) If the Federal Court is satisfied, on the balance of probabilities, that a person has contravened a civil penalty provision, the Court may order the person to pay the Commonwealth such fine, by way of civil penalty, in respect of the contravention as the Court determines to be appropriate.

(2) In determining the civil penalty, the Court must have regard to the following matters:

(a) the nature and extent of the contravention;

(b) the nature and extent of any loss or damage suffered as a result of the contravention;

(c) the circumstances in which the contravention took place;

(d) whether, in proceedings under this Act, the person has previously been found to have engaged in similar conduct.

The Court may also have regard to any other matters it considers relevant.

(3) The civil penalty payable under subsection (1) must not exceed:
   (a) in the case of a body corporate—5,000 penalty units; or
   (b) in the case of an individual—500 penalty units.

   Note: See section 4AA of the *Crimes Act 1914* for the current value of a penalty unit.

(4) The Federal Court may make such declarations or orders as it considers appropriate in relation to the proceedings, including:
   (a) a declaration that the person did not contravene a civil penalty provision; and
   (b) an order as to costs.

82 Procedure

(1) The Minister may, by application, take proceedings in the Federal Court for the payment of a civil penalty mentioned in section 81.

(2) The proceedings must be commenced within 6 years after the contravention.

(3) In hearing and determining the proceedings, the Federal Court is to apply the rules of evidence and procedure that it applies in hearing and determining civil matters.

83 Not an offence to contravene civil penalty provision

A person is not guilty of an offence merely because the person has contravened a civil penalty provision.

Part 7—Investigation of accidents
Division 1—Scope of Part
84 Scope of Part

This Part applies if an accident (see section 85) or an incident (see section 86) involving a space object occurs during:
(a) the liability period for the launch of the space object from a launch facility located in Australia; or
(b) the liability period for the return of the space object to a place in Australia.

85 Meaning of *accident*

An *accident* involving a space object occurs if:
(a) a person dies or suffers serious injury as a result of the operation of the space object; or
(b) the space object is destroyed or seriously damaged or causes damage to property (other than in the circumstances prescribed by the regulations).

86 Meaning of *incident*

An *incident* is an occurrence associated with the operation of a space object that affects or could affect the safety of the operation of the space object or that involves circumstances indicating that an accident nearly occurred.

Division 2—Investigations
87 Object of Division

(1) The object of this Division is, by establishing a system of investigating the circumstances surrounding any accident or incident, to prevent other accidents and incidents occurring.

(2) It is not the object of this Division:
(a) to provide a way of apportioning blame for an accident or incident; or
(b) to provide a way of determining the liability of any person in respect of an accident or incident.

88 Appointing an Investigator

(1) If an accident occurs, the Minister must appoint a person as the Investigator of the accident.

(2) If an incident occurs, the Minister may appoint a person as the Investigator of the incident.

(3) Before appointing a person under this section, the Minister must be satisfied that the person has suitable qualifications and experience to be an Investigator.

89 Investigator to investigate accident or incident

(1) An Investigator appointed under section 88 must investigate the circumstances surrounding the relevant accident or incident.

(2) In particular, the Minister may determine the terms of reference of the investigation.

90 Investigator may invite assistance

(1) An Investigator may invite other persons to assist him or her in performing any or all of his or her functions under this Division.

(2) A person who gives such assistance is entitled to be paid fees and allowances for expenses, as determined under the regulations.

91 Investigator's powers to gather information

(1) In conducting an investigation under this Division, the Investigator may, by written notice:
  (a) require a person to attend before the Investigator and answer questions about matters relevant to the investigation; and
  (b) require the person to give the Investigator a specified document or record, a specified part or component of a space object or any other thing relevant to the investigation.

(2) A notice under subsection (1) must be signed by the Investigator and must specify the time and place at which the person is required to attend or to give the relevant thing.

(3) The Investigator may require the person to answer questions mentioned in paragraph (1)(a) on oath or

affirmation. For that purpose, the Investigator may administer an oath or affirmation to the person.

(4) The Investigator may:
   (a) retain a thing given in accordance with a requirement under subsection (1) for as long as is reasonably necessary for the purposes of the investigation; and
   (b) if the thing is a document or record—make copies of, or take extracts from, the document or record.

(5) If a person answers a question in accordance with subsection (1), the answer, and any information or thing obtained directly or indirectly as a result, is not admissible in evidence against the person in any proceeding (other than a proceeding in respect of the falsity of the answer).

(6) If a person gives a thing in accordance with subsection (1), the thing, and any information or thing obtained directly or indirectly as a result, is not admissible in evidence against the person in a criminal proceeding or in a proceeding for the recovery of a penalty.

(7) A person who attends before the Investigator under this section is entitled to be paid fees and allowances for expenses, as determined under the regulations.

92 Offences relating to section 91 requirements

(1) A person to whom a requirement under subsection 91(1) is given and who:
   (a) fails to attend before the Investigator in accordance with the requirement; or
   (b) refuses to take an oath or make an affirmation when required by the Investigator to do so; or
   (c) refuses or fails to answer a question lawfully put to the person by the Investigator; or
   (d) fails to give the Investigator a thing in accordance with the requirement, if it would have been reasonably practicable to have done so;
   is guilty of an offence.

Maximum penalty: 30 penalty units.

Note 1: Chapter 2 of the *Criminal Code* sets out the general principles of criminal responsibility.

Note 2: See section 4AA of the *Crimes Act 1914* for the current value of a penalty unit.

(2) However, a person is not required to answer a question or give a thing if doing so might tend to incriminate the person or expose the person to a penalty.

(3) A person to whom a requirement under subsection 91(1) is given and who:
   (a) gives information to the Investigator in answering a question lawfully put to the person by the Investigator; and
   (b) does so knowing that the information is false or misleading in a material particular;
is guilty of an offence.

Maximum penalty: Imprisonment for 12 months.

Note: Chapter 2 of the *Criminal Code* sets out the general principles of criminal responsibility.

(4) A person to whom a requirement under subsection 91(1) is given and who:
   (a) gives a document or record to the Investigator in accordance with the requirement; and
   (b) does so knowing that the document or record is false or misleading in a material particular;
is guilty of an offence.

Maximum penalty: Imprisonment for 12 months.

Note: Chapter 2 of the *Criminal Code* sets out the general principles of criminal responsibility.

(5) Subsection (4) does not apply if, when the person gave the document or record to the Investigator, the person informed the Investigator that it was false or misleading in a material particular and specified in what respect it was false or misleading.

93 Report of investigation

(1) When an investigation is completed, the Investigator must give the Minister a written report of the investigation and, if the Minister requires, any relevant documents, records or other things.

(2) Subject to subsection (3), no part of a report or other document given to the Minister under this section may be published without the Minister's written approval.

(3) The Minister may cause to be published any information contained in a report or document given to the Minister under this section if he or she considers that publishing the information is desirable in the interest of promoting safety in the space industry.

94 Custody of space object etc.

(1) If an accident occurs, the space object or the space object wreckage concerned and any thing in the space object or wreckage is taken to be in the Minister's custody until an Investigator is appointed for the accident. The things are then taken to be in the Investigator's custody.

(2) When it is no longer necessary to retain any such thing for the purposes of the investigation, the Investigator must release custody of the thing to its owner or to a person the owner authorises to receive it.

(3) A person who removes or otherwise interferes with a thing that is in the custody of the Minister or Investigator under subsection (1), except:
   (a) with the permission of the Minister or Investigator; or
   (b) as mentioned in subsection (4);
   is guilty of an offence.

   Maximum penalty: Imprisonment for 6 months.

   Note: Chapter 2 of the *Criminal Code* sets out the general principles of criminal responsibility.

(4) Subsection (3) does not prevent any action necessary for all or any of the following:
   (a) extracting persons (including deceased persons) from the wreckage of a space object;

(b) protecting the wreckage from being destroyed by fire or other cause;

(c) preventing immediate danger to the safety of persons or property;

(d) moving the space object or the wreckage and its contents to a safe place when the object crashes on water or is wrecked on water.

95 Automatic suspension of launch permit etc. after accident

(1) Immediately after an accident occurs, the launch permit, exemption certificate or section 43 authorisation under which the relevant launch or return was carried out is taken to be suspended, until the Minister revokes the suspension.

(2) The permit, certificate or authorisation has no effect while suspended, but the period for which it remains in force continues to run despite the suspension.

(3) The permit, certificate or authorisation may be revoked or varied even while it is suspended.

96 Disclosure of safety records

(1) An investigation officer (see subsection (9)) must not, except for the purposes of this Part, directly or indirectly:

(a) disclose a safety record (see subsection (9)) to any person or a court; or

(b) give a safety record to any person or a court.

(2) A person who contravenes subsection (1) is guilty of an offence.

Maximum penalty: 30 penalty units.

Note 1:   Chapter 2 of the *Criminal Code* sets out the general principles of criminal responsibility.

Note 2:   See section 4AA of the *Crimes Act 1914* for the current value of a penalty unit.

(3) Subsection (1) does not apply to criminal proceedings, investigations relating to a criminal offence or a proceeding relating to bail.

(4) Subsection (1) does not apply to the disclosure of a safety record to the Minister under section 93.

(5) Subsection (1) does not prohibit an investigation officer from disclosing or giving a safety record to a court if an order is made under subsection (7).

(6) A person may apply to a court for an order that a safety record must be disclosed or given to the court.

(7) If the court is satisfied that the disclosure or production of the safety record is in the public interest, having regard to:
(a) the adverse impact disclosure or production may have on the investigation to which the record relates or to any future investigations; and
(b) any other relevant matter;
the court must order the disclosure or production.

(8) If the court makes such an order, then the court must also make an order that restricts access to the safety record to:
(a) the person or persons constituting the court; and
(b) the parties to the proceeding (including any interveners); and
(c) the parties' legal representatives; and
(d) specified witnesses for the purposes of the proceeding;
unless the court is satisfied that such an order would not be in the interests of justice or would not be desirable in the interests of the court performing its functions.

(9) In this section:

investigation officer means a person who is or has been:
(a) the Minister; or
(b) an Investigator; or
(c) any other person who performs functions or provides services in relation to an investigation under this Part.

safety record means all or any of the following:

(a) all statements (whether oral or written) an Investigator takes from persons in the course of an investigation under this Part, including any record of such a statement;

(b) all communications between persons involved in operating a space object that is involved in an accident or incident;

(c) medical or personal information about persons (including deceased persons) involved in an accident or incident;

or any part of such a thing.

97 Relationship with other powers

The powers and functions of a Commonwealth agency or a person (other than a member of the Australian Federal Police) under another law of the Commonwealth that would allow the agency or person to investigate any matters relating to an accident or incident must be exercised and performed subject to this Part.

Division 3—Accident site powers

98 Accident sites and accident site premises

In this Division:

accident site means:

(a) a site where an accident has occurred; or

(b) a site on which there is an impact point caused by a space object that has been involved in an accident; or

(c) a site on which there is a space object that has been involved in an accident;

together with such area around the site as the Investigator of the accident determines to be reasonably necessary to facilitate the investigation of the accident and securing of the site.

accident site premises means:

(a) premises on which there is an accident site; or

(b) premises that it is necessary to enter to get to premises on which there is an accident site.

99 Power of entry to accident site

(1) An Investigator may:
   (a) with the consent of the occupier of accident site premises; or
   (b) subject to this Division, without the consent of the occupier of accident site premises;

   enter the premises and do any or all of the following for the purposes of investigating a particular accident:
   (c) leave and re-enter the accident site premises at any time during the access period (see subsection (2));
   (d) take control of and secure the accident site during the access period;
   (e) search the accident site;
   (f) take photographs, video recordings or sketches of the accident site or the space object or any other thing on or in the site;
   (g) inspect or examine a thing;
   (h) take samples of a thing;
   (i) measure a thing;
   (j) take equipment to the accident site and operate the equipment;
   (k) remove the space object, the space object wreckage or any other thing from the accident site premises and exercise any of the powers mentioned in paragraphs (g), (h) and (i), take photographs or video recordings or subject the thing to testing.

(2) In this section, the **access period** is the period beginning when the Investigator first enters the accident site premises and ending on the day that the Investigator specifies in a written determination as the last day of the access period.

(3) That day must be no later than is reasonably necessary for investigating the accident and in any case no later than 28 days after the day on which the access period begins.

(4) However, the Minister may, by written determination, extend or further extend the access period beyond that 28 day limit, if the Minister considers it is reasonably necessary for investigating the accident.

100 Procedure before entry

(1) Before an Investigator or a person authorised to assist the Investigator under section 102 enters accident site premises, the Investigator must:
   (a) announce that this Division authorises him or her to enter the premises; and
   (b) give any occupier at the premises an opportunity to allow entry.

(2) When requesting an occupier's consent, the Investigator must tell the person that the Investigator has powers of entry and search under this Division even if the occupier refuses to give his or her consent.

101 Identity cards

(1) The Minister must issue an Investigator a card identifying the holder as an Investigator.

(2) An identity card must include a recent photograph of the holder.

(3) An Investigator or is not entitled to exercise any powers under this Part if:
   (a) the occupier of the relevant premises has required the Investigator to show his or her identity card; and
   (b) the Investigator fails to comply with the requirement.

(4) As soon as practicable after a person ceases to be an Investigator, the person must return his or her identity card to the Minister.

(5) A person who fails to do so is guilty of an offence.

   Maximum penalty: 1 penalty unit.

   Note 1: Chapter 2 of the *Criminal Code* sets out the general principles of criminal responsibility.

   Note 2: See section 4AA of the *Crimes Act 1914* for the current value of a penalty unit.

102 Availability of assistance and use of force in entering accident site premises

In entering accident site premises without the consent of the occupier of the premises:
(a) an Investigator may get such assistance as is necessary and reasonable; and
(b) the Investigator or a person assisting may use such force against the occupier and things as is necessary and reasonable.

103 Offence of entering etc. an accident site without permission

If:
(a) an accident site has been secured under subsection 99(1); and
(b) a person enters or remains on the site without the Investigator's permission;
the person is guilty of an offence.

Maximum penalty: 10 penalty units.

Note 1: Chapter 2 of the *Criminal Code* sets out the general principles of criminal responsibility.

Note 2: See section 4AA of the *Crimes Act 1914* for the current value of a penalty unit.

Part 8—Miscellaneous

104 Delegation

The Minister may, by signed writing, delegate to another person any or all of his or her powers under this Act, if the Minister considers that the person is suitably qualified to exercise the powers concerned.

105 Operation of other laws

Nothing in this Act limits or excludes the operation of other laws of the Commonwealth, except to the extent (if any) that they are inconsistent with this Act.

106 Immunity

A person is not subject to any liability to any person in respect of anything done, or omitted to be done, in good faith in connection with the exercise or performance of powers, functions or duties under this Act.

107 Compensation—constitutional safety net

(1) If:
  (a) apart from this section, the operation of this Act would result in the acquisition of property from a person otherwise than on just terms; and
  (b) the acquisition would be invalid because of paragraph 51(xxxi) of the Constitution;
  the Commonwealth is liable to pay compensation of a reasonable amount to the person in respect of the acquisition.

(2) If the Commonwealth and the person do not agree on the amount of the compensation, the person may take proceedings in the Federal Court for the recovery from the Commonwealth of such reasonable amount of compensation as the Court determines.

(3) In this section:

acquisition of property has the same meaning as in paragraph 51(xxxi) of the Constitution.

just terms has the same meaning as in paragraph 51(xxxi) of the Constitution.

108 Severability: additional effect of Act

(1) Without limiting its effect apart from this section, this Act also has effect as provided by this section.

(2) This Act also has the effect it would have if its operation were expressly confined to:
  (a) giving effect to the UN Space Treaties; and
  (aa) giving effect to specified space cooperation agreements; and
  (b) matters external to Australia; and
  (c) matters of international concern.

(3) This Act also has the effect it would have if:
  (a) the operation of Part 3 were expressly confined to acts or omissions of corporations to which paragraph 51(xx) of the Constitution applies; and

(b) the operation of Part 4 were expressly confined to cases in which the responsible party, for the launch or return of a space object, is such a corporation.

(4) This Act also has the effect it would have if its operation were expressly confined to acts or omissions taking place in the course of, or in relation to, trade or commerce:
   (a) between Australia and places outside Australia; or
   (b) among the States; or
   (c) within a Territory, between a State and a Territory or between 2 Territories.

(5) This Act also has the effect it would have if its operation were expressly confined to acts or omissions taking place in a Territory.

(6) This Act also has the effect it would have if its operation were expressly confined to acts or omissions taking place in a place acquired by the Commonwealth for public purposes.

109 Application of Act: pre-existing agreement

(1) Subject to this section, this Act does not apply in relation to:
   (a) launches or returns, or activities related to launches or returns; or
   (b) the operation of a launch facility or the doing of anything directly connected with the operation of a launch facility;
   in accordance with any agreement made between the Commonwealth and another person before 11 November 1998.

(2) However:
   (a) any term or condition of such an agreement that relates to the launch or return of a space object is taken, for the purposes of this Act, to be a condition (but not a standard launch permit condition) of a launch permit held by the person; and
   (b) any other term or condition of such an agreement is taken, for the purposes of this Act, to be a condition of a space licence held by the person.

(3) If a person launches or returns a space object purportedly in accordance with an agreement mentioned in subsection (1) and:
 (a) the launch or return is conducted in a way that is likely to cause substantial harm to public health or public safety or to cause substantial damage to property; or
 (b) the space object is or contains a nuclear weapon or a weapon of mass destruction of any other kind; or
 (c) the space object contains any fissionable material and the Minister's written approval for this has not first been obtained; or
 (d) the launch or return does not comply with a term or condition of the agreement that requires insurance cover to be obtained in connection with the launch or return;
the person is guilty of an offence punishable on conviction by:
 (e) in the case of a body corporate—a fine not exceeding 100,000 penalty units; or
 (f) in the case of an individual—imprisonment for a term not exceeding 10 years, or a fine not exceeding 600 penalty units, or both.

 Note 1: Chapter 2 of the *Criminal Code* sets out the general principles of criminal responsibility.

 Note 2: See section 4AA of the *Crimes Act 1914* for the current value of a penalty unit.

(4) The Minister may take civil proceedings under Part 6 against a person who is alleged to have committed an offence against subsection (3), as an alternative to prosecution.

(5) An application may be made to the Administrative Appeals Tribunal for review of any decision made under an agreement mentioned in subsection (1) (including a decision made before this Act commenced):
 (a) refusing to authorise activities covered by paragraph (1)(a) or (b); or
 (b) varying, revoking or suspending such an authorisation; or

(c) imposing a particular condition or conditions on the conduct of such activities.

For this purpose, the decision is treated as though it had been made in the exercise of a power conferred by this Act.

(6) Subsection (1) does not apply to Part 5 (which deals with the Register of Space Objects) or to Part 7 (which deals with investigating accidents and incidents).

110 Regulations

(1) The Governor-General may make regulations prescribing matters:
   (a) required or permitted by this Act to be prescribed; or
   (b) necessary or convenient for carrying out or giving effect to this Act.

(2) The regulations may make provision for or in relation to a matter by applying, adopting or incorporating (with or without modification) any matter contained in a written instrument or other document, as in force at a particular time or as in force from time to time.

AUSTRIA

Austrian Federal Law on the Authorization of Space Activities and the Establishment of a National Space Registry (Austrian Outer Space Act, adopted by the National Council on 6 December 2011, entered into force on 28 December 2011)[51]

Scope of Application

§ 1. (1) This Federal Law is applicable to space activities carried out

1. on Austrian territory,

2. on board of vessels or airplanes, registered in Austria or

3. by a natural person with Austrian citizenship or legal persons seated in Austria.

(2) Entitlements under private law are covered by this Federal Law only if Austrian law is applicable according to the rules of private international law.

Definitions

§ 2. Unless otherwise specified, the following definitions shall apply for the purpose of this Federal Law:

1. "Space activity": the launch, operation or control of a space object, as well as the operation of a launch facility;

---

[51] Unofficial translation

2. "Space object": an object launched or intended to be launched into outer space, including its components;

3. "Operator": a natural or juridical person that carries out or undertakes to carry out space activities.

Authorization

§ 3. Space activities require authorization by the Minister for Transport, Innovation and Technology.

Authorization requirements under other provisions than under this Federal Law remain unaffected.

Conditions for authorization

§ 4. (1) The authorization according to § 3 shall be issued if

1. the operator possesses the necessary reliability, capability and expertise to carry out the space activity,

2. the space activity does not pose any immediate threat to the public order, to the safety of persons and property and to public health,

3. the space activity does not run counter to national security, Austria's obligations under international law or Austrian foreign policy interests,

4. appropriate provision has been made for the mitigation of space debris according to § 5,

5. the space activity does not cause harmful contamination of outer space or celestial bodies or adverse changes in the environment,

6. the operator fulfils the requirements of the ITU concerning orbital positions and frequency assignments,

7. the operator has taken out an insurance according to subparagraph 4, and 2

8. the operator has made provision for the orderly termination of the space activity.

(2) The operator of the space activity has to submit all necessary documents for the assessment of the conditions laid down in subparagraph 1.

(3) The authorization may contain conditions and obligations. The Minister for Transport, Innovation and Technology decides on the request for authorization without undue delay and no later than six months after the request has been filed.

(4) In order to cover liability for damages caused to persons and property, the operator is under the obligation to take out an insurance covering a minimum amount of € 60 000 000 per insurance claim. Run-off liability may not be excluded or limited. If the space activity is in the public interest, the Minister for Transport,

Innovation and Technology may determine a lower sum or release the operator from the insurance requirement by administrative decision, taking into account the risks connected to the activity and the operator's financial capacity. Space activities are in the public interest if they serve science, research or education. Taking out insurance is not necessary if the Federal State itself is the operator.

Mitigation of Space debris

§ 5. The operator has to make provision for the mitigation of space debris in accordance with the state of the art and in due consideration of the internationally recognized guidelines for the mitigation of space debris.

Especially measures limiting debris released during normal operations have to be taken.

Modification or termination of the Space activity

§ 6 (1) The operator is under the obligation to notify immediately all incidents which delay or render impossible the carrying out of the space activity authorized under § 4 or which may require the modification or revocation of the authorization according to § 7.

(2) The operator must notify immediately the planned or imminent termination of the activity to the Minister for Transport, Innovation and Technology. The Minister for Transport, Innovation and Technology may issue instructions with regard to the safe termination of the space activity.

Revocation and modification of the authorization

§ 7 (1) The authorization is to be withdrawn whenever the requirements of § 4 (1) are no longer met or the conditions and obligations of § 4 (3) are not complied with.

(2) In the cases of subparagraph 1, the authorization may also be modified as to its content.

(3) In the case of withdrawal of the authorization, measures for the temporary continuation or the safe termination of the activity may be prescribed to the operator. If the operator does not comply with these instructions, control over the space activity shall be conferred to another operator by administrative decision of the Minister for Transport, Innovation and Technology.

Transfer

§ 8. A change of the operator requires the authorization of the Minister for Transport, Innovation and Technology. The change of the operator shall be authorized under the conditions set out under § 4. 3

Registry

§ 9 (1) The Minister for Transport, Innovation and Technology maintains a registry for space objects.

(2) All space objects for which Austria is considered to be the launching State according to Art I of the Convention on Registration of Objects Launched into Outer Space (BGBl. Nr. 163/1980) shall be entered into this registry.

(3) If other States also qualify as launching States aside from Austria, the agreement according to Art II (2) of the Convention on Registration of Objects Launched into Outer Space (BGBl. Nr. 163/1980) is relevant for the registration in Austria.

(4) During the presence in outer space and on celestial bodies, a registrable space object as well as its personnel remain under the jurisdiction and control of Austria.

Registration and Information

§ 10 (1) The following information shall be entered in the registry:

1. Name of the launching State or States;

2. an appropriate designation of the space object, its registration number and the ITU frequency

allocation number;

3. the date and territory or location of launch;

4. the main orbital parameters, including

a) nodal period,

b) inclination,

c) apogee,

d) perigee,

5. general function of the space object;

6. the manufacturer of the space object;

7. the owner and operator of the space object;

8. further information, which the Minister for Transport, Innovation and Technology may determine, if necessary, in light of the technological state of the art, the international legal obligations or relevant decisions of international organizations.

(2) The operator shall submit the information set out in subparagraph 1 to the Minister for Transport, Innovation and Technology after the launch of the space object without delay.

(3) Similarly, the operator shall submit all modifications relevant to the information set out under subparagraph 1 without delay.

(4) The Minister for Transport, Innovation and Technology shall communicate to the Secretary General of the United Nations the information contained in subparagraph 1, letters 1 to 5. The same applies with regard to the information contained in subparagraph 3.

Recourse

§ 11 (1). In the case that the Republic of Austria has compensated damage caused by a space activity in accordance with international law, the Federal Government has the right of recourse against the operator.

(2) For damage caused on the surface of the Earth or to aircraft in flight, the right of recourse comprises an amount up to the sum of the insured risk, but no less than the minimum amount of insurance set out under

§ 4. This limitation does not apply if the damage is due to fault by the operator or his agents or if the operator has infringed the provisions of § 3 or § 4. 4

Ordinance

§ 12. The following shall be set out in more detail in an ordinance issued by the Minister for Transport,

Innovation and Technology:

1. requirements for the authorisation under § 4 (1);

2. the relevant documents and technical specifications that have to be attached to the request for authorisation as set out under § 4 (2);

3. fees covering the cost of the proceeding to be carried out under the present law;

4. a lump sum to compensate the costs caused to the Federal Government as a consequence of the verification of the operator's reliability according to § 4 (1) subparagraph 1 being determined by the average expenses of the security authorities;

5. information necessary for registration according to § 10 (1) and (3).

Supervision and competent authorities

§ 13 (1) Operators of space activities are subject to supervision by the Minister for Transport, Innovation and Technology with regard to matters covered by the present Federal Law.

(2) The operator is obliged to grant the organs of the supervisory authority access to all business premises and plants, allow them to inspect relevant documents and provide them with information.

(3) The security authorities shall cooperate in the verification process of the operator's reliability provided for in § 4 (1) subparagraph 1. If the operator is a juridical person, the reliability of the authorised representative shall be verified. During the verification process, the security authorities shall have the right to use person-related data gathered in the execution of federal or provincial laws and to transmit the result of the verification to the Minister for Transport, Innovation and Technology.

(4) If the business premises and plants or the documents relevant for a space activity are located within a military estate, the responsible commander of the casern shall be informed in the case of subparagraph 2 before the entering of the military estate. For important reasons concerning military security , the commander may deny access or make the access subject to certain conditions.

Sanctions

§ 14. Everyone who infringes provisions of the present Federal Law or the respective ordinances, commits an administrative offence and will be fined up to € 100 000, unless the action represents a criminal offence falling within the competence of the courts. Everyone who carries out a space activity without the authorisation provided for in § 3 and § 7 will be fined minimum € 20 000.

Transitional provision

§ 15. This Federal Law applies to space activities carried out after its entry into force. For space activities commissioned before entry into force of the present Federal Law, the authorisation requirement provided for in the §§ 3 to 5 shall be substituted by a notification obligation of the operator. The operator shall provide all documents necessary for the verification of the conditions contained in § 4 (1). § 11 does not apply to space activities commissioned before the entry into force of the present Federal Law. 5

Linguistic nondiscrimination

§ 16. To the extent that the terms used in this Federal Law relate to natural persons, the form chosen applies to both sexes. When applying these terms to specific natural persons, the respective gender-specific form shall be used.

Implementation

§ 17 (1). The Minister for Transport, Innovation and Technology is entrusted with the implementation of the present Federal Law.

(2) The implementation of § 4, subparagraph 1, letter 2, is entrusted to the Minister for Transport, Innovation and Technology in agreement with the Minister of the Interior.

(3) The implementation of § 4, subparagraph 1, letter 3, is entrusted to the Minister for Transport, Innovation and Technology in agreement with the Minister for European and International Affairs and the Minister of

Defence and Sports.

(4) The implementation of § 4, subparagraph 4, is entrusted to the Minister for Transport, Innovation and Technology in agreement with the Minister of Justice.

(5) The implementation of § 11 is entrusted to the Minister for Transport, Innovation and Technology in agreement with the Minister of Finance and the Minister of Justice.

(6) The implementation of § 12, subparagraphs 3 and 4, is entrusted to the Minister for Transport, Innovation and Technology in agreement with the Minister of Finance.

THE RUSSIAN FEDERATION

LAW of the RUSSIAN FEDERATION ABOUT SPACE ACTIVITY

Decree No. 5663-1 of the Russian House of Soviets

The exploration of outer space, which began in Russia, opens up new prospects for global civilization. In Russian Federation the exploration and use of outer space, including the Moon and other celestial bodies, is one of the most important directions of activities in the interests of citizens, society and state. The present Law is intended to provide legal regulation for space activities and stimulates the application of the potential of space science and industry for solving socio-economic, scientific, technical and defense task of Russian Federation.

Section 1. GENERAL PROVISIONS

Article 1. Legislation of Russian Federation on Space Activity

1. The present Law shall lay down legal and organization foundations of space activities under the jurisdiction of Russian Federation.

2. Space activities under the jurisdiction of Russian Federation shall also be regulated by other laws and normative acts of Russian Federation issued in accordance with the Constitution of Russian Federation and this Law.

Article 2. The Concept of Space Activity

1. For purposes of this Law space activity shall be defined as any activity immediately connected with operations to explore and use outer space, including the Moon and other celestial bodies. Space activity shall include:

- space researches;
- remote sensing of the Earth from outer space, including environmental monitoring and meteorology;
- use of navigation, topographical and geodesic satellite systems;
- piloted space missions;
- manufacturing of materials and other products in outer space;
- other kinds of activity performed with the aid of space technology.

2. Space activity comprises creating (including development, manufacture and test), as well as using and transferring of space techniques, space technology, other products and services necessary for carrying out space activity.

Article 3. Goals and Purposes of Space Activity

1. Space activity shall be carried out with the goal of promoting the well-being of the citizens of Russian Federation, the development of Russian Federation and ensuring its security, as well as solving global problems of mankind.

2. Main tasks of space activity under the jurisdiction of Russian Federation shall be:

- providing access to outer space;

- studying of the Earth and outer space;
- developing science, techniques and technologies, enhancing economic efficiency;
- ensuring defense capabilities of Russian Federation and control over the implementation of international treaties concerning armaments and armed forces.

Article 4. The Principles of Space Activity

1. Space activity shall be carried out in conformity with the following principles:

- the equal right of the organizations and citizens of Russian Federation to participate in space activity;
- access to information about space activity;
- use of the results of space activity in the interests of customers with due regard to the rights of organizations and citizens participating in space activity;
- introduction of the achievements of space science and technology into national economy;
- restriction of monopolistic activity and the development of entrepreneurial activity;
- independence of expertise on issues of space activity;
- provision of safety in space activity, including protection of the environment;
- promotion of international cooperation in the field of space activity;
- international responsibility of the state for space activity performed under its jurisdiction.

2. In order to ensure strategic and ecological security it is prohibited in Russian Federation:

- to put into the orbit around the Earth or to deploy in outer space otherwise nuclear weapons and any other kinds of weapons of mass destruction;
- to test nuclear weapons and any other kinds of weapons of mass destruction in outer space;
- to use space objects and other space technology as a tool to influence the environment for military and other hostile purposes;
- to use the Moon and other celestial bodies for military purposes;
- to create deliberate immediate threat to safety of space activity, including safety of space objects;
- to create harmful contamination of outer space which leads to unfavourable changes of the environment, including deliberate elimination [destruction?] of space objects in outer space.

Other space activity under the jurisdiction of Russian Federation, which is prohibited by international treaties of Russian Federation, is not allowed as well.

3. Space activity, as well as dissemination of information on space activity shall be carried out with the observation of the requirements, stipulated by the legislation of Russian Federation, on the protection of intellectual property rights, state (including military) and commercial secret.

4. General information about space activity, which is subject to point 3 of present Article, including the data:

- about plans of launching of space objects and their changes;
- about space projects and the course of their realization;
- about budget allocations for space activities;
- about incidents and accidents while carrying out space activity and the damage because of such accidents shall be disseminated without restrictions.

Section II. ORGANIZATION of SPACE ACTIVITY

Article 5. Competence of Bodies of State Power and Administration

1. In Russian Federation space activity pertains to the competence of federal bodies of state power and administration.

2. The Supreme Soviet of Russian Federation shall determine the space policy of Russian Federation, including:

- adoption of legislative acts, regulating space activity;
- adoption of the Federal Space Program of Russia;
- exercising control over the fulfilment of the Federal Space Program of Russia and spending the state means allotted for space activity;
- ratification of international treaties of Russian Federation on issues of space activity;
- resolve other issues, within its competence, arising in the pursuit of space activity.
- The President of Russian Federation shall be responsible for the implementation of space policy of Russian Federation, including:

- issuing of Edicts and executive orders necessary for carrying out space activity;
- supervising of activities of Council of Ministers - the Government of Russian Federation to implement the Federal Space Program of Russia and on other issues related to carrying out of space activity;
- resolving, within his competence, other issues arising in the pursuit of space activity.

4. Council of Ministers - the Government of Russian Federation shall ensure the supervision of space activity, including:

- issuing of Decrees and Executive Orders necessary for carrying out of space activity;
- considering of the draft Federal Space Program of Russia as proposed by the Russian Space Agency, the Ministry of Defence of Russian Federation, the Russian Academy of Sciences and other state customers for works to create and use space technology;
- submit to the Supreme Soviet of Russian Federation the draft Federal Space Program of Russia and proposals on financing of space activity;
- approve the Regulations of Russian Space Agency;
- undertake measures to protect interests of Russian Federation, as well as Russian organizations and citizens in the field of space activity;
- resolve within its competence other issues arising in the pursuit of space activity.

5. Republics within Russian Federation, autonomous region, autonomous areas, territories, regions and cities of Moscow and St.Peterburg shall participate in the exercise of powers to regulate space activity provided for by this Law.

Article 6. The Russian Space Agency

1. The Russian Space Agency shall be a body of federal executive power responsible for carrying out space activity in scientific and national-economy purposes under the jurisdiction of Russian Federation in accordance with the space policy of Russian Federation.

2. The Russian Space Agency shall, within its competence:

- elaborate a draft Federal Space Program of Russia in coordination with the Ministry of Defence of Russian Federation, the Russian Academy of Sciences and other state customers of works in creation and use of space technology;
- form and place a state order for works in creation and use of space technology for scientific and national- economy purposes, including works under international space projects;
- participate in coordination with the Ministry of Defence of Russian Federation in placing the state order for works in creation and use of space technology, used both for scientific and national-economy purpose and for purposes of defence and security of Russian Federation;
- ensure, in coordination with the Ministry of Defence of Russian Federation and other ministries and departments of Russian Federation the exploitation, maintenance and development of ground and other objects of space infrastructure for scientific and national-economy purposes;
- issue licenses for the types of space activity;
- organize certification of space technology ;
- provide space activity with necessary normative technical documentation;
- ensure, in conjunction with corresponding state services, the safety of space activity;
- interact with the organizations and agencies of foreign states, as well as international organizations on questions

of space activity and enter into appropriate international agreements;

- perform other functions, as defined by Council of Ministers - the Government of Russian Federation.

3. The Russian Space Agency may create its territorial agencies in order to fulfil its functions, taking into account interests of subjects of Russian Federation in use of results of space activity.

Article 7. Space Activity for Purposes of Defense and Security of Russian Federation.

1. Space activity for purposes of defense and security of Russian Federation shall be pursued by the Ministry of Defense of Russian Federation which shall be responsible for the implementation of the long-term program and annual plans of works to create and use military space technology in conjunction with other ministries and departments of Russian Federation.

2. The Ministry of Defence of Russian Federation shall within its competence:

- elaborate draft program and annual plans of works to create and use military space technology and, in conjunction with the Russian Space Agency of space technology applied for both scientific and national-economy purposes and for the purposes of defense and security of Russian Federation;

- form and place the state order for works to create and use military space technology and, in conjunction with the Russian Space Agency space technology applied both for scientific and national-economy purposes and for purposes of defense and security of Russian Federation;

- use space technology for purposes of defense and security of Russian Federation;

- perform exploitation of space technology for scientific and national-economy purposes on a contractual basis;

- ensure, jointly with the Russian Space Agency and other ministries and departments of Russian Federation, the maintenance and development of ground and other objects of space infrastructure;

- provide space activity with necessary normative technical documentation;

- participate in the certification of space technology on a contractual basis;

- ensure, in conjunction with corresponding state services, safety of space activity;

- perform other functions established by Council of Ministers - the Government of the Russian Federation.

4. The Ministry of Defence of Russian Federation shall have the right to temporarily transfer idle objects of space infrastructure under its jurisdiction to the Russian Space Agency on a contractual basis to be used for space activity for scientific and national-economy purposes.

Article 8. Federal Space Program of Russia

1. The Federal Space Program of Russia shall be the document on the basis of which the state order for the creation and use of space technology for scientific and national-economy purposes shall be formed. The procedure of interaction of the Russian Space Agency and the Ministry Defence of Russian Federation in elaboration and approval of the Federal Space Program of Russia and the long-term program and annual plans of works to create and use military space technology shall be determined by the legislation of Russian Federation.

2. The Federal Space Program of Russia shall be elaborated taking into account:

- established goals, tasks and principles of space activity;
- interests of the subject of Russian Federation;
- economic situation in the country;
- condition of space science and industry;
- need for a comprehensive development of the space and the ground segments of space infrastructure;
- interests of users and producers of space technologies;
- situation and trends in the development of cosmonautics;
- conditions in the world space market;
- international obligations of Russian Federation and the task to expand international cooperation.

3. The Federal Space Program of Russia shall be elaborated in accordance with the results of a competition of space projects submitted by the ministries and departments of Russian Federation, organizations and citizens concerned.

The procedure and terms for holding competitions of space projects for scientific and national-economy purposes shall be determined by the Russian Space Agency with the participation of the Russian Academy of Sciences and other customers of works in creation and use of space technology.

4. General information about the Federal Space Program of Russia and annual reports on its implementation shall be published in the press.

Article 9. Licensing of Space Activity

1. This Law shall establish a licensing (permission) procedure for the pursuit of space activity in scientific and national-economy purpose.

2. Subject to licensing shall be space activity of organizations and citizens of Russian Federation or space activity of foreign organizations and citizens under the jurisdiction of Russian Federation, if such activity includes tests, manufacture, storage, preparation for launching and launching of space objects, as well as control over space flights.

3. Types, forms, and terms of licenses, the conditions and procedures for their issue, withholding, suspension or termination, as well as other questions of licensing shall be regulated by the legislation of Russian Federation.

4. Carrying out space activity by an organization or a citizen without a license or in wilful violation of the terms of the license shall be punishable by virtue of the legislation of Russian Federation.

5. The actions of the state bodies to license space activity may be claimed in the court of law or in the arbitration tribunal.

Article 10. Certification of Space Technology

1. Space technology, including space objects, ground and other objects of space infrastructure created for scientific and national-economy purposes, shall be checked for the compliance with the requirements establish by the legislation of Russian Federation (certification).

Equipment used in the creation and use of space technology may also be subject to certification.

2. Upon the completion of the certification procedure a certificate shall be issued to each sample of space technology.

The types, forms and terms of certificates, the terms and procedures for the issue, withholding, suspension or termination thereof, as well as other questions of certification shall be regulated by the legislation of Russian Federation.

3. The certification agencies, manufacturers of space technology and corresponding officials violating the rules of certification of space technology shall be responsible by virtue of the legislation of Russian Federation.

Article 11. Expertise on Issues of Space Activity

1. Decisions on the following issues connected with the pursuit of space activity shall be taken on the basis of expertise:

- inclusion of a project into the Federal Space Program of Russia;
- adoption of the Federal Space Program of Russia;
- issuing of licenses for space activity;
- issuing of certificates for samples of space technology as well as equipment used in the creation and use of space technology ;
- categorizing space technologies as products whose export shall be banned or restricted;
- review of competitions of space projects;
- identification of the cause of accidents in the pursuit of space activity;
- other questions as determined by Council of Ministers - the Government of Russian Federation.

2. For the purposes of expertise the Supreme Soviet of Russian Federation, Council of Ministers - the Government of Russian Federation, the Russian Space Agency or other body making a decision on issues connected with space activity shall form expert commissions from amongst specialists not concerned about the result of the expertise

3. The procedure for the formation and work of expert commissions shall be determined by the legislation of Russian Federation.

4. The conclusion of an expert commission shall not be binding on the body making a decision on issues connected with space activity.

The responsibility for such decision that does not accord with the conclusion of the expert commission shall rest with the chief executive officer of the body making the decision.

The members of the expert commission shall be responsible for the accuracy and validity of their findings

Section III. ECONOMIC CONDITIONS OF SPACE ACTIVITY

Article 12. Financing of Space Activities and Foreign Investments

1. Financing of space activity for scientific and national-economy purposes shall be executed from the republican budget of Russian Federation in accordance with the Federal Space Program of Russia and figured in the republican budget of Russian Federation as a separate item.

Financing of space activity for purposes of defence and security of Russian Federation shall be provided by the republican budget of Russian Federation as a part of defense expenditures.

2. Space activity shall be financed from the republican budget of Russian Federation in purpose-oriented manner through state customers of works in creation and use of space technology and shall be distributed between contractors in accordance with state contracts.

The state customer and the contractor shall have the right to resort to non-budget sources of financing, including their own resources, provided this does not contradict to objectives of the space project.

3. Organizations and citizens involved in the implementation of space projects shall be, according to the established procedures, granted with state guarantees, soft credits, tax exemptions and other necessary privileges.

4. Foreign investments into space activity falling within the framework of the Federal Space Program of Russia, shall be guaranteed by the budget of Russian Federation, as well as by the assets and other property of Russian Federation.

Foreign investments in space activity of organizations and citizens of Russian Federation shall be guaranteed by their assets or by their intellectual or other property.

Article 13. The Russian Space Fund

1. The Russian Space Fund shall be established with the aim to support and promote space science and industry.

2. The assets of the Russian Space Fund shall be provided by:

- allocations from the republican budget of Russian Federation granted on a purpose-oriented basis as part of the financing of the Federal Space Program of Russia;

- extra-budgetary funds created by state customers for works to create and use space technology ;

- part of the profit received by organizations and citizens at the expense of tax exemption granted in connection with space activity;

- profit resulting from the realization of space projects financed by the Russian Space Fund;

- insurance payments made by organizations and citizens involved in space activity in the form of obligatory or voluntary insurance;

- voluntary contributions of Russian and foreign organizations and citizens.

The order of accumulation and spending of the resources of the Russian Space Fund shall be laid down in the Statutes of the Russian Space Fund.

3. The resources of the Russian Space Fund shall be directed towards financing the Federal Space Program of Russia in coordination with the Russian Space Agency and other customers for works to create and use space technology, towards supporting space projects involving innovation and military conversion, as well as towards projects to use of the results of space activity, among others, for promoting science, education and culture.

In the distribution of the resources of the Russian Space Fund priority shall be given to ground-breaking research projects and high efficiency economic, social and other projects.

The resources of the Russian Space Fund shall also be employed to ensure risks connected with space activity and to eliminate the after-effects of accidents that may result from such activity.

4. The Russian Space Fund shall operate in accordance with the Statutes approved by Council of Ministers - the Government of Russian Federation in coordination with the Supreme Soviet of Russian Federation

Article 14. Creation of Space Technology

1. The state order for the creation of space technology shall be formed and placed in accordance with the Federal Space Program of Russia and the long-term program and annual plans of works to create and use military space technology.

2. The works under the state order shall be carried out in accordance with the technical assignment approved by the state customer, which shall form grounds for the conclusion of the state contract between the state customer and the contractor.

3. Property rights over space technology shall be transferred to the customer from the moment of signing the acceptance certificate, unless otherwise stipulated by the relevant agreement.

The rights of organizations and citizens involved in the creation of space technology to further utilize such technology shall be specified in agreements, concluded by these organizations and citizens with the customer of the works

4. Mixed companies shall be allowed to act as contractors under the state order, provide that the share of foreign capital in their statutory fund does not exceed 49 percent.

Contractors under the state order shall be allowed to involve foreign organizations and citizens as subcontractors, and shall be responsible for fulfilment of their obligations by the latters.

Article 15. Use and Transfer of Space Technology

1. Space technology shall be allowed to be used according to its purpose, pending on its putting into exploitation.

The order of using space technology for testing and the order of its putting into exploitation shall be stipulated by the legislation of Russian Federation.

2. The use of space technology shall be effected by the proprietor of such technology or by other organizations and citizens upon agreement with the proprietor.

3. Components of space technology may belong to several organizations and citizens, unless this disrupts the operational regime of the functioning of such space technology.

Procedures for the use of space technology, components of which belong to several organizations and citizens, shall be governed by contracts between such organizations and citizens.

4. An organization exploiting space technology, which is in federal ownership shall provide, on a contractual basis, opportunities for the use of such technology by any interested organization and citizen. In concluding agreements for the use of space technology, which is in federal ownership preference shall be given to project under the Federal Space Program of Russia, and also to organizations and citizens of Russian Federation that offer more beneficial terms of such use.

5. Space technology taken out of operation may be transferred to organizations whose main line of activities is directed at using the results of space activity in purposes of education and culture. Such technology may also be sold to organizations or citizens on a contractual basis.

Article 16. Use of Space Technologies and Results of Space Activity

1. The use and transfer of space technology shall be effected with respect to the rights of intellectual property that are protected by the legislation of Russian Federation.

2. The fulfilment of the works to create space technology, including those under the state order, shall not bind the contractor to transfer technologies to the customer, unless otherwise specified by the agreement between the contractor and the customer.

3. Procedures and terms of the use of technologies developed while fulfilling the works in creation and use of space technology, legal protection of which is not stipulated by the legislation of Russian Federation, shall be established under agreements between the interested organizations and citizens.

4. The property rights over the physical product created in outer space shall belong to the organizations and citizens possessing property rights in the components of space technology, with the use of which such product has been created, unless otherwise specified by relevant agreements.

The property rights over the information product created as a result of space activity shall belong to the organizations and citizens, that have created such information product, unless otherwise specified by relevant agreements.

The property rights of other organizations and citizens participating in space activity, in particular by providing transportation and other services, shall be stipulated by relevant agreements.

Section IV. SPACE INFRASTRUCTURE

Article 17. Space Objects

1. Space objects of Russian Federation shall be subject to registration and shall have markings certifying their appurtenance to Russian Federation.

2. Russian Federation shall retain jurisdiction and control over space objects registered in it, during the ground time of such objects, at any stage of a space flight or stay in outer space, on celestial bodies and also on return to the Earth outside the jurisdiction of any state.

3. The rights of ownership over space objects shall remain unaffected, during the ground time of such objects, at any stage of a space flight or stay in outer space, on celestial bodies and also on return to the Earth, unless otherwise specified in international treaties of Russian Federation.

4. If a space object is designed and manufactured by Russian organizations and citizens jointly with foreign organizations and citizens or international organizations, the issues of the registration of such object, the jurisdiction and control thereover and also the issues of the rights of ownership thereof shall be decided on the basis of the appropriate international treaties.

5. The rights of jurisdiction and control over space objects, as well as of ownership thereof shall not affect the legal status of the area of outer space or the surface or subsoil of a celestial body occupied by it. In direct proximity to a space object of Russian Federation within the zone minimally necessary for ensuring safety of space activity, rules may be established that shall be binding for Russian and foreign organizations and citizens.

Article 18. Ground and Other Objects of Space Infrastructure

1. The ground and other objects of space infrastructure in Russian Federation shall consist of:

- cosmodromes;
- launching complexes and installations;
- instrumentation and command complexes;
- space objects flight control centers and points;
- space equipment storage bases;
- areas of fallout of separating parts of space objects;
- space objects landing grounds and runways;
- experimental base facilities for the creation of space technology ;
- cosmonaut training centers and equipment;
- any other ground facilities and equipment used for carrying out of space activities.

Ground and other objects of space infrastructure, including mobile, shall be considered as such to the extent that they are used for ensuring or carrying out space activity.

2. The ground and other objects of space infrastructure, which are in federal property, shall be under the authority of state organizations in charge of their operation.

The transfer of ground and other objects of space infrastructure, which are in federal property, under the authority, ownership or leaseholding of other organizations shall only be permitted in the manner specified by the legislation of Russian Federation.

3. The allotment of slots of land for ground and other objects of space infrastructure and the right-of-way zones adjacent thereto shall be made by bodies of state power and administration of relevant subjects of Russian Federation, as well as by local authorities in accordance with the legislation of Russian Federation.

The procedure and terms of use of such slots of land shall be laid down by agreements between relevant bodies of state power and administration and the organizations responsible for the operation of the ground and other objects of space infrastructure.

4. Activities involving the utilization of ground and other objects of space infrastructure by organizations and citizens of Russian Federation outside the jurisdiction of any state shall be carried out in accordance with this Law.

Such activities by organizations and citizens of Russian Federation within the territories, which are under the jurisdiction of a foreign state shall be carried out in accordance with the legislation of this state, unless it is contrary to this Law.

Article 19. Space Flight Control

1. Space flight control at all stages from the launching of a space object of Russian Federation to completion of the flight shall be

exercised by the organizations in charge of the ground and other objects of space infrastructure.

2. The launch and landing of space objects of Russian Federation shall be carried out in preset area under an arrangement made with the appropriate bodies of state power and administration.

In case of accidents, including failures and crashes, while conducting space activity the landing of space objects of the Russian Federation can be made in other regions with the notice of appropriate bodies of a state authority and management.

3. Manoeuvring of space objects in the air space of the Russian Federation is executed in view of the requirements of the legislation, regulating use of the air space of the Russian Federation.

4. The space object of a foreign state can execute a single innocent flight [passage?] through the air space of the Russian Federation with the purpose to insert such an object into an orbit around the Earth or further in outer space, as well as with the purpose to return it to the Earth under the condition of advance noting of appropriate services of the Russian Federation about time, place, trajectory and other conditions of such flight.

5. The Russian Space Agency and the Ministry of Defence of the Russian Federation informs about launching and landing of space objects of the Russian Federation appropriate bodies of a state authority and management of the Russian Federation, and in case of necessity - interested foreign states and international organizations as well.

In case of launching, landing or terminating of existence of space objects of the Russian Federation beyond its boundaries the appropriate services of the Russian Federation execute their functions as agreed with competent bodies of the interested foreign states.

Article 20. Cosmonauts and crews of piloted space objects

1. Citizens of the Russian Federation, who expressed desire to participate in space flights and meet the established professional and medical requirements, are selected for preparation and realization of space flights on the basis of competition.

The order and conditions of competition shall be determined by the Russian Space Agency and the Ministry of Defence of the Russian Federation with the participation of other customers of works in creation and use of space technology and published in the press.

2. The order of preparation cosmonauts, of formation of crews of piloted space objects and approval of the flight program, as well as rights and responsibilities of cosmonauts, payment of their labour and other conditions of their professional activity shall be determined by the contracts pursuant to the legislation of the Russian Federation.

3. The commander of a crew of a piloted space object of the Russian Federation can be nominated a citizen of the Russian Federation.

The commander of a crew of a piloted space object of the Russian Federation shall be vested with all completeness of authority, necessary for realization of the space flight, for management of crew and other persons, participating in the flight.

The commander of a crew of a piloted space object of Russian Federation shall within the scope of his authority bear responsibility for the fulfilment of the flight program, the safety of the crew and other persons participating in the flight and the preservation of the space object and the property within it.

4. Russian Federation shall retain jurisdiction and control over any crew of a piloted space object registered in it, during the ground time of such object, at any stage of a space flight or stay in outer space, on celestial bodies, including extra-vehicular stay, and on return to the Earth, right up to the completion of the flight program, unless otherwise specified in international treaties of Russian Federation.

5. Citizens of foreign states who take a space flight training course in Russian Federation or are involved in a flight on a piloted space object of Russian Federation shall be obliged to observe the legislation of Russian Federation, unless otherwise specified in international treaties of Russian Federation

Article 21. Personnel at the Ground and Other Objects of Space Infrastructure

1. Personnel to be regarded as personnel at the ground and other objects of space infrastructure shall be specialists performing duties in the sphere of testing, storage and operation of space technology , as well as any other duties involving the provision of operational regime of the functioning of the ground and other objects of space infrastructure.

2. The functional duties of personnel at the ground and other objects of space infrastructure shall be determined by the organizations in charged of the operation thereof.

Personnel at the ground and other objects of space infrastructure shall be subject to appraisal for adequacy in the established professional standards.

3. The size of the pay and the additional material remuneration of personnel at the ground and other objects of space infrastructure shall be established by the contracts of employment concluded with the organizations using such objects.

The procedure of payment and personal equipment for personnel at the ground and other objects of space infrastructure, who are in military service shall be laid down in the appropriate legislation of Russian Federation.

4. Members of personnel at the ground and other objects of space infrastructure, whose professions are connected with hazardous or harmful conditions of work shall be given additional benefits in accordance with the legislation of Russian Federation and the conditions of the appropriate contracts.

5. Persons enlisted in the performance of space accident or disaster clean-up operations shall enjoy the same privileges as attending to the ground and other objects of space infrastructure.

Section V. SAFETY of SPACE ACTIVITY

Article 22. Ensuring Safety of Space Activity

1. Any space activity shall be carried out with the observance of the safety requirements laid down by the legislation of Russian Federation.

Overall guidance of the work to ensure the safety of space activity shall be laid down upon the Russian Space Agency and the Ministry of Defence of Russian Federation.

Carrying out the safety measures in space activity shall be laid down upon the appropriate state services, as well as upon the organizations and citizens that are engaged in carrying out such activity

The bodies of state power and administration of Russian Federation and of subjects of Russian Federation, as well as organizations and citizens shall be obliged to take all necessary measures to ensure safety of space activity.

The Russian Space Agency and the Ministry of Defence of Russian Federation upon request of interested organizations and citizens shall provide the information on the threat arising while carrying out space activity.

With origination of a threat to public safety and the environment the Russian Space Agency shall immediately inform the appropriate bodies of state power and administration, as well as organizations and citizens, about this.

Article 23. Investigation of Space Incidents

1. Incidents, including accidents and disasters, while carrying out space activity shall be subject to investigation, the procedure of which shall be set in the legislation of Russian Federation.

2. The manner of conducting and the substantiation of the results of an investigation of accidents, including accidents and disasters, may be appealed against in courts of law.

Article 24. Search-and-Rescue, Clean-up of Accidents

1. Search-and-rescue works, as well as clean-up of an accident while carrying out space activity shall be accomplished by appropriate state services with the participation of bodies of state power and

administration of relevant subjects of Russian Federation, local authorities, organizations and citizens.

2. Clean-up of accidents while carrying out space activity shall consist of the restoration and reconstruction of the industrial and other plants that have suffered as a result of the accidents, necessary environmental measures and compensation for damage to relevant subjects of Russian Federation, organizations and citizens.

Article 25. Insurance of Space Activity

1. The organizations and citizens, which exploit space technology or to whose order the creation and use of space technology in scientific and national-economy purpose is carried out, shall take compulsory insurance coverage in the amount set by legislation of Russian Federation.

Compulsory insurance shall be affected against damage to the life and health of the cosmonauts and the personnel at the ground and other objects of space infrastructure, as well as against property damage to third parties.

Compulsory insurance premiums shall be transferred to the Russian Space Fund or other insurance companies which have obtained a license for the insurance of space activity, and shall be used to compensate for damage as a result of accidents while carrying out space activity on the basis of contracts of insurance with organizations and citizens carrying out such activity.

2. Organizations and citizens carrying out space activity may effect voluntary insurance of space technology, as well as risks connected with such activity.

Section VI. INTERNATIONAL COOPERATION

Article 26. International Obligations in the Field of Space Activity

1. International treaties of Russian Federation on issues of space activity shall be subject to ratification by the Supreme Soviet of Russian Federation.

2. If rules are laid down in an international treaty ratified by the Supreme Soviet of Russian Federation other than those contained in this Law and other legislative acts of Russian Federation governing space activity, the rules of the international treaty shall preempt.

3. Russian Federation shall ensure the fulfillment of the obligations it has assumed in the field of space activity, and specially under the Treaty on Principles Governing the Activity of States in the Exploration and Use of Outer Space, including the Moon and Other Celestial Bodies.

4. Russian Federation shall promote the development of international cooperation in the field of space activity, as well as the solution of international legal problems that may arise in the exploration and use of outer space.

Article 27. The Legal Regime for Foreign Organizations and Citizens

1. Foreign organizations and citizens carrying out space activity under the jurisdiction of Russian Federation shall enjoy the legal regime established for organizations and citizens of Russian Federation to the extent that such regime is provided by the appropriate state to organizations and citizens of Russian Federation.

2. The Russian Federation shall ensure the legal protection of the technologies and commercial secrets of foreign organizations and citizens carrying out space activity under the jurisdiction of Russian Federation in accordance with the legislation of Russian Federation.

Any other protection of the technologies and commercial secrets of foreign organizations and citizens carrying out space activity under the jurisdiction of Russian Federation that may be required shall be provided on a reciprocal basis.

3. Foreign organizations and citizens engaged in carrying out space activity under the jurisdiction of Russian Federation shall effect the insurance of space technology and also risks involved in space activity in the manner specified by this Law.

Article 28. The Legal Regulation of International Cooperation

1. The organizations and citizens of Russian Federation involved in carrying international projects in the field of space activity shall conclude agreements with foreign organizations and citizens in accordance with the legislation of Russian Federation, unless otherwise specified in these agreements.

2. In case of a conflict of the rules of the legislation of Russian Federation and that of a foreign state applicable to space activity with the participation of organizations and citizens of Russian Federation, the legislation of Russian Federation shall prevail, unless otherwise specified in international treaties signed by Russian Federation.

Section VII. LIABILITY

Article 29. Responsibility of Officials, Organizations and Citizens

State bodies and their officials, other organizations and their officials, as well as citizens guilty of violation of this Law and other legislative acts governing space activity shall be held responsible in accordance with legislation of Russian Federation.

Article 30. Liability for Damage

1. Russian Federation shall guarantee full compensation for direct damage inflicted as a result of accidents while carrying out space activity in accordance with legislation of Russian Federation.

2. Compensation for damage inflicted as a result of accidents while carrying out space activity shall be paid by the organizations and citizens responsible for operation of the space technology involved.

If such damage is the result of errors committed at the creation and use of space technology, liability for damages shall be partly of fully laid upon the appropriate organizations and citizens.

3. Liability for damages inflicted by a space object of Russian Federation within the territory of Russian Federation or outside the jurisdiction of any state, except outer space, shall arise regardless of the fault of the inflictor thereof.

If in any place, apart from the Earth surface, damage has been inflicted on a space object of Russian Federation or on property on board of such object by another space object, the liability of organizations and citizens shall emerge with their being at fault and in proportion to their fault.

Should liability for damage inflicted by a space object of Russian Federation attach to several organizations and citizens, the injured party may claim for a compensation to all such organizations and citizens or to any of them.

In the latter case, the organization or the citizen that has indemnified for the damage shall have the right of recourse against the correspondents, whose liability shall be apportioned according to the degree of their fault, and if it is impossible to establish the fault - equally.

4. The liability of organizations and citizens participating in the creation and use of space technology for damage inflicted as a result of accidents while carrying out space activity shall be limited to the amount of the insured sum or insurance indemnity provided in contracts of insurance of space technology and risks involved in space activity.

If the insured sum or insurance indemnity is insufficient for compensation for the damage inflicted as a result of accidents while carrying out space activity, recourse may be taken against the property of relevant organizations and citizens in the manner specified in the legislation of Russian Federation.

**The President of
Russian Federation**

UKRAINE

Ordinance Of The Supreme Soviet Of Ukraine, On Space Activity
Law of Ukraine of 15 November 1996[52]
(VVRU, 1997, p. 2)

Section I. GENERAL PROVISIONS

Article 1. Use of terms and concepts

For the purposes of this Law the terms and concepts listed below shall have the following meanings:

"Space activity" shall mean scientific space research, the design and application of space technology and the use of outer space;

"Space facilities (space technology)" shall mean material objects produced by piecework which are designed, manufactured and operated both in outer space (space segment, space infrastructure) and on the Earth◆s surface (ground segment, ground infrastructure) for the purpose of exploring and using outer space;

"Subjects of space activity" shall mean enterprises, institutions and organizations, whether domestic, international or foreign, which engage in space activity;

"Space technologies and services" shall mean the results of scientific development, methods, means and services required for the pursuit of space activity and for obtaining and making use of the results of such activity;

"Incident" shall mean an event related to space activity which has led to a threat to the life or health of persons or damage to or

[52] Unofficial translation

destruction of the property of citizens, enterprises, institutions or organizations, or damage to the environment;

"Emergency" shall mean an event related to space activity which has led to the death of persons or to serious bodily injury, or to destruction of the property of citizens, enterprises, authorities or organizations, or substantial damage to the environment;

"Rules of space activity" shall mean special rules, technical norms and standards which regulate space activity and its safety;

"Personnel of space facilities" shall mean the staff of enterprises, institutions or organizations which are involved in the manufacture, testing or operation of space facilities and the clean-up of incidents and emergencies, as well as specialists working for enterprises, institutions or special units of military units involved in performing such work;

"Compliance certificate" shall mean a document attesting to the fulfilment by a space facility of the operating requirements of space technology, as regulated by the relevant regulatory texts in force in Ukraine.

Article 2. Legislation on space activity in Ukraine

Relations in the area of space activity shall be regulated by this Law and by other legislative acts of Ukraine adopted in conformity therewith.

Article 3. Aims of space activity

Space activity shall be conducted with the following aims:

- Furthering the socio-economic development and scientific progress of Ukraine and promoting the welfare of its citizens;
- Contributing to the solution of the general problems facing humankind;

- Developing space science and engineering and space-related services and technologies apt to assist in bringing about the stable development of the national economy;
- Creating an extensive export potential in the space sector;
- Ensuring access to outer space and the conduct of scientific investigations of the Earth and outer space;
- Establishing and maintaining space systems to ensure modern State information coverage;
- Safeguarding the long-term interests of the State in relation to national security and defence capabilities;
- Fostering the development of education;
- Assisting in the monitoring of conformity with international security agreements to which Ukraine is a party.

Article 4. Principles of space activity

The space activity of Ukraine shall be conducted in accordance with the following principles:

- State regulation;
- Progressive development and systematic reform of State policy in relation to the exploration and use of outer space;
- Practical exploitation of the scientific and technical potential of Ukraine and of possibilities created by space activity in the interests of the national economy, scientific advancement and State security and for commercial purposes;
- Furtherance of international cooperation and the maintenance and development of existing relations in matters related to space with due regard for national interests.

Section II. ORGANIZATION OF SPACE ACTIVITY

Article 5. State regulation and management of space activity

State regulation and management of space activity in Ukraine shall be effected by means of the following:

- Legislative definition of the basic principles, standards and rules governing space activity;
- Elaboration of the conceptual bases of State policy in relation to the exploration and use of outer space for peaceful purposes and in the interests of State security;
- Establishment of the Ukrainian All-State (National) Space Programme;
- Specialized training of personnel to be covered by the Ukrainian National Budget;
- The application of a licensing (authorization) system in relation to such activity, as well as other rules and regulations in conformity with legislation currently in force.

The Ukrainian National Space Agency shall be the specially authorized central executive authority responsible for implementing State policy in relation to space activity.

Article 6. Competences of the Ukrainian National Space Agency

The Ukrainian National Space Agency shall, within its competence:

- Formulate the conceptual basis of State policy in relation to the exploration and use of outer space for peaceful purposes and in the interests of national security;
- Provide for the organization of space activity in Ukraine and under the jurisdiction of Ukraine outside its borders;
- Prepare, in collaboration with ministries, other central executive authorities and the Ukrainian National Academy of Sciences, the Ukrainian All-State (National) Space Programme and ensure its implementation;
- Direct the management and coordination of the work of enterprises, institutions and organizations in the space and related sectors;
- Act as the general State customer placing orders for scientific research relating to the exploration and exploitation of outer space and to scientific research and design and engineering studies for the design, manufacture and testing of space technology, including in connection with international space projects;

- Arrange, in collaboration with ministries and other central authorities of Ukraine, for the operation, maintenance and improvement of space facilities;
- Arrange for licensing of space activity in Ukraine and the licensing of such activity under the jurisdiction of Ukraine outside its borders;
- Arrange for the development and operation of the Ukrainian Space Technology Certification System (UkrSSKT);
- Ensure that subjects of space activity in Ukraine are furnished with the requisite regulatory texts;
- Carry out the registration of space technology;
- Arrange for cooperation between Ukraine and other States and international organizations in space-related matters, and ensure the maintenance and development of existing international relations in the area of space activity;
- Undertake action aimed at improving the foreign trade relations of Ukraine with other States in the area of space activity;
- Participate in the preparation of international treaties to be concluded by Ukraine;
- Perform other functions in the area of space activities in conformity with legislation currently in force.

Article 7. Ukrainian All-State (National) Space Programme

Space activity in Ukraine shall be pursued on the basis of the Ukrainian All-State (National) Space Programme, which shall be prepared for periods of five years and submitted by the Cabinet of Ministers of Ukraine to the Supreme Soviet of Ukraine for its approval.

The Ukrainian All-State (National) Space Programme shall be drawn up by the Ukrainian National Space Agency in collaboration with the competent central executive authorities and the Ukrainian National Academy of Sciences on the basis of the aims and basic principles of space activity in Ukraine.

The Ukrainian All-State (National) Space Programme shall serve as the basis for the following:

- Determination of civil, defence and dual-use space technology requirements and the conclusion of contracts in conformity with current legislation for the performance of scientific research work (hereinafter referred to as space technology orders) and the release of space technology for the current year, subject to approval by the Cabinet of Ministers of Ukraine;
- Assignment of funds from the Ukrainian National Budget for the financing of space activity in accordance with State orders;
- The training of personnel to be covered by the Ukrainian National Budget and the provision of social welfare coverage for personnel of space facilities;
- Maintenance and improvement of space facilities forming part of the ground infrastructure and maintenance of the requisite safety standards in space activity;
- Conduct of international cooperation in space-related matters, including the involvement of Ukraine in international space projects.

Article 8. Regulations governing space activity

The regulations governing space activity in Ukraine include operating standards for space facilities, and standards and regulatory texts governing procedures for the following:

- Licensing of space activity;
- Certification and registration of space facilities;
- Organization, execution and ensuring of space launches and flights;
- Supervision and monitoring of the safety of space launches and flights and of the operation of space technology;
- Environmental protection in the course of space activity;
- Conduct of search and rescue operations in connection with space activities;
- Conduct of official investigations of incidents and emergencies;
- Construction, operation, maintenance and repair of installations and equipment of infrastructural ground facilities;
- Training of the personnel of space facilities;
- Implementation of measures to protect space activity from unlawful intrusion.

The regulations governing space activity also include other regulatory acts governing space-related activities and their safety, as well as compliance with the requirements of intellectual property protection and State, military and commercial secrecy.

The regulations governing space activity shall be established by the relevant State authorities of Ukraine within their competence and shall be binding upon all subjects of space activity.

Article 9. Prohibitions on and restrictions of space activity

The following shall be prohibited in connection with the conduct of space activity in Ukraine:

- Insertion into orbit and placing in space by whatsoever means of nuclear weapons or any other types of weapons of mass destruction, or the testing of such weapons;
- The use of space technology as a means of producing effects upon the environment for military purposes or other purposes posing a threat to humankind;
- The use of the Moon and other celestial bodies for military purposes;
- The presenting of a direct threat to the life and health of human beings and the causing of damage to the environment;
- The violation of international norms and standards regarding pollution of outer space;
- Other acts related to space activity which are not permissible under international law.

Space activity conducted under a specific project which has led to the loss of human lives, substantial material damage or substantial damage to the environment may be restricted or prohibited in conformity with the legislation of Ukraine currently in force.

Article 10. Licensing of space activity

Any space facility engaging or intending to engage in space activity in Ukraine or under the jurisdiction of Ukraine outside its borders shall be required to have a licence from the Ukrainian National Space Agency for the pursuit of such activity.

The list of the types of space activity subject to licensing shall be established by the laws of Ukraine.

The procedures for the licensing of space activity in Ukraine shall be established by the Cabinet of Ministers of Ukraine.

Article 11. Financing of space activity

Space activity pursued for scientific or economic purposes for which the State is the customer shall be financed on the basis of the Ukrainian All-State (National) Space Programme and shall be covered by a special item in the Ukrainian National Budget.

Space activity for the purposes of the defence and security of Ukraine shall be financed from the Ukrainian National Budget in respect of defence expenditure.

Financing shall be effected through State customers of works for the design and use of space technology and shall be allocated among contractors in accordance with State contracts.

Foreign credits and investments in space activity related to implementation of the Ukrainian All-State (National) Space Programme shall be guaranteed by the State in conformity with Ukrainian legislation currently in force.

Section III. GENERAL REQUIREMENTS IMPOSED ON SPACE FACILITIES

Article 12. Certification of space facilities

Any space facility in Ukraine shall be subject to certification attesting to its compliance with operating requirements established by the regulatory texts in force in Ukraine, with subsequent issuance of a compliance certificate.

Procedures for the certification of space technology in Ukraine shall be determined by the Ukrainian Space Technology Certification System, which shall operate as part of the State Certification System (UkrSEPRO).

Procedures for the testing and certification of imported space facilities or space facilities to be exported from Ukraine and for the preparation of the respective certification documents shall be established by the Regulations for the Certification of Space Technology in Ukraine, subject to approval by the Cabinet of Ministers of Ukraine.

Article 13. Registration of space facilities

Space facilities shall be subject to mandatory State registration in the State Register of Space Facilities of Ukraine in accordance with Regulations Governing the Registration of Space Facilities in Ukraine, subject to approval by the Cabinet of Ministers of Ukraine. If a space facility has been designed jointly with corporate entities of other countries or with international organizations, the question of its registration shall be decided in accordance with the international agreements (contracts) concluded.

A space facility registered in the State Register of Space Facilities of Ukraine shall be issued with a registration certificate.

Following the registration of a space facility in the State Register of Space Facilities of Ukraine, any entries in respect of such facility previously made in registers of space facilities of other States shall not be recognized by Ukraine.

The registration of a space facility in the register of space facilities of another State shall not be recognized by Ukraine unless that facility is also registered in the State Register of Space Facilities of Ukraine.

Article 14. Removal of space facilities from the State Register

A space facility shall be removed from the State Register of Space Facilities by the Ukrainian National Space Agency if:

- It is withdrawn from operation;
- It is physically destroyed;
- It is transferred in accordance with established procedure to another State or to an international or foreign enterprise, institution or organization.

If a space facility is removed from the State Register of Space Facilities of Ukraine, the relevant registration certificate shall be rendered invalid.

Article 15. Clearance, restriction and prohibition of the operation of space facilities

A space facility shall be cleared for operation if it has been issued with a compliance certificate and registered in the State Register of Space Facilities of Ukraine. The Ukrainian National Space Agency may restrict or prohibit the operation of space facilities if:

- No compliance certificate has been issued or the period of validity of the compliance certificate has elapsed;
- The operation of the space facility is in violation of Ukrainian legislation currently in force; or
- The operation of the space facility is in violation of the requirements established by the technical operating documentation for that facility.

Article 16. Leasing of a space facility

The procedures and rules for leasing a space facility to an international or foreign subject of space activity shall be governed by the legislation currently in force, unless otherwise provided by international agreements to which Ukraine is a party which have been concluded in the form of a law.

Section IV. PARTICIPATION BY UKRAINE IN INTERNATIONAL SPACE-RELATED COOPERATION

Article 17. Ukraine as a subject of international space law

As a subject of international space law, Ukraine shall pursue its space activities on the basis of equality with other States in the light of its national interests.

Ukraine shall ensure the fulfillment of all its international obligations in the field of space activity and shall bear responsibility under generally recognized standards of international law and the provisions of international treaties to which it is a party.

Article 18. Principles of international space activity

International space activity in Ukraine shall be conducted in accordance with the following fundamental principles:

- Strengthening of national sovereignty;
- Observance of generally recognized principles and standards of international law;
- Maintenance and further development of existing international links;
- Fostering of the integration of Ukraine in the global economy;
- Freedom of foreign-economic enterprise;
- The legal equality of subjects of space activity; and
- Protection of the interests of subjects of space activity in the territory of Ukraine and outside its borders.

Article 19. Settlement of disputes

Disputes arising in the course of international space-related cooperation shall be subject to examination in the courts of Ukraine, unless otherwise provided by the international treaties to which Ukraine is a party.

Section V. ENSURING THE SAFETY OF SPACE ACTIVITY

Article 20. State supervision of the safety of space activity

State supervision of compliance with safety requirements in respect of space activity, as well as the training and certification of persons responsible for monitoring compliance with space regulations and verifying the necessary level of safety of space activity and of persons investigating incidents and emergencies shall be the responsibility of the Ukrainian National Space Agency, the Ministry of Defence of Ukraine and other executive authorities within their competence.

Article 21. Public safety and environmental protection

In the pursuit of space activity, subjects of space activity shall comply with safety requirements with regard to the life and health of the public, the property of citizens, enterprises, institutions and organizations and protection of the environment.

Subjects of space activity shall ensure that the necessary measures are taken in order to prevent environmental damage as the result of space activity in accordance with Ukrainian legislation currently in force.

Article 22. Transport of space technology

For the purposes of the transport of space technology presenting a threat to the life or health of the population or to the environment, use shall mandatorily be made of special means of transport under guard.

Procedures for organizing the guarding and transport of space technology shall be established by special regulations, subject to approval by the Cabinet of Ministers of Ukraine.

Article 23. Notification of incidents and emergencies

Subjects of space activity shall be under a compulsory requirement to furnish full information to executive authorities on any incidents or emergencies.

The Ukrainian National Space Agency, ministries and other central executive authorities shall be required to furnish prompt and reliable information on the danger posed by the conduct of space activity, as well as on measures aimed at ensuring the necessary levels of safety for the public, property and the environment, to the duly authorized State authority, enterprises, institutions and organizations, as well as to citizens at their request.

Should there arise in the course of space activity a threat to the population of Ukraine or to its environment or to foreign States, the Ukrainian National Space Agency shall, in conformity with legislation currently in force, immediately inform the competent State authorities of Ukraine of such threat and shall also take the necessary measures to ensure public safety and the safety of the property of citizens, enterprises, institutions and organizations and of the environment.

Article 24. Compulsory insurance in the pursuit of space activity in Ukraine

The list of types of compulsory insurance to be taken out in connection with the pursuit of space activity shall be established by the Ukrainian legislation currently in force.

Procedures for compulsory insurance shall be established by the Cabinet of Ministers of Ukraine.

Article 25. Liability for damage sustained in the course of space activity, and compensation therefor

Liability for damage sustained in the course of space activity, as well as procedures for determining the extent of such damage for which compensation shall be payable, shall be established in conformity with Ukrainian legislation currently in force.

Section VI. SPACE ACTIVITY RELATED TO THE DEFENCE AND SECURITY OF UKRAINE

Article 26. Conduct of space activity related to defence and national security

Space activity related to defence and national security shall be conducted by the Ministry of Defence of Ukraine, which shall be responsible, jointly with the relevant ministries and other central executive authorities, for implementation of the Ukrainian All-State (National) Space Programme in respect of the use of military and dual-use space technology.

Article 27. Cooperation of the Ministry of Defence of Ukraine with the Ukrainian National Space Agency in relation to space activity

Procedures for cooperation between the Ministry of Defence of Ukraine and the Ukrainian National Space Agency in the conduct of space activity shall be defined by a statute, subject to approval by the Cabinet of Ministers of Ukraine.

Article 28. Competence of the Ministry of Defence of Ukraine in relation to space activity

The Ministry of Defence of Ukraine, within its competence, shall:

- Formulate the conceptual basis of national space policy and of the Ukrainian All-State (National) Space Programme in respect of the part relating to the design and use of military space technology, and, in conjunction with the Ukrainian National Space Agency, of dual-use space technology;
- Prepare orders and arrange for the respective work to be performed in relation to the design and use of military space technology and, in conjunction with the Ukrainian National Space Agency, of dual-use space technology on the basis of the Ukrainian All-State (National) Space Programme;
- Provide for the use of space technology for the purposes of the defence of Ukraine;
- In conjunction with the Ukrainian National Space Agency, ensure the operation and development of ground and space infrastructural facilities;
- Participate in the process of the certification of military space technology.

Section VII. FINAL PROVISIONS

Article 29. Liability for offences under the legislation on space activity in Ukraine

Offences under the legislation on space activity in Ukraine shall be punishable by disciplinary, civil-law or criminal penalties in conformity with Ukrainian legislation currently in force.

On Procedures For The Entry Into Force Of The Law Of Ukraine On Space Activity

Ordinance of the Supreme Soviet of Ukraine of 15 November 1996 No. 503/96-VR (VVRU), 1197, No. 1, p. 3)

The Supreme Soviet of Ukraine orders that:

1. The Law of Ukraine on Space Activity shall enter into force on the day of its publication.

2. The Cabinet of Ministers of Ukraine shall, within a period of three months:

Submit to the Supreme Soviet of Ukraine for its consideration proposals for the harmonization of legislative acts of Ukraine with this Law; Harmonize decisions of the Government of Ukraine with the Law of Ukraine on Space Activity; Ensure the review and revocation by ministries and government departments of Ukraine of their regulatory acts not in harmony with this Law.

3. The Cabinet of Ministers of Ukraine shall, in the first half of 1997, submit to the Supreme Soviet of Ukraine for approval the draft Ukrainian All-State (National) Space Programme.

On The Amendment Of Particular Legislative Acts Of Ukraine Regarding The Activities Of Communications Enterprises

Law of Ukraine of 20 December 1996
No. 626/96-VR (VVRU, 1997, No. 9, p. 71)

The Supreme Soviet of Ukraine orders that:

I. Amendments be made in the following legislative acts of Ukraine:

1. In article 4 of the Law of Ukraine on Entrepreneurial Activity (*Gazette of the Supreme Soviet of the Ukrainian Soviet Socialist Republic*, 1991, No. 14, p. 168; Gazette of the Supreme Soviet of Ukraine, 1992, No. 51, p. 680; 1993, No. 30, p. 322, p. 324, No. 51, p. 481, p. 482; 1994, No. 3, p. 13, No. 28, p. 234, No. 33, p. 301, No. 40, p. 366, No. 49, p. 434; 1995, No. 7, p. 47, No. 10, p. 64, No. 30, p. 232, No. 45, p 334, p. 335, p. 336; 1996, No. 2, p. 4, No. 31, p. 144)

1) The following wording shall be added to the first part:

"Activity relating to the technical maintenance and operation of primary networks (except for local networks) and satellite telephone communications systems in general-use communications networks (except for satellite telephone communications systems in general-use networks in which there is a ground tracking station in the territory of Ukraine and which are established or developed with the aid of national carrier rockets or national spacecraft), together with the dispatch of money transfers, letters of up to 20 (twenty) grams or postcards, the payment and delivery of pensions, and the furnishing of financial assistance to citizens of limited means, shall be carried out exclusively by State enterprises and communications associations";

2) In the second part:

(a) Paragraphs 27 and 28 shall be redrafted as follows:

"Construction and technical maintenance of general-use data transmission and documentary communications networks and the provision of services using such networks;

"Construction and technical maintenance of relay stations in satellite communications networks and the provision of services relating to their use";

(b) In paragraph 30, the words "postal correspondence" shall be replaced with the words "postal dispatches";

(c) Paragraph 31 shall be deleted;

(d) This part shall be supplemented by the following new paragraphs:

"Construction and technical maintenance of television, radio and wire broadcasting networks;

"Construction and technical maintenance of international, inter-city and local telephone communications networks and the provision of services using such networks;

"Construction and technical maintenance of mobile communications networks and the provision of services related to their use".

2. In article 11 of the Law of Ukraine on Communications (*Gazette of the Supreme Soviet of Ukraine*, 1995, No. 20, p. 143), after the first part a new part shall be added as follows:

"The first part of this article shall not apply to general-use satellite telephone communications systems which have a ground tracking station in the territory of Ukraine and are established or developed with the aid of national carrier rockets or national spacecraft".

In this connection, the second and third part shall be deemed the third and fourth part respectively.

3. In Decree No. 9-93 of the Cabinet of Ministers of Ukraine of 21 January 1993 "on the association of State communications enterprises and the licensing of particular types of activity related to communications" (*Gazette of the Supreme Soviet of the Ukraine*, 1993, No. 13, p. 115):

1) The title of the Decree shall be worded as follows:

"On the association of State communications enterprises";

2) Article 2 shall be deleted.

II. This Law shall enter into force on the day of its publication.

JAPAN

Law Concerning The National Space Development Agency Of Japan[53]
(Law No. 50 of June 23, 1969, as amended)

Chapter I: General Provisions

ARTICLE 1. (Purpose)

The National Space Development Agency shall be established with a view to conducting in an integrated, systematic and effective manner the development, launching and tracking of artificial satellites and rockets for the launching of artificial satellites, exclusively for peaceful purposes, thereby contributing to the promotion of space development and utilization.

ARTICLE 2. (Status as Judicial Person)

The National Space Development Agency (hereinafter referred to as the "Agency") shall be a judicial person.

ARTICLE 3. (Offices)

1. The Agency shall have its main offices in Tokyo.

2. The Agency, upon authorization from the Prime Minister, may establish subordinate offices at necessary places.

---

[53] Unofficial translation

ARTICLE 4. (Capital)

1. The capital of the Agency shall consist of the sum of the following amounts:

(1) 500,000,000
(2) The amount that is deemed to have been the contributed by the Government under the provisions of Article 3, Paragraph 2 of the Supplementary Provisions.
(3) The amounts that are to be contributed by persons other than the Government on the occasion of establishment of the Agency.

2. The Government, on the occasion of establishment of the Agency, shall contribute the 500,000,000 referred to in Item I of the preceding Paragraph.

3. The Agency, whenever necessary, may increase its capital upon authorization from the competent Ministers.

4. When the Agency is to increase its capital under the provisions of the preceding Paragraph, the Government may, within the scope of amount to be determined under the budget, make a contribution to the Agency.

5. The Government, when making contributions to the Agency, may use land, buildings and fixtures on land or articles (hereinafter referred to as "land, etc.") for purposes of making its contribution.

6. The values of land, etc. which are to be contributed under the provisions of the preceding Paragraph shall be the values that are appraised by the Appraisal Committee on the basis of the prices prevailing as of the date of the contribution.

7. The Appraisal Committee referred to in the preceding Paragraph and the other necessary matters concerning the appraisal shall be prescribed by a Cabinet Order.

ARTICLE 5. (Investment Bonds)

1. The Agency shall issue investment bonds for the contributions.

2. The investment bonds shall be in non-bearer form.

3. The necessary matters concerning the investment bonds other than those which are stipulated in the preceding Paragraph shall be prescribed by a Cabinet Order.

ARTICLE 6. (Prohibition of Refundment of Holdings, Etc.)

1. The Agency shall not be able to refund to the contributors their holdings.

2. The Agency shall be able neither to acquire holdings of the contributors nor receive the same for the purposes of establishing the right of pledge.

ARTICLE 7. (Registration)

1. The Agency shall have to effect registration in accordance with the provisions of a Cabinet Order.

2. On the matters that ought to be registered under the provisions of the preceding Paragraph, the Agency shall not be able to set up them against third parties unless the registration has been completed.

ARTICLE 8. (Restrictions on the Use of Appellation)

No one other than the Agency shall be able to use the appellation "National Space Development Agency."

ARTICLE 9. (Mutatis Mutandis Application of Civil Code)

The provisions of Article 44 (Corporation's Capacity for Assuming Responsibility for illegal Acts) and Article 50 (Address of Corporation) of the Civil Code (Law No. 89 of 1896) shall apply mutatis mutandis to the Agency.

Chapter II: Executives, Etc.

ARTICLE 10. (Executives)

1. The Agency shall have one President, one Vice President, no more than five Executive Directors and two General Auditors as executives.

2 . The Agency may have no more than two part-time Executive Directors as executives in addition to the Executive Directors referred to in the preceding Paragraph.

ARTICLE 11. (Duty and Authority of Executives)

1. The President shall represent the Agency and preside over its overall business.

2. The Vice President shall represent the Agency and shall, as determined by the President, manage the business of the Agency in assistance with the President, temporarily take over the duties of the President when he is unable to perform his duties, and carry out the duties of the President when that position is vacant.

3. The Executive Directors (with the exception of the part-time Executive Directors) shall, as determined by the President, manage the business of the Agency in assistance with the President and the Vice President, temporarily take over the duties of the President and the Vice President when they are unable to perform their duties, and

carry out the duties of the President and the Vice President when their positions are vacant.

4. The part-time Executive Directors shall, as determined by the President, manage the business of the Agency in assistance with the President and the Vice President.

5. The General Auditors shall audit the business of the Agency.

6. The General Auditors may submit opinions to the President or the competent Ministers (the Director-General of the Science and Technology Agency for the Prime Minister in the event that the former is delegated under the provisions of Article 40. The same is applicable under Article 41, Paragraph 2 and Article 43, Item l), wherever they deem it necessary, on the basis of the findings of an audit.

ARTICLE 12. (Appointment of Executives)

1. The President shall be appointed by the Prime Minister with the concurrence of the Space Activities Commission.

2. The Vice President and Executive Directors shall be appointed by the President with the authorization of the Prime Minister.

3. The General Auditors shall be appointed by the Prime Minister after obtaining the opinion of the Space Activities Commission.

ARTICLE 13. (Term of Office of Executives)

1. The term of office of the President and Vice President shall be four years and the term of office of the Executive Directors and General Auditors two years.

2. The executives may be reappointed.

ARTICLE 14. (Disqualification for Executives)

Those persons who fall under any one of the following Items shall not be able to become executives:

(1) Officials of the Government or local public bodies (except those educational public servants who are prescribed by a Cabinet Order and part-time officials).
(2) Persons who engage in the business of production or sales of commodities or contracting construction and have close interests with the Agency in business deals or, if such persons are judicial persons, their executives (including those persons who have authority or controlling power which is equivalent to or higher than that of such executives, regardless of their title).
(3) Executives of the organizations of the entrepreneurs referred to in the preceding Item (including those persons who have authority or controlling power which is equivalent to or higher than that of such executives, regardless of their title).

ARTICLE 15. (Removal of Executives)

1. The Prime Minister or the President shall remove any executive appointed by him when such executive falls under any one of the Items of the preceding Article.

2. The Prime Minister or the President may remove any executive appointed by him, in the manner set forth in Article 12, when such executive falls under either of the following Items or when the Prime Minister or the President otherwise considers that such executive is not fit to remain an executive:

(1) When it is recognized that he is no longer able to execute his duties due to his mental or physical problems.
(2) When he has violated the duties of his office.

ARTICLE 16. (Prohibition of Concurrent Posts by Executives)

An executive shall neither become an executive of a profit-making organization nor engage in any Profit-making business by himself; provided however, that this provision is not applicable when approval has been secured from the Prime Minister.

ARTICLE 17. (Restrictions on Right of Representation)

On the matters for which there exists conflict of interests between the Agency and the President or the Vice President, such person shall not have the right of representation. In such case, the General Auditors shall represent the Agency.

ARTICLE 18. (Appointment of Agents)

The President and the Vice President may appoint from among the Executive Directors or staff members of the Agency the agents who are empowered to take all actions in court or out of court, in connection with matters concerning the business of subordinate offices of the Agency.

ARTICLE 19. (Advisors)

1. Advisors may be assigned to the Agency to take part in the planning of important matters concerning the management of its business.

2. Advisors shall be appointed by the President from among men of learning and experience with the authorization of the Prime Minister.

ARTICLE 20. (Appointment of Staff Members)

Staff members of the Agency shall be appointed by the President.

ARTICLE 21. (Status of Executives, Etc. as Public Servants)

The executives, Advisors and staff members shall be regarded as staff members who engage in public services by law insofar as the application of the Criminal Code (Law No. 45 of 1907) and other penal regulations are concerned.

Chapter III: Business

ARTICLE 22. (Scope of Business)

1. The Agency shall conduct the following business in order to achieve the purpose referred to in Article 1:

(1) The development of artificial satellites and rockets for the launching of artificial satellites (hereinafter referred to as "artificial satellites, etc.") and development of facilities and equipment necessary therefor.
(2) The launching and tracking of artificial satellites, etc. developed by it and development of means, facilities and equipment necessary therefor.
(3) The development referred to in Item 1, the launching and tracking of artificial satellites, etc. and the development of means, facilities and equipment necessary therefor, which are conducted pursuant to entrustment thereof.
(4) Business incidental to those businesses mentioned in the preceding three Items.
(5) Business required to accomplish the purpose referred to in Article 1 other than the business mentioned in each of the foregoing Items.

2. The Agency, in carrying out the following business, shall comply with the guidelines which it prescribes with authorization from the competent Ministers:

(1) The launching of artificial satellites, etc. referred to in Item 2 of the preceding Paragraph.
(2) Business referred to in Item 3 of the preceding Paragraph.

3. The Agency shall have to secure authorization from the competent Ministers when it is to carry out the business referred to in Paragraph l, Item 5.

4. In addition to carrying out those businesses which are referred to In Paragraph I, the Agency may, in accordance with the guidelines which it prescribes with authorization from the competent Ministers, offer the facilities and equipment which are to be established by it for development, for the use of those who carry out space development.

ARTICLE 23. (Entrustment of Business)

The Agency may, in accordance with the guidelines which it prescribes with authorization from the competent Ministers, entrust part of its business.

ARTICLE 24. (Guidelines for Business Management)

The business of the Agency shall be conducted in accordance with a basic plan for space development which is to be stipulated by the Prime Minister after resolution by the Space Activities Commission.

Chapter III-2: Compensation for Damages due to Launch of Artificial Satellites, Etc.

ARTICLE 24-2. (Conclusion of Insurance Contracts)

1. The Agency shall not launch an Artificial Satellite, Etc., until and unless it has entered into an insurance contract by which it can secure such amount as is necessary to compensate for damages incurred by others as a result of the launch of the Artificial Satellite, Etc.

2. The amount secured under the insurance contract set forth in the preceding Paragraph shall be determined by the competent Ministers, in order for such amount to be appropriate from the viewpoint of the protection of victims, etc., taking into account the amount that insurers can underwrite and other factors.

3. In the event that the launch of an Artificial Satellite, Etc. is to be performed by the Agency as a result of the consignment set forth in Article 22, Paragraph 1, Item 3 (hereinafter referred to as the ◆Consigned Launch◆), the insurance contract set forth in Paragraph 1 hereof may, notwithstanding the provision of said Paragraph, be entered into by a person or entity which has consigned the launch of such Artificial Satellite, Etc., (hereinafter referred to as the ◆Consignor◆) for and on behalf of the Agency.

ARTICLE 24-3. (Special Arrangements for the Consigned Launch)

1. In the event that the Agency enters into an agreement with a Consignor with respect to the Consigned Launch, the Agency may, upon the approvals of the competent Ministers, enter into the following special arrangements with respect to its liability for compensation for damages caused by the Consigned Launch incurred by any persons or entities other than those related to the Consigned Launch:

(i) If the Agency is held liable for compensation for damages caused by the Consigned Launch incurred by any persons or entities other than those related to the Consigned Launch, and any of those related to the Consigned Launch are also liable for compensation for such damages, the Agency shall assume all of the liabilities for compensation for damages owed by those related to the Consigned Launch; and

(ii) In the preceding Item, if such damages are caused by a willful misconduct of any of those related to the Consigned Launch, the Agency shall have the right to have such person reimburse the damages already paid by the Agency.

2. For the purpose of the preceding Paragraph, "those related to the Consigned Launch" means the Consignor and any person or entity designated by the Agency and the Consignor in accordance with the said special arrangements as the persons or entities which are related to the Consigned Launch.

3. When the Agency enters into the special arrangements set forth in Paragraph 1 hereof, the insurance contract set forth in the first Paragraph of the immediately preceding Article shall, notwithstanding the provisions of said first Paragraph and the third Paragraph of the immediately preceding Article, be entered into by the Consignor for and on behalf of the Agency.

Chapter IV: Finance and Accounting

ARTICLE 25. (Fiscal Year)

The fiscal year of the Agency shall commence on April 1 of every year and terminate on March 31 of the following year.

ARTICLE 26. (Authorization of Business Plan. Etc.)

In each fiscal year the Agency shall prepare a business plan, a budget and a fund plan and secure authorization from the competent Ministers prior to the beginning of the fiscal year concerned. The same shall also be applicable in the event that Agency is to amend such plans or budget.

ARTICLE 27. (Settlement of Accounts)

The Agency shall complete a settlement of accounts for each fiscal year not later than May 31 of the following fiscal year.

ARTICLE 28. (Financial Statements)

1. In each fiscal year the Agency shall prepare a general inventory, a balance sheet and a statement of profit and loss (referred to as "financial statements" in this Article and in the following Article), submit them to the competent Ministers within one month after completion of the settlement of accounts and secure the approval from such Ministers.

2. When the Agency submits the financial statements to the competent Ministers under the provisions of the preceding Paragraph it shall affix to the financial statements a business report for the fiscal year concerned, a statement of accounts prepared according to the budget classification, and the opinion of the General Auditors on the financial statements and the statement of accounts.

3. When the Agency obtains approval of the competent Ministers set forth in the first Paragraph of this Article it shall, without delay make its financial statements public in the Official Gazette (Kanpo), and maintain such financial statements and supplemental schedules, and the business report, statement of accounts and the opinion of General Auditors referred to in the immediately preceding Paragraph, at each of its offices and make the same available for public inspection for the period stipulated by an ordinance of the competent Ministries.

ARTICLE 29. (Transmittal of Documents)

When the Agency has secured authorization or approval under the provisions of Article 26 or Paragraph 1 of the preceding Article, it shall transmit the documents pertinent to the business plan, budget and fund plan or the financial statements under such authorization or approval to those persons, other than the Government, who have made contributions to the Agency.

ARTICLE 30. (Disposition of Profit and Loss)

1. In the event that a profit is made according the accounting of profit and loss for a fiscal year, the Agency shall use it to make up for the loss carried over from the previous fiscal year, and, if there still remains a surplus settle it as a reserved fund.

2. In the event that a loss is incurred according to the accounting of profit and loss for a fiscal year, the Agency shall settle it by reducing the reserve fund stipulated in the preceding Paragraph, and, if there still remains a shortage, settle it as a loss to be carried over to the following fiscal year.

ARTICLE 31. (Short-Term Loans)

1. The Agency may secure short-term loans upon authorization from the Prime Minister.

2. The short-term loans stipulated in the preceding Paragraph shall be repaid within the fiscal year concerned; provided, however, that in the event that the repayment cannot be made due to a lack of funds, only that amount which cannot be repaid may be converted into a new loan, upon authorization from the Prime Minister.

3. A short term loan which has been converted into a new loan under the proviso of the preceding Paragraph shall be repaid within one year.

ARTICLE 32. (Operation of Surplus Funds)

The Agency shall not operate surplus business funds with the exception of the following manners:

(1) Acquisition of national bonds and other securities designated by the Prime Minister.
(2) Deposits with banks or other financial institutions designated by the Prime Minister or postal savings.
(3) Money trust to banks engaging in trust business or trust firms.

ARTICLE 33. (Restrictions on Disposal of Property, Etc.)

The Agency shall secure authorization from the competent Ministers when it is to loan, transfer, or offer as security such important property exchange as prescribed by an ordinance of the competent Ministries.

ARTICLE 34. (Guidelines for Payment of Wages and Severance Allowances)

The Agency shall, secure approval from the Prime Minister when it is to establish guidelines for the payment of wages and severance allowances to its executives and staff members. The same shall also be applicable when the Agency is to amend such guidelines.

ARTICLE 35. (Mandate to Ordinance of Competent Ministries)

The necessary matters concerning the finance and accounting of the Agency other than those stipulated in this Law shall be prescribed by an ordinance of the competent Ministries.

Chapter V: Supervision

ARTICLE 36. (Supervision)

1. The competent Ministers shall exercise supervision over the Agency.

2. The competent Ministers may issue an order to the Agency concerning its business required for the supervision thereof, when they deem it necessary for the implementation of this Law.

ARTICLE 37. (Acquisition of Report and On-Spot Inspection)

1. The competent Ministers when they deem it necessary for the implementation of this Law, may cause the Agency to file a report on its business or have their staff members enter the offices and other places of business of the Agency and inspect the conditions of the business or the books, documents and other necessary objects.

2 . When staff members are to carry out an on-spot inspection under the preceding Paragraph, they shall carry a certificate which identifies them and show it to the persons concerned.

3. The authority to enter and inspect, stipulated in Paragraph l, shall not be construed as being recognized for criminal investigation.

Chapter VI: Miscellaneous Provisions

ARTICLE 38. (Dissolution)

1. In the event of dissolution of the Agency, there remain assets after the Agency has paid its obligations, the Agency shall distribute them to each contributor within the limit of the amount of his contribution.

2. Matters concerning the dissolution of the Agency other than that which is stipulated in the preceding Paragraph, shall be prescribed by a separate law.

ARTICLE 39. (Competent Ministers and Ordinance of Competent Ministries)

1. The competent Ministers in this Law shall be the prime Minister, the Minister of Posts and Telecommunications and the Ministers who are in charge of matters concerning to the development of artificial satellites, etc. and designated by a Cabinet Order.

2. The ordinances of the competent Ministries in this Law shall be Ministerial Ordinances issued by the competent Ministers.

ARTICLE 40. (Delegation to Director-General of the Science and Technology Agency)

1. The Prime Minister may delegate the following authorities to the Director-General of the Science and Technology Agency:

(1) The authorization under the provisions of Article 3, Paragraph 2; Article 4, paragraph 3; Article 22, Paragraphs 2 through 4; Article 23; Article 24-3, Paragraph 1; Article 26; Article 31, Paragraph 1 or the proviso of Paragraph 2; or Article 33.
(2) The approval under the provisions of the proviso of Article 16; Article 28, Paragraph 1; or Article 34.
(3) The determination of the amount secured under the insurance contract under the provisions of Article 24-2, Paragraph 2.
(4) The designation under the provisions of Article 32, Item 1or 2.
(5) The acquisition of report and conduct of on-spot inspection under the provisions of Article 37, Paragraph 1.

ARTICLE 41. (Consultations with Minister of Finance)

1. The Prime Minster, (Director-General of the Science and Technology Agency when he is delegated under the provisions of the preceding Article. The same is applicable under Article 43, Item 1.) shall have prior consultations with the Minister of Finance in the following cases:

(1) When he is to formulate the basic plan referred to in Article 24.
(2) When he is to give authorization under the provisions of Article 31, Paragraph 1 or the proviso of Paragraph 2.
(3) When he is to make designation under the provisions of Article 32, Item l or 2.
(4) When he is to give approvals under the provisions of Article 34.

2. The competent Ministers shall have prior consultations with the Minister of Finance in the following cases

(1) When they are to give authorization under the provisions of Article 4, Paragraph 3; Article 22, Paragraph 2, Item 2 or Paragraph 3; Article 24-3, Paragraph 1; Article 26 or Article 33.
(2) When they are to determine the amount secured under the insurance contract under the provision of Article 24-2, Paragraph 2.
(3) When they are to give approvals under the provisions of Article 28, Paragraph 1.
(4) When they are to formulate an ordinance of the competent Ministries under the provisions of Article 33 or Article 35.

Chapter VII: Penal Provisions

ARTICLE 42. (Penal Provisions)

In the event of the failure to file a report or filing of a false report under Article 37, Paragraph 1, or refusal, interference or evasion of the inspection under the same Paragraph, the executive or the staff member of the Agency who has committed such violation shall be subject to a fine not exceeding ◆200,000.

ARTICLE 43.

In any of the following events, the executive of the Agency who has committed such violation shall be subject to an administrative fine not exceeding ◆200,000.

(1) Failure to secure the authorization or approval in case the authorization or approval must be secured from the Prime Minister or the competent Ministers under this Law.
(2) Failure to make the registration in violation of the provisions of the Cabinet Order referred to in Article 7, Paragraph l.
(3) Conducting business other than that referred to in Article 22, Paragraphs 1 and 4.
(4) Launching an Artificial Satellite, Etc., without entering into an insurance contract, in breach of the provision of Article 24-2, Paragraph 1.
(5) Operating surplus business funds in violation of the provisions of Article 32.
(6) Violating an order of the competent Ministers under in Article 36, Paragraph 2.

ARTICLE 44.

A person who has violated the provisions of Article 8 shall be subject to an administrative fine not exceeding ◆100,000.

Supplementary Provisions

ARTICLE l. (Date of Enforcement)

This Law shall come into force as of the day of promulgation.

ARTICLE 2. (Establishment of Agency)

1. The Prime Minister shall designate the persons who will become President or General Auditors of the Agency in the manner set forth in Article 12, Paragraph 1 or Paragraph 3.

2. The persons who will be President or General Auditors designated under the preceding Paragraph shall be deemed as being appointed President or General Auditors under the provisions of this Law at the time of establishment of the Agency.

3. The Prime Minister shall appoint the Establishment Committee and cause it to handle business pertinent to the establishment of the Agency.

4. The Establishment Committee shall raise contributions to the Agency from persons other than the Government.

5. The Establishment Committee, when the raising of contributions referred to in the preceding Paragraph is completed, shall apply to the competent Ministers for the authorization of the establishment of the Agency.

6. Upon securing the authorization referred to in the preceding Paragraph, the Establishment Committee shall request the Government and those persons, other than the Government, who have agreed to make contributions, to pay their contributions.

7. On the day the contributions are paid in, the Establishment Committee shall turn over its business to the person who will be President designated under the provisions of Paragraph 1.

8. The person who will be President designated under the provisions of Paragraph 1 shall effect registration for the establishment without delay in accordance with the provisions of a Cabinet Order, when the business referred to in the preceding Paragraph has been turned over to him.

9. The Agency shall be brought into existence upon the completion of the registration under the preceding Paragraph.

ARTICLE 3. (Succession of Rights and Obligations, Etc.)

1. Among the rights and obligations actually owned or owed by the State at the time of establishment of the Agency, those which are relevant to the business handled by the Space Development Office of the Science and Technology Agency under the provisions of Article 20-2, Paragraph 1 of the Law Concerning the Establishment of the Science and Technology Agency (Law No. 49 of 1956) and the business (limited to that concerning the development of artificial satellites for the observation of the ionosphere) handled by the Radio Research Laboratories of the Ministry of Posts and Telecommunications under the provisions of Article 17-2 of the Law Concerning the Establishment of the Ministry of Posts and Telecommunications (Law No. 244 of 1948) and which are prescribed by a Cabinet Order, shall be succeeded by the Agency as of its establishment.

2. When the Agency has succeeded the rights and obligations owned or owed by the State under the preceding Paragraph, an amount equivalent to the total of the value of the land, buildings, articles and other assets which are relevant to the rights to be succeeded and which are prescribed by a Cabinet Order, shall be deemed as having been contributed to the Agency by the Government upon such succession.

3. The value of the assets referred to in the preceding Paragraph which will be deemed as having been contributed by the Government under the provisions of the preceding Paragraph shall be the value to be assessed by the Appraisal Committee on the basis of prices prevailing as of the date of establishment of the Agency.

4. The necessary matters concerning the Appraisal Committee referred to in the preceding Paragraph and other necessary matters concerning the appraisal shall be prescribed by a Cabinet Order.

5. In the event that the Agency has succeeded the rights of the State under the provisions of Paragraph l, the registration license tax and the real estate acquisition tax shall not be levied on the registrations accompanying such succession or on the acquisition of immovable properties relevant to such succession.

Supplementary Provisions

ARTICLE 1. (Date of Enforcement)

This Law shall come into force as of the date of promulgation.

ARTICLE 2. (Transitional Measures Pertaining to the Term of Office of Executives)

The term of office of the persons who are actually the Executive Directors at the time of enforcement of this Law shall be a s previously prescribed by this Law.

ARTICLE 3. (Transitional Measures Pertaining to the Penal Provisions)

Application of the penal provisions to conducts that have been done before the enforcement of this Law shall be as previously prescribed by this Law.

NORWAY

Act on launching objects from Norwegian territory etc. into outer space[54]

13 June. No. 38. 1969

1 Without permission from the Norwegian Ministry concerned[55], it is forbidden to launch any object into outer space from:

a) Norwegian territory, also including Svalbard, Jan Mayen and the Norwegian external territories.

b) Norwegian vessels, aircrafts etc.

c) Areas that are not subject to the sovereignty of any state, when the launching is undertaken by a Norwegian citizen or person with habitual residence in Norway.

Certain terms can be set for such permission as described in paragraph one.

2 The Ministry can issue regulations on control etc. of activities as described in 1.

3 This act enters into force immediately.

---

[54] Unofficial translation
[55] Ministry of Trade and Industry (our note)

REPUBLIC OF KAZACHSTAN
Law of the Republic of Kazakhstan on Space Activities 6 January, 2012 No. 528-IV

The present Law regulates public relations on space activities in the Republic of Kazakhstan.

Chapter 1. General provisions Article 1. Basic definitions used in the present Law

In the present Law the following basic definitions are used:

1) cosmodrome - a complex of technical facilities, devices, buildings, constructions and land plots that is intended to provide preparation and implementation of space objects launches;

2) spacecraft - a technical device designed to be launched into outer space with the purpose of exploration and (or) the use of outer space;

3) national operators of space systems - legal entities that carry out the management of space systems and their operation;

4) space system - a set of functionally-related orbital and ground technical facilities that is intended to solve tasks in outer space;

5) space rocket complex - a set of carrier rocket and technical facilities, constructions, technological equipment and Communications, that provides reception, storage, preparation for launching and the launch of the carrier rocket with the spacecraft;

6) outer space - a space extending beyond the airspace at an altitude of more than one hundred kilometers above the sea level;

7) space activities - activities aimed at exploration and use of outer space for achieving the scientific, economic, environmental, defense, information and commercial purposes;

8) participants of the space activities - individuals and (or) legal entities performing space activities on the territory of the Republic of Kazakhstan, as well as in outer space in accordance with the present Law;

9) project in the field of space activities - a set of arrangements to create space engineering and technologies, aimed to carry out the space activities;

10) project in the field of dual-use space activities - a project in the field of space activities implemented to solve the social and economic tasks as well the purposes of defense and security;

11) authorized body in the field of space activities - the central executive body responsible for the management of the space activities, as well as inter-sectoral coordination within the limits stipulated by the legislation of the Republic of Kazakhstan;

12) space object - a spacecraft and (or) a device and its components to be launched into outer space;

13) objects of space sector - manufacturing facilities, buildings, constructions and other real estates of the participants of space activities used to perform the space activities;

14) space services - services provided by using space engineering and technologies;

15) high-accuracy satellite navigation system - funcţional supplements to global navigation satellite system that includes technical facilities of ground and (or) space basing;

16) global navigation satellite system - a space system designed to determine the coordinate-and time parameters (geographical coordinates and altitudes, speed and direction of movement, time) of ground, water and air objects;

17) Earth remote sensing - the process of obtaining information about the Earth's surface by observing and measuring its own and the reflected radiation of elements of land, ocean and atmosphere from outer space;

18) cosmonaut candidate of the Republic of Kazakhstan (hereinafter - the cosmonaut candidate) - a citizen of the Republic of Kazakhstan, pre-selected and assigned to have trainings in order to obtain the cosmonaut qualification;

19) cosmonaut of the Republic of Kazakhstan (hereinafter - the cosmonaut) -a citizen of the Republic of Kazakhstan, who has been trained and received the cosmonaut qualification documents (test-cosmonaut, cosmonaut-researcher, instructor-cosmonaut) and the status of the cosmonaut;

20) satellite navigation - the problem solving process of the navigation by using the global navigation satellite system to determine the coordinate and time parameters of objects;

21) satellite navigation services - activities aimed at the satisfaction of needs in additional (according to the standard services provided by the global navigation satellite systems) services on determination of coordinate-and time parameters of objects;

22) carrier rocket - a technical device designed for inserting the spacecrafts into outer space;

23) drop area for carrier rocket's separated parts - the land plot, where the exhausted and separated elements and (or) fragments of carrier rockets fall (land) in flight;

24) transponder of the spacecraft - a set of radio-transmitting devices installed on the spacecraft and designed for retransmission the Earth - space - the Earth signals;

25) launch services - a set of activities aimed to organize and implement the launching of carrier rockets in order to insert spacecrafts into outer space;

26) launch vehicle - a carrier rocket, an upper stage rocket, an aviation space-rocket system intended that is designed to insert the spacecrafts into outer space.

Article 2. Legislation of the Republic of Kazakhstan in the field of space activities

1. The legislation of the Republic of Kazakhstan in the field of space activities is based on the Constitution of the Republic of Kazakhstan and consists of the present Law and other regulator/legislative acts of the Republic of Kazakhstan.
2. If an internațional treaty that ratified by the Republic of Kazakhstan establishes other rules than contained in the present Law, then the rules of internațional treaty are applied.

Article 3. Principles of implementation of space activities

The principles of implementation of space activities are:
1) compliance with național interests, provision of defense and național security of the Republic of Kazakhstan during the implementation of space activities;
2) support of the priority directions of space activities development;
3) economic stimulation of space activities;

4) compensation for harm to health of individuals, damage to the environment, property of individuals and legal entities, the state arising out of the implementation of space activities;
5) compliance with ecological requirements, requirements in the field of technical regulation and provision of sanitary and epidemiological wellbeing of population;
6) compliance with the internațional law norms in the field of space activities;
7) efficient and rațional use of outer space and space infrastructure of the Republic of Kazakhstan;

8) stimulation for attraction of investments in the development of space activities in compliance with the state interests of the Republic of Kazakhstan.

Article 4. Directions of space activities

The space activities in the Republic of Kazakhstan are carried out in the following directions:
1) creation and use of space sector objects;
2) exploration of outer space, planets and solar-terrestrial relations;
3) Earth remote sensing;
4) coordinate-and time and navigation provision;
5) creation and use of space communication systems;
6) implementation of space objects launches;

7) development of the national market of space services and the expansion of the space services in the world market;
8) international cooperation of the Republic of Kazakhstan in the field of exploration and use of outer space for peaceful purposes.

Article 5. Types of space activities for creation and use of space infrastructure

In order to create and use space infrastructure in the Republic of Kazakhstan, the following types of space activities are carried out:
1) scientific research developments;
2) design-engineering and technological developments;
3) manufacturing and testing experimental, prototype and commercial
models of space engineering;

4) technical operation, maintenance and upgrading of space engineering;
5) utilization of space objects and technical facilities;
6) rendering space services to end users.

Article 6. Material and human resource bases of space activities

Material and human resource bases of space activities of the Republic of Kazakhstan are:
1) scientific, scientific technological and scientific experimental bases;
2) design-engineering and industrial bases;
3) basis for the operation of space engineering;
4) basis for rendering space services to end users;
5) personal staff of the participants of space activities.

Article 7. Financing space activities

The space activities are financed from the budgetary funds and other sources of money, which are not prohibited by the legislation of the Republic of Kazakhstan.

Chapter 2. State regulation and control in the field of space activities

Article 8. Competence of the Government of the Republic of Kazakhstan in the field of space activities

The Government of the Republic of Kazakhstan:

1) develops the main directions of state policy in the field of space activities and organizes their implementation;

2) coordinates items of international cooperation of the Republic of Kazakhstan in the field of space activities;

3) approves coordination and decision-making procedures on space objects launches from the territory of the Republic of Kazakhstan, as well as outside the territory in case of their implementation by the Kazakhstan's participants of space activities;

4) approves selection procedure of a cosmonaut candidate and assignment of the status of the cosmonaut candidate, the cosmonaut;

5) makes decisions on space objects launches from the territory of the Republic of Kazakhstan, as well as outside the territory in case of their implementation by the Kazakhstan's participants of space activities;

6) deflnes the payment procedures of one-time indemnification to the cosmonaut candidate, to the cosmonaut at the establishment of the disability, occurred as a result of injury, mutilation, disease, obtained in the course of duty, as well as in case of his/her loss (death) in connection with execution in the course of duty;

7) approves technical regulations in the field of space activities;

8) defines arrangements for the development and economic support of the "Baikonur" cosmodrome;

9) approves procedures of provision of spacecrafts' transponders for individuals and (or) legal entities;

10) defines planning procedures of space imaging, reception, processing and distribution of Earth remote sensing data by the national operator of Earth remote sensing space system;

11) defines the organizational procedure and provision of satellite navigation services by the national operator of high-accuracy satellite navigation system;

12) defines provision of the național operators of space systems by an authorized body in the field of the space activities, as well as their tasks and functions;

13) approves the rules of creation and operation (application) of space systems in the territory of the Republic of Kazakhstan, as well as in outer space, the rules of creation and operation (application) of space rocket complexes on the territory of the Republic of Kazakhstan;

14) defines procedure of utilization of space objects and technical facilities, taken out of operation;

15) approves qualifying requirements claimed to the activities in the field of outer space use;

16) defines performance procedure of sectoral expertise of the projects in the field of space activities by authorized body in the field of space activities;

17) approves the procedure of state registration of space objects and rights for them;

18) approves the form of register of space objects;

19) performs other functions assigned to it by the Constitution, the present Law, other laws of the Republic of Kazakhstan and acts of the President of the Republic of Kazakhstan.

Article 9. Competence of an authorized body in the field of space activities

1. Authorized body in the field of space activities (hereinafter - the authorized body):

1) ensures the realization of state policy in the field of space activities;

2) ensures the realization of projects and programs in the field of space activities, including carrying out of scientific research and development works;

3) carries out state regulation in the field of space activities;

4) develops the coordination and decision-making procedures on space objects launches from the territory of the Republic of Kazakhstan, as well as outside the territory in case of their implementation by the Kazakhstan's participants of space activities;

5) develops the selection procedure of a cosmonaut candidate and assignment of the status of the cosmonaut candidate, the cosmonaut;

6) develops the payment procedures of the one-time indemnification to the cosmonaut candidates, to the cosmonaut at the establishment of the disability, occurred as a result of an injury, mutilation, disease, obtained in the course of duty, as well as in case of his/her loss (death) in connection with execution in the course of duty;

7) carries out the licensing in the field of use of outer space;

8) develops the qualifying requirements claimed to the activities in the field of outer space use;

9) carries out the state control in the field of space activities;

10) carries out the sectoral expertise of the projects in the field of space activities;

11) develops the procedure of state registration of space objects and rights for them;

12) carries out the state registration of space objects and rights for them;

13) carries on the register of space objects;

14) carries out the organization and coordination activities on preparation, retraining and professional development of cosmonauts, as well as on retraining and professional development of specialists in the field of space activities;

15) develops and approves the regulation on team of cosmonauts of the Republic of Kazakhstan;

16) develops and accepts within its competence the legal regulatory acts in the field of space activities;

17) carries out international cooperation in the field of space activities and represents the interests of the Republic of Kazakhstan in the international organizations and foreign states;

18) organizes the development of technical regulations and state standards in the field of space activities according to the legislation of the Republic of Kazakhstan on technical regulation;

19) develops the procedure of provision of spacecrafts' transponders for individuals and (or) legal entities;

20) develops planning procedure of space imaging, reception, processing and distribution of Earth remote sensing data by the national operator of Earth remote sensing space system;

21) develops the organizational procedure and provision of satellite navigation services by the national operator of the high-accuracy satellite navigation system;

22) represents the list of legal bodies for the definition of national operators of space systems, as well as their tasks and functions to the Government of the Republic of Kazakhstan;

23) develops the rules of creation and operation (application) of space systems on the territory of the Republic of Kazakhstan, as well as in outer space, rules of creation and operation (application) of space rocket complexes on the territory of the Republic of Kazakhstan;

24) develops the utilization procedure of space objects and technical facilities, taken out of operation;

25) establishes the procedure of acceptance of results on completed projects in the field of space activities;

26) participates within its competence in management of search, rescue and salvage operations, as well as in investigation of accidents during the implementation of space activities;

27) carries out other authorities stipulated by the present Law, other laws of the Republic of Kazakhstan, acts of the President

of the Republic of Kazakhstan and the Government of the Republic of Kazakhstan.

2. Functions of the authorized body on realization of projects in the field of space activities of dual purpose are realized together with the Ministry of Defense of the Republic of Kazakhstan.

Article 10. Sectoral expertise of projects in the field of space activities

1. Projects in the field of space activities are subject to obligatory industrial expertise.

2. Sectoral expertise of projects in the field of space activities is carried out by an authorized body for the purposes of definition of expediency, technical possibilities, economic efficiency, as well as conformity to the legislation of the Republic of Kazakhstan, technical regulations and standards in the field of space activities.

3. Sectoral expertise of projects in the field of space activities is carried out within the time limit, not exceeding thirty working days from the date of provision of project materials to an authorized body.

After the elimination of remarks revealed by the authorized body during the implementation of initial expertise, a repeated sectoral expertise of projects in the field of space activities is carried out within the time limit, not exceeding twenty working days.

4. Realization of the projects in the field of space activities is forbidden without the positive resolution of sectoral expertise.

Article 11. State registration of space objects and rights for them

1. The space objects are subject to a state registration:
1) that belong to the individuals or to legal entities of the Republic of Kazakhstan, as well as the rights to the given space objects;

2) that belong to the foreign individuals or to legal entities, launching into outer space from the territory of the Republic of Kazakhstan.

2. State registration of space objects and the rights for them specified in subclause 1) of clause **1** of the present article, is a record of space objects, the certificate of acknowledgement and confirmation by the state of occurrence, amendment or termination of the rights (the encumbrance of rights) for space object according to the civil legislation of the Republic of Kazakhstan.

State registration of space objects specified in subclause 2) of clause 1 of the present article is a record in the register of space objects without the state registration of the rights for them.

3. The space objects specified in clause 1 of the present article are subject to the state registration according to the procedure of state registration of space objects and the rights for them.

The state registration is carried out by an authorized body within fifteen working days from the date of statement receipt.

4. The rights for space objects arise from the moment of their state registration and are proved by the certificate of state registration, given out by an authorized body.

In case of loss of the certificate of state registration, the authorized body gives out the duplicate of the mentioned document to the applicant. The duplicate of the certificate of state registration is given out according to the procedure of state registration of space objects and rights for them.

5. To get a state registration and issue of the duplicate of the certificate of state registration, a duty is collected following the procedure and rate defined by the tax legislation of the Republic of Kazakhstan.

6. For the state registration of a space object and the rights for it the following documents are provided to an authorized body:

1) A statement;

2) a copy of the title document on space object (notarized copy in case of failure to provide the original copy for verification);

3) a copy of the license for the right of realization of activities in the sphere of outer space use (notarized copy in case of failure to provide the original copy for verification);

4) a document confirming the payment of the duty sum into the budget for the state registration of a space object and the rights for it.

7. Reasons for refusal in the state registration of a space object and the rights for it are:

1) provision of an incomplete set of documents necessary for the state registration by the applicant;

2) provision of documents unconformable with the requirements of the legislation of the Republic of Kazakhstan by the applicant;

3) presence of the encumbrance of rights for the space object, limiting or excluding the disposal of space object;

4) decision of the court, that has entered into force, limiting or excluding the right of disposal of space object.

8. In case of refusal in a state registration, an authorized body sends a written answer to an applicant indicating the reasons of refusal no later than fifteen working days from the date of statement receipt.

9. Refusal in the state registration of a space object and the rights for it can be appealed in court following the procedures established by the legislation of the Republic of Kazakhstan.

10. In case of eliminating the reasons for refusal in the state registration, the statement on the state registration can be submitted repeatedly.

11. Once the state registration is completed, as well as the applicant provides the documents confirming the fact of destruction

or utilization of a space object to an authorized body, the authorized body makes corresponding record in the register of space objects.

Article 12. State control in the field of space activities

State control in the field of space activities is carried out by an authorized body in the form of verification in accordance with the Law of the Republic of Kazakhstan «On the state control and supervision in the Republic of Kazakhstan».

Chapter 3. Implementation of space activities

Article 13. Licensing activities in the field of use of outer space

The activity of individuals and legal entities in the field of outer space use is carried out on the basis of license issued in accordance with the legislation of the Republic of Kazakhstan on licensing.

Article 14. Scientific researches in the field of the space activities

1. Scientific researches in the field of space activities include fundamental and applied researches and space experiments aimed at scientific support of space activities and development of models of space engineering and technologies.

Scientific researches in the field of space activities are carried out within the framework of scientific and technical projects and programs that are coordinated by an authorized body in science field. Scientific and technical projects and programs are developed and implemented under the supervision of an authorized body with the assistance of scientists, qualified specialists and scientific workers, scientific and social organizations, institutes of higher education of the Republic of Kazakhstan.

2. The legal protection of intellectual property obtained during the development of space engineering and technologies is carried out according to the procedures determined by the Civil Code of the Republic of Kazakhstan and other laws of the Republic of Kazakhstan.

Article 15. Creation of space systems and space rocket complexes

Creation of space systems and space rocket complexes includes the scientific development, designing, manufacturing, assembling, construction, testing of space systems and space rocket complexes, its components, as well as operation.

Article 16. Usage of space communication system

1. Regulation of use of space communication system is the package of legal, economic, organizational and technical measures directed to its effective use.

2. Space communication system is intended to provide spacecrafis' transponders for the needs of individuals and legal entities.

3. National operator of space communication system ensures technical operation of the space communication system and

renders the services on provision with the spacecrafts' transponders to individuals and legal entities according to the procedures approved by the Government of the Republic of Kazakhstan.

4. National operator of space communication system, as agreed with authorized body in the field of communication, interacts with foreign operators of space communication for the purpose of reservation of the naţional spacecrafts'transponders, as well as for the purpose of extending the coverage area by the naţional spacecrafts outside the territory of the Republic of Kazakhstan.

Article 17. Usage of Earth remote sensing space system

1. Earth remote sensing space system is intended for acquisition of spaţial data concerning the surface and the surface structure of the Earth; description of nature and temporal variability of natural environmental parameters and phenomena, natural resources, environmental and anthropogenic factors and generations for the solution of scientific, social-economic, environmental and defense tasks through the space imaging.

2. National operator of the Earth remote sensing space system plâns the space coverage; receives, processes and distributes the Earth remote sensing data to individuals and (or) legal entities, state authorities of the Republic of Kazakhstan according to the procedures determined by the Government of the Republic of Kazakhstan.

Article 18. Usage of high-accuracy satellite navigation system

1. High-accuracy satellite navigation system is intended to provide users with the data concerning the integrity of the global navigation satellite system, as well as the information, which allows

enhancing the accuracy of definition of coordinate and time parameters.

2. National operator of the high-accuracy satellite navigation system renders the satellite navigation services in the territory of the Republic of Kazakhstan according to the procedures determined by Government of the Republic of Kazakhstan.

Article 19. Usage of space-rocket complexes

1. The space-rocket complexes are intended to launch the space objects into outer space.

2. Launches of space objects with the use of space-rocket complexes are performed in the presence of positive decision of the Government of the Republic of Kazakhstan made in accordance with the approval and decision-making procedures on the launch of space objects from the territory of the Republic of Kazakhstan, as well as outside of it in case they are implemented by Kazakhstan's the participants of the space activities.

Chapter 4. Space infrastructure

Article 20. Objects of space infrastructure of the Republic of Kazakhstan

1. The objects of space infrastructure of the Republic of Kazakhstan form the basis of its space sector and include:
   1) objects of ground space infrastructure;
   2) space objects.

3. The objects of space infrastructure are the strategic objects.

Article 21. The objects of ground space infrastructure

The objects of ground space infrastructure are:
1) scientific and experimental base for space researches;
2) production facilities of space engineering and space-rocket complexes designed for space activities;
3) cosmodromes;
4) drop areas for the separated components of carrier rockets;
5) ground complexes for the control of space objects;
6) dedicated ground facilities for data reception from space objects, its processing and distribution.

For the purpose of safe and secure operations of objects of ground space infrastructure, the proiective land zone areas are established excluding drop areas for separated components of carrier rockets, within the frame of which the activities are limited or forbidden inconsistent with the purposes of zone establishment.

Article 22. Facilities for space engineering production

1. Facilities of space engineering production are special design-technological bureaus of space engineering and assembly testing complex.

2. The list of state orders for the production of space technologies, created for the Republic of Kazakhstan, is approved by the Government of the Republic of Kazakhstan under provision of it by an authorized body.

Article 23. «Baikonur» cosmodrome

1. The «Baikonur» cosmodrome is a constituent part of space infrastructure and includes technical, launching, landing

complexes; ground areas intended to prepare and implement space objects launches.

2. The «Baikonur» cosmodrome is a strategic object and is the property complex not subject to privatizați on.

Article 24. Marking of space objects of the Republic of Kazakhstan

The space objects of the Republic of Kazakhstan launching into outer space shall have the marking defined by the authorized body in accordance with the international standards and legislation of the Republic of Kazakhstan.

Article 25. Utilization of space objects and technical facilities

The space objects and technical facilities that are out of service are subject to utilization according to the procedures determined by the Government of the Republic of Kazakhstan and international treaties.

Article 26. Lend-lease of space sector object

The procedure for lend-lease of a space sector object to international or foreign participant of space activities is governed by the legislation of the Republic of Kazakhstan, unless otherwise provided by international treaties ratified by the Republic of Kazakhstan.

Chapter 5. Safety of space activities

Article 27. Safety assurance of space activities

1. The space activities are carried out on the assumption of provision of people's health and environment protection, security of property of individuals and legal entities.

Safety of space activities is provided by the authorized body according to the established safety rules, as well as by other state bodies within the competence established by the legislation of the Republic of Kazakhstan.

2. Indemnification for harm to the health of individuals, damage to the environment, property of individuals and legal entities, the state, which have arisen
from the implementation of the space activities, is made voluntary or under the court decision according to the laws of the Republic of Kazakhstan.

Hazard is subject to indemnification in full taking into account the degree of disability of an injured; expenses for his/her treatment and health recovery, expenses for the care of patient.

3. Before the performance of staff launch of space object, the participants of space activities send the coordinates of drop areas for separated parts of the carrier rocket located in the territory of the Republic of Kazakhstan to the authorized body in the field of preservation of the environment.

4. In case of death of people or animals, as well as damnification to citizens and environment as a result of the performed launch of space object, the participants of space activities should indemnify the caused damage according to clause 2 of the present article.

5. A space object belonging to the foreign individual or legal entity can perforai the safe flight through the airspace of the Republic of Kazakhstan during the process of its injection into the outer space or returning to the Earth on the assumption of preliminary agreement with the Ministry of Defense of the Republic of Kazakhstan, by the authorized bodies in the field of emergency situations of natural and anthropogenic character, environment protection.

Article 28. Investigation of accidents during the implementation of space activities

Accidents, which have led to the occurrence of anthropogenic emergency situations , are subject for investigation following the procedures established by the legislation of the Republic of Kazakhstan in the field of emergency situations of natural and anthropogenic character.

Article 29. Ecological control of the environment and level of health of population in regions, subject to influence of space activities

1. State monitoring of the environment and natural resources during the realization of space activities is conducted by authorized state bodies in the field of environmental protection, management of land resources within the limits of the Unified state system for monitoring of the environment and natural resources together with the specially authorized state bodies.

2. The participants of space activities are obliged to exercise industrial ecological control of the environment following the procedures established by the ecological legislation of the Republic of Kazakhstan.

3. State control in the field of environmental protection and health of population during the implementation of the space activities is carried out by the authorized bodies in the field of environmental protection and public health services.

4. The information on environmental protection and emergency situations is opened in connection with realization of space activities on the territory of the Republic of Kazakhstan, and it is a subject to distribution through mass media by using of the system of notifications and Communications.

Article 30. Interdictions and restrictions in the space activities

1. During the implementation of space activities the following actions is prohibited:
    1) creation of immediate threat to life and health of people;
    2) injection into the orbit, deployment of mass destruction weapon in the outer space;
    3) use of space engineering and (or) celestial bodies for negative influence on the environment;
    4) infringement of the international norms and standards on pollution of outer space.
2. Space activities within the limits of a separate project at the occurrence of threat to life and health of people, cause damage to property or damage to the environment is limited or is prohibited according to the ecological legislation of the Republic of Kazakhstan.

Chapter 6. Legal status and social security measures of cosmonaut candidate, cosmonaut

Article 31. Status of cosmonaut candidate, the cosmonaut. Preparation of cosmonaut candidate, cosmonaut

1. The status of a cosmonaut candidate, a cosmonaut is assigned by the Government of the Republic of Kazakhstan on provision by the authorized body.

2. Cosmonauts are formed into the team of cosmonauts of the Republic of Kazakhstan. The team of cosmonauts of the Republic of Kazakhstan acts on the basis of regulation on the team of cosmonauts of the Republic of Kazakhstan.

3. The government ensures preparation, retraining of cosmonaut candidates, cosmonauts.

4. Preparation and performance of the space flight by a cosmonaut are realized on the basis of a contract concluding with the corresponding participant of the space activities (the customer carrying out space flight testing and (or) scientific researches and experiments in case of implementation of the space flight), in which obligations of the parties are defined.

5. The time period when a cosmonaut candidate, a cosmonaut is being on preparation, retraining, as well as his/her time at work in the field of the space activities is included in the work experience of the cosmonaut candidate, the cosmonaut.

Article 32. Guarantees in case of reception of mutilation, diseases or destructions (death) of cosmonaut candidates, cosmonaut

1. In case of establishment of the disability, occurred as a result of injury, mutilation, disease, obtained in the course of duty, one-time indemnification is paid at the expense of budgetary funds to a cosmonaut candidate, a cosmonaut in
the amounts of:
    1) to a disabled person of 1st group - 3000 monthly calculation indices;

2) to a disabled person of 2nd group - 2000 monthly calculation indices;
3) to a disabled person of 3rd group - 1000 monthly calculation indices.

2. In case of loss (death) of a cosmonaut candidate, a cosmonaut in the course of duty the one-time indemnification is paid to his/her heirs from budgetary funds in the amount of 6000 monthly calculation indices.

3. Payment of the one-time indemnification provided by clause 1 or 2 of the present article, is carried out according to the procedures defined by the Government of the Republic of Kazakhstan.

4. The one-time indemnification is not paid, if it is proven in accordance with the established procedures that the loss (death), mutilation or disease of a cosmonaut candidate, a cosmonaut occurred in connection with the circumstances, not connected on duty.

5. In case of loss (death) of a cosmonaut candidate, a cosmonaut in the course of duty, the state assures the transition of one property into heirs' ownership of the lost (died) from the state residential properties or gratuitous transfer of the employer's apartment provided before to the cosmonaut candidate, to the cosmonaut of into heirs' ownership of the lost (died) or granting similar property in a settlement of the Republic of Kazakhstan from the state residential properties at the discretion of heirs of the lost (died), if earlier provided employer's apartment to the cosmonaut candidate, to the cosmonaut is located in the territory of other state no later than six months from the date of loss (death) of the designated person.

6. Regulation of clause 5 of the present article is applied under the condition of absence of the own property of a cosmonaut

candidate, a cosmonaut and his/her heirs in the territory of the Republic of Kazakhstan.

Article 33. Indemnification of expenses on burial

Burial of the lost (died) cosmonaut candidate, cosmonaut is made domiciliary or at will of his/her relatives in another place of the Republic of Kazakhstan. The expenses related to the preparation for body transportation, body transportation, burial, manufacturing and installation of a gravestone monument, are compensated at the expense of budgetary funds in the amount of 80 monthly calculation indices.

Article 34. Medical and sanatorium service to cosmonaut candidate, cosmonaut

1. A cosmonaut candidate, a cosmonaut on the assumption of his/her permanent residence on the territory of the Republic of Kazakhstan, in accordance with the established procedures by the Government of the Republic of Kazakhstan is assured with annual preventive examinations, medical and sanatorium treatment.

2. Regulations of clause 1 of the present article apply to cohabiting members of the family of a cosmonaut candidate , a cosmonaut.

3. Regulations of clause 1 of the present article do not apply to cosmonaut candidate, cosmonaut, who has lost the citizenship of the Republic of Kazakhstan.

Article 35. Endowment of cosmonauts awarded a title of honor "The pilot-cosmonaut of Kazakhstan"

The cosmonauts awarded a title of honor "The pilot-cosmonaut of Kazakhstan" are assigned with the multiplying factor in the amount of 2.9 to the official salary.

Chapter 7. Final provisions

Article 36. Liability for infringement of the legislation of the Republic of Kazakhstan in the field of space activities

Infringement of the legislation of the Republic of Kazakhstan in the field of space activities is subject to responsibility according to the laws of the Republic of Kazakhstan.

Article 37. Corning into force procedure of the present Law

The present Law comes into effect after ten calendar days of its first official publication.

SWEDEN

Act on Space Activities (1982:963)[56]

Section 1

This Act applies to activities in outer space (space activities).

In addition to activities carried on entirely in outer space, also included in space activities are the launching of objects into outer space and all measures to manoeuvre or in any other way affect objects launched into outer space.

Merely receiving signals or information in some other form from objects in outer space is not designated as space activities according to this Act. Nor is launching of sounding rockets designated as space activities.

Section 2

Space activities may not be carried on from Swedish territory by any party other than the Swedish State without a licence. Nor may a Swedish natural or juridical person carry on space activities anywhere else without a licence.

Section 3

A licence to carry on space activities is granted by the Government.

A licence may be restricted in the way deemed appropriate with regard to the circumstances. It may also be subject to required conditions with regard to control of the activity or for other reasons. Inspection of the space activities of licence holders is exercised by the authority decided by the Government.

Section 4

[56] Unofficial translation

A licence may be withdrawn if the conditions of the licence have been disregarded or if there are other particular reasons for it.

The Government decides on withdrawal of licences to carry on space activities. Pending a final decision on its withdrawal, a licence may be withdrawn temporarily.

Section 5

Any person who wilfully or through negligence carries on space activities without the necessary licence shall be sentenced to a fine or to imprisonment for at most one year. The same applies to any person who wilfully or through negligence disregards the conditions laid down as a prerequisite for obtaining a licence.

Any person who has committed outside the country a crime as referred to in paragraph one shall be sentenced, if he is in this country, according to this Act and the Swedish Penal Code and at a Swedish court, even though Chapter 2 section 2 or 3 of the said Code is not applicable and notwithstanding Chapter 2 section 5a first and second paragraphs of the said Code. Legal proceedings for a crime as referred to in paragraph one may be taken only with the Government's consent.

Section 6

If the Swedish State on account of undertakings in international agreements has been liable for damage which has come about as a result of space activities carried on by persons who have carried on the space activity shall reimburse the State what has been disbursed on account of the above-mentioned undertakings, unless special reasons tell against this.

SPAIN

ROYAL DECREE NO. 278/1995 OF 24 FEBRUARY 1995 [57]P RIME MINISTER S CHANCELLERY

Space Exploration. Establishment in Spain of the Registry of Objects Launched into Outer Space as provided for in the Convention adopted by the United Nations General Assembly on 12 November 1974 (RCL 1979, 269 and ApNDL 8191).

Following the accession of Spain on 20 December 1978 to the Convention on Registration of Objects Launched into Outer Space, adopted by the United Nations General Assembly on 12 November 1974 (*Official State Gazette* No. 25 of 29 January 1979) (RCL 1979, 269 and ApNDL 8191), appropriate internal measures must be adopted to enable Spain to comply with the terms of that Convention, especially with regard to the establishment of a registry of objects launched into outer space and to the notifications that have to be made to the Secretary-General of the United Nations.

The recent placing in orbit of the Spanish Hispasat 1A and 1B satellites offers a further reason not to delay the setting up of this registry.

By virtue thereof, at the proposal of the Minister for Foreign Affairs and the Minister of Industry and Energy, following approval by the Minister for Public Authorities, with the agreement of the Council of State and after discussion by the Council of Ministers at its meeting on 24 February 1995, I hereby order the following:

Article 1

The Spanish Registry of Objects Launched into Outer Space, hereinafter referred to as the "Spanish Registry", shall be established.

Article 2

[57] Unofficial translation

The Spanish Registry shall be kept by the Division of Multilateral Economic Relations and Development of the Department of International Economic Relations of the Ministry of Foreign Affairs.

Article 3

Full and free access shall be provided to the information contained in the Spanish Registry in accordance with the provisions of article 37 of Law No. 30/1992 (RCL 1992, 2512, 2775 and RCL 1993, 246) on the Legal Regime Governing Public Authorities and Common Administrative Procedures and any regulations adopted in implementation thereof.

Article 4

The term "space object" includes component parts of a space object as well as the launch vehicle and parts thereof.

Article 5

Entries shall be made in the Spanish Registry in respect of space objects that have been launched or whose launching has been procured by the Spanish State or that have been launched from Spain or from a Spanish facility.

If, in addition to Spain, one or more States, hereinafter referred to as "launching State or States" are competent to make an entry, the procedure to be followed shall be as laid down in article II, paragraph 2, of the Convention on Registration of Objects Launched into Outer Space adopted on 12 November 1974.

Article 6

The registration of each space object shall contain the following information:

(a) Name of launching State or States;
(b) An appropriate designator of the space object or its registration number;

(c) Date and territory or location of launch;
(d) Basic orbital parameters, including:
(I) Nodal period;
(II) Inclination;
(III) Apogee;
(IV) Perigee;
(e) General function of the space object.

Any other additional information deemed useful may also be included.

Article 7

Enterprises and institutions in possession of the information referred to in the previous article shall be obliged to communicate it to the Department of Industrial Technology of the Ministry of Industry and Energy, which may, in turn, extract from it any supplementary information that it considers necessary to make the entry and the mandatory notification to the Secretary-General of the United Nations in accordance with the Convention.

The Department of Industrial Technology of the Ministry of Industry and Energy shall transmit any information that it receives to the Department of International Economic Relations of the Ministry of Foreign Affairs and the Department of International Economic Relations shall enter this information in the Spanish Registry and arrange for its formal notification to the Secretary-General of the United Nations with a view for its inclusion in the latter's Register.

The notifications referred to in this article shall also include any modifications to data concerning registered space objects and, in particular cases where space objects have ceased to be in Earth orbit. Such modifications shall form the subject of a prior entry in the Spanish Registry in accordance with the provisions of the preceding article.

Single additional clause

The Department of International Economic Relations of the Ministry of Foreign Affairs shall arrange for the formal notification to the Secretary-General of the United Nations of the establishment of the Spanish Registry.

Single provisional clause

The Department of International Economic Relations of the Ministry for Foreign Affairs shall arrange for the entry and subsequent formal notification to the Secretary-General of the United Nations of any space objects that were launched before the establishment of the Spanish Registry and of any space objects for which Spain is the launching State.

First final clause

The Minister for Foreign Affairs and the Minister of Industry and Energy may enact the necessary provisions for the execution and implementation of this Royal Decree.

Second final clause

By order of the Minister in charge of the Prime Minister's Chancellery, issued at the proposal of the Minister for Foreign Affairs and the Minister of Industry and Energy, the Spanish Registry may be kept by a body within these ministries other than that specified in article 2 of this Royal Decree.

Third final clause

This Royal Decree shall enter into force on the day following its publication in the *Official State Gazette*.

UNITED KINGDOM OF GREAT BRITAIN AND NORTHERN IRELAND

Outer Space Act 1986
1986 CHAPTER 38

An Act to confer licensing and other powers on the Secretary of State to secure compliance with the international obligations of the United Kingdom with respect to the launching and operation of space objects and the carrying on of other activities in outer space by persons connected with this country.

[18th July 1986]

Be it enacted by the Queen's most Excellent Majesty, by and with the advice and consent of the Lords Spiritual and Temporal, and Commons, in this present Parliament assembled, and by the authority of the same, as follows:—

Application of Act

1 Activities to which this Act applies.

This Act applies to the following activities whether carried on in the United Kingdom or elsewhere—

(a) launching or procuring the launch[58] of a space object;

(b) operating a space object;

(c) any activity in outer space.

---

[58] It is very difficult to define the expression *"a State procuring the launching"* as nowadays a finished product is often the result of many components manufactured globally and many states might be involved in the launching, starting from production of space objects to the final registration. Therefore, we should consider an "active and substantial participation" in the launch in order for a State to be considered as one of the launching States.

2 Persons to whom this Act applies.

(1)This Act applies to United Kingdom nationals, Scottishfirms, and bodies incorporated under the law of any part of the United Kingdom[59].

(2)For this purpose "United Kingdom national" means an individual who is—

(a)a British citizen, a British Dependent Territories citizen, a British National (Overseas), or a British Overseas citizen,

(b)a person who under the British Nationality Act 1981 is a British subject, or

(c)a British protected person within the meaning of that Act.

(3)Her Majesty may by Order in Council extend the application of this Act to bodies incorporated under the law of any of the Channel Islands, the Isle of Man or any dependent territory.

Licensing of activities

3 Prohibition of unlicensed activities.

(1)A person to whom this Act applies shall not, subject to the following provisions, carry on an activity to which this Act applies except under the authority of a licence granted by the Secretary of State.

(2)A licence is not required—

(a)by a person acting as employee or agent of another; or

(b)for activities in respect of which it is certified by Order in Council that arrangements have been made between the United Kingdom and another country to secure compliance with the international obligations of the United Kingdom.

This is a unique approach. The law applies to the launch or procuring the launch of a space object, operating a space object or any activity in outer space, whether carried out in the United Kingdom or elsewhere and restrict its applicability to nationals of the United Kingdom only. Thus, a foreign national that conducts space activities in the United Kingdom would not be subject to regulation under the legislation. If a foreign national launches a space object from the United Kingdom that causes damage to third parties outside the United Kingdom it will not be reliable.

(3)The Secretary of State may by order except other persons or activities from the requirement of a licence if he is satisfied that the requirement is not necessary to secure compliance with the international obligations of the United Kingdom.

(4)An order shall be made by statutory instrument which shall be subject to annulment in pursuance of a resolution of either House of Parliament.

4 Grant of licence.

(1)The Secretary of State may grant a licence if he thinks fit.

(2)He shall not grant a licence unless he is satisfied that the activities authorised by the licence—

(a)will not jeopardise public health or the safety of persons or property,

(b)will be consistent with the international obligations of the United Kingdom, and

(c)will not impair the national security of the United Kingdom.

(3)The Secretary of State may make regulations—

(a)prescribing the form and contents of applications for licences and other documents to be filed in connection with applications;

(b)regulating the procedure to be followed in connection with applications and authorising the rectification of procedural irregularities;

(c)prescribing time limits for doing anything required to be done in connection with an application and providing for the extension of any period so prescribed;

(d)requiring the payment to the Secretary of State of such fees as may be prescribed.

5 Terms of licence.

(1)A licence shall describe the activities authorised by it and shall be granted for such period, and may be granted subject to such conditions, as the Secretary of State thinks fit.

(2)A licence may in particular contain conditions—

(a)permitting inspection by the Secretary of State of the licensee's facilities, and inspection and testing by him of the licensee's equipment;

(b)requiring the licensee to provide the Secretary of State as soon as possible with information as to—

(i)the date and territory or location of launch, and

(ii)the basic orbital parameters, including nodal period, inclination, apogee and perigee,

and with such other information as the Secretary of State thinks fit concerning the nature, conduct, location and results of the licensee's activities;

(c)permitting the Secretary of State to inspect and take copies of documents relating to the information required to be given to him;

(d)requiring the licensee to obtain advance approval from the Secretary of State for any intended deviation from the orbital parameters, and to inform the Secretary of State immediately of any unintended deviation;

(e)requiring the licensee to conduct his operations in such a way as to—

(i)prevent the contamination of outer space or adverse changes in the environment of the earth,

(ii)avoid interference with the activities of others in the peaceful exploration and use of outer space,

(iii)avoid any breach of the United Kingdom's international obligations, and

(iv)preserve the national security of the United Kingdom;

(f)requiring the licensee to insure himself against liability incurred in respect of damage or loss suffered by third parties, in the United Kingdom or elsewhere, as a result of the activities authorised by the licence;

(g)governing the disposal of the payload in outer space on the termination of operations under the licence and requiring the licensee to notify the Secretary of State as soon as practicable of its final disposal; and

(h)providing for the termination of the licence on a specified event.

6 Transfer, variation, suspension or termination of licence.

(1)A licence may be transferred with the written consent of the Secretary of State and in such other cases as may be prescribed.

(2)The Secretary of State may revoke, vary or suspend a licence with the consent of the licensee or where it appears to him—

(a)that a condition of the licence or any regulation made under this Act has not been complied with, or

(b)that revocation, variation or suspension of the licence is required in the interests of public health or national security, or to comply with any international obligation of the United Kingdom.

(3)The suspension, revocation or expiry of a licence does not affect the obligations of the licensee under the conditions of the licence.

Other controls

7 Register of space objects.

(1)The Secretary of State shall maintain a register of space objects.

(2)There shall be entered in the register such particulars of such space objects as the Secretary of State considers appropriate to comply with the international obligations of the United Kingdom.

(3)Any person may inspect a copy of the register on payment of such fee as the Secretary of State may prescribe.

8 Power to give directions.

(1)If it appears to the Secretary of State that an activity is being carried on by a person to whom this Act applies—

(a)in contravention of section 3 (licensing requirement), or

(b)in contravention of the conditions of a licence,

he may give such directions to that person as appear to him necessary to secure compliance with the international obligations of the United Kingdom or with the conditions of the licence.

(2)He may, in particular, give such directions as appear to him necessary to secure the cessation of the activity or the disposal of any space object.

(3)Compliance with a direction may, without prejudice to other means of enforcement, be enforced on the application of the Secretary of State by injunction or, in Scotland, by interdict or by order under section 91 of the Court of Session Act 1868.

Warrant authorising direct action.

(1)If a justice of the peace is satisfied by information on oath that there are reasonable grounds for believing—

(a)that an activity is being carried on by a person to whom this Act applies in contravention of section 3 (licensing requirement) or in contravention of the conditions of a licence, and

(b)that a direction under section 8 has not been complied with, or a refusal to comply with such a direction is apprehended, or the case is one of urgency,

he may issue a warrant authorising a named person acting on behalf of the Secretary of State to do anything necessary to secure compliance with the international obligations of the United Kingdom or with the conditions of the licence.

(2)The warrant shall specify the action so authorised.

(3)The warrant may authorise entry onto specified premises at any reasonable hour and on production, if so required, of the warrant.

(4)The powers conferred by the warrant include power to use reasonable force, if necessary, and may be exercised by the named person together with other persons.

(5)A warrant remains in force for a period of one month from the date of its issue.

(6)In Scotland the reference in subsection (1) to a justice of the peace shall be construed as a reference to a justice of the peace or a sheriff and the reference to information shall be construed as a reference to evidence.

10 Obligation to indemnify government against claims.

(1)A person to whom this Act applies shall indemnify Her Majesty's government in the United Kingdom against any claims brought against the government in respect of damage or loss arising out of activities carried on by him to which this Act applies.

(2)This section does not apply—

(a)to a person acting as employee or agent of another; or

(b)to damage or loss resulting from anything done on the instructions of the Secretary of State.

General

11 Regulations.

(1)The Secretary of State may make regulations—

(a)prescribing anything required or authorised to be prescribed under this Act, and

(b)generally for carrying this Act into effect.

(2)Regulations under this Act shall be made by statutory instrument which shall be subject to annulment in pursuance of a resolution of either House of Parliament.

12 Offences.

(1)A person commits an offence who—

(a)carries on an activity in contravention of section 3 (licensing requirement);

(b)for the purpose of obtaining a licence (for himself or for another) knowingly or recklessly makes a statement which is false in a material particular;

(c)being the holder of a licence, fails to comply with the conditions of the licence;

(d)fails to comply with a direction under section 8;

(e)intentionally obstructs a person in the exercise of powers conferred by a warrant under section 9; or

(f)fails to comply with such of the regulations under this Act as may be prescribed.

(2)A person committing an offence is liable on conviction on indictment to a fine and on summary conviction to a fine not exceeding the statutory maximum.

(3)Where an offence committed by a body corporate is proved to have been committed with the consent or connivance of, or to be attributable to neglect on the part of, a director, secretary or other similar officer of the body corporate, or a person purporting to act in any such capacity, he as well as the body corporate is guilty of the offence and liable to be proceeded against and punished accordingly.

In this subsection "director", in relation to a body corporate whose affairs are managed by its members, means a member of the body corporate.

(4)Proceedings for an offence committed outside the United Kingdom may be taken, and the offence may for incidental purposes be treated as having been committed, in any place in the United Kingdom.

(5)In proceedings for an offence under paragraph (a), (c), (d) or (f) of subsection (1) it is a defence for the accused to show that he used all due diligence and took all reasonable precautions to avoid the commission of the offence.

(6)A person other than a person to whom this Act applies is not guilty of an offence under this Act in respect of things done by him outside the United Kingdom, except—

(a)an offence of aiding, abetting, counselling or procuring, conspiracy or indictment in relation to the commission of an offence under this Act in the United Kingdom; or

(b)an offence under subsection (3) (liability of directors, officers, &c.) in connection with an offence committed by a body corporate which is a person to whom this Act applies.

(7)Section 2 (person to whom this Act applies) shall not be construed as restricting the persons against whom proceedings for an offence may be brought.

13 Minor definitions.

(1)In this Act—

- "dependent territory" means—

(a)a colony, or

(b)a country outside Her Majesty's dominions in which Her Majesty has jurisdiction in right of Her Government in the United Kingdom;

- "outer space" includes the moon and other celestial bodies;

and

- "space object" includes the component parts of a space object, its launch vehicle and the component parts of that.

(2) For the purposes of this Act a person carries on an activity if he causes it to occur or is responsible for its continuing.

14 Index of defined expressions.

The following Table shows provisions defining or otherwise explaining expressions used in this Act (other than provisions defining or explaining an expression used in the same section):—

activities to which this Act applies	section 1
carrying on an activity	section 13(2)
dependent territory	section 13(1)
outer space	section 13(1)
person to whom this Act applies	section 2
prescribed	section 11(1)(a)
space object	section 13(1)

15 Short title, commencement and extent.

(1) This Act may be cited as the Outer Space Act 1986.

(2) This Act comes into force on such day as the Secretary of State may appoint by order made by statutory instrument.

(3) The Secretary of State may appoint a later day for the commencement of so much of section 2(2)(a) as refers to the status of British National (Overseas).

(4) Activities to which this Act applies begun before the commencement of this Act may be carried on without a licence

under section 3 for six months after commencement; but sections 8 and 9 (directions and action to secure compliance with international obligations) apply to such activities as they apply to activities carried on in contravention of that section.

(5)This Act extends to England and Wales, Scotland and Northern Ireland.

(6)Her Majesty may by Order in Council direct that this Act shall apply, subject to such exceptions and modifications as may be specified in the Order, to the Channel Islands, the Isle of Man or any dependent territory.

INDEX

A

accident · xvi, xvii, 40, 47, 93, 111, 139, 142, 144, 146, 148, 150, 168, 218, 219, 222, 223, 225, 226, 227, 228, 267, 268, 371, 378
    assistance · 32
    astronauts · 40
    emergency landing · 32
    personnel of a spacecraft (return to representatives) · 43
    search and rescue operations · 42
    states responsabilities (spacecraft personnel) · 41
aircraft · 49, 51, 52, 155, 209, 238, 368, 369, 370, 372, 377, 379, 380, 381, 382, 383
astronauts
    assistance · 40

C

Celestial Bodies · vi, viii, 23, 24, 26, 27, 29, 30, 38, 40, 44, 49, 54, 59, 66, 67, 68, 70, 75, 81, 84, 85, 96, 101, 103, 104, 106, 111, 113, 114, 116, 117, 129, 155, 172, 270
Charter of the United Nations · 30, 31, 37, 38, 45, 54, 61, 76, 77, 92, 95, 96, 97, 101, 106, 114, 116, 117
claim · 29, 31, 53, 54, 55, 56, 58, 60, 64, 81, 92, 114, 129, 130, 131, 137, 138, 212, 213, 235, 273, 375
compensation · 49, 50, 51, 52, 53, 54, 55, 56, 58, 60, 65, 113, 114, 129, 130, 136, 137, 138, 152, 153, 158, 159, 166, 199, 208, 209, 210, 211, 212, 213, 229, 269, 272, 273, 288, 303, 304, 320, 369, 377
    claim · 55

how it will be determined · 56
payment · 56
procedure · 55
cooperation
principle of ~ shall guide the space exploration · 34

D

damage · xv, 29, 34, 39, 49, 50, 51, 52, 53, 54, 55, 56, 59, 60, 65, 66, 69, 84, 93, 114, 121, 125, 127, 129, 130, 131, 136, 137, 138, 139, 142, 143, 144, 145, 152, 153, 158, 159, 166, 167, 168, 179, 184, 185, 189, 193, 194, 197, 199, 200, 207, 208, 209, 210, 211, 212, 213, 216, 218, 231, 238, 247, 269, 272, 273, 275, 276, 281, 286, 288, 320, 336, 338, 345, 352, 354, 356, 357, 369, 377
definition · 50
responsability for a tier · 52
states are liable for any ~ · 34
diplomatic relations · 55, 85
disputes · ix, x, 40, 97, 105, 114, 286
distress · 32, 40, 41, 42, 43, 47, 81, 93, 371
due diligence · 55, 212, 358

E

Earth · ix, x, xv, xix, 27, 30, 31, 32, 34, 43, 48, 49, 51, 67, 69, 94, 95, 99, 100, 103, 104, 109, 110, 111, 112, 113, 121, 122, 123, 130, 133, 134, 170, 171, 183, 192, 200, 208, 209, 214, 238, 244, 245, 246, 261, 264, 266, 272, 275, 277, 319, 321, 323, 326, 332, 337, 348, 374, 375, 376, 381, 390
emergency · xv, 32, 39, 40, 41, 42, 43, 47, 83, 93, 147, 148, 203, 337, 338, 371
extraterrestrial matter
affecting the environment of the earth · 79
contamination · 34
responsability · 34

H

high seas · 32, 41, 42, 43, 47, 93

I

international cooperation
    dissemination of the space activities · 35
    observation · 35
    on moon · 80
    reciprocity · 35
    space vehicles inspections · 35

J

jurisdiction
    hazardous or deleterious spacecraft parts · 44
    search and rescue operations · 42
    spacecrafts parts · 43

L

launching
    includes attempted launching · 50
launching authority · 40, 41, 42, 43, 44, 47, 48, 66
launching State · 41, 49, 50, 51, 52, 53, 54, 55, 56, 57, 59, 67, 68, 73, 83, 106, 107, 110, 111, 112, 113, 152, 153, 169, 184, 189, 193, 207, 214, 236, 237, 347, 349, 369, 377, 378, *See* launching authority
    definition · 50, 67
    obligations on object launch · 67
liability
    compensation · 52
    exoneration · 53
    joint liability · 52
    No exoneration · 53
liable · 29, 34, 39, 49, 51, 52, 53, 55, 56, 60, 93, 114, 124, 129, 131, 137, 159, 167, 178, 181, 186, 190, 195, 198, 209, 210, 211, 213, 229, 304, 345, 357, 358, 369, 377, 378

M

mankind · 29, 30, 32, 38, 39, 47, 49, 66, 77, 81, 89, 91, 92, 93, 103, 117, 244, 371, 385, 386, 387
military

bases · 32
installations · 32
military bases · 32
military bases on the moon, prohibition · 77
military manoeuvres · 32
military personnel
   use for scientific research, prohibition · 77
moon
   activities, exploration and use · 76
   claim of sovereignty · 81
   collecting samples, obligations · 79
   common heritage of mankind · 81
   cooperation between states working on the same orbit around the moon · 78
   equitable sharing of resources · 82
   establishing manned or unmanned stations, obligations · 80
   exploration and use · 77
   exploration and use, principle · 77
   exploration on or below its surface, obligations · 80
   freedom of scientific investigation · 78
   not fulfilling the obligations · 84
   obligation to inform about the exploration and use · 78
   obligation to inform on anything that could endagerhuman life or health · 78
   protecting its environment · 79
   use of force, hostile act · 77
   used for peaceful purposes · 77
Moon · vi, viii, ix, 23, 24, 26, 27, 29, 30, 31, 32, 33, 34, 35, 36, 38, 39, 40, 44, 49, 54, 59, 66, 67, 68, 70, 75, 81, 84, 85, 89, 96, 101, 103, 104, 106, 111, 113, 114, 116, 117, 121, 129, 133, 155, 172, 243, 244, 246, 270, 281, 371, 386, 392

N

national activities
   responsibility · 33
national appropriation · 29, 31, 38, 39, 81, 92, 375, 382
natural disasters · 103
nuclear power · 105, 106, 107, 108, 110, 111, 112, 113, 114
nuclear reactors · 109

O

object launched

control · 34
jurisdiction · 34
return to the Earth · 34
outer space
experiment · 35
exploration · 31
weapons · 31
Outer space
sovereignty · 31
ownership of objects · 34, 93

P

phenomena
states obligation to inform of any ~ · 32
prejudice · 53, 68, 79, 82, 97, 104, 121, 356
public announcement
accident · 41

R

radioactive materials · 111
radiological hazards · 107
reciprocity
all stations shall be opened to representatives of other states · 36
rescue operations · 42, 280
responsibility
governmental agencies · 33
international organization · 33
non-governmental entities · 33
on activities on moon by governamental or non-guvernamental entities · 83
states are responsible to carry out any activity respecting the treaty · 33

S

search and rescue operations · 42
accident, spacecraft personnel · 42
jurisdiction · 42
space accident
obligation for each state to do the following · 41

space debris · 124, 234, 235
space object · xiii, xvii, 40, 41, 43, 44, 46, 47, 50, 51, 52, 53, 54, 59, 65, 67, 68, 69, 73, 74, 83, 100, 106, 110, 111, 112, 113, 114, 121, 122, 123, 124, 125, 126, 127, 128, 129, 130, 131, 134, 136, 142, 143, 146, 148, 153, 154, 169, 170, 171, 172, 173, 175, 176, 177, 180, 182, 183, 184, 185, 186, 188, 189, 190, 192, 193, 194, 195, 200, 201, 207, 209, 210, 211, 212, 213, 214, 218, 219, 222, 223, 225, 226, 230, 231, 233, 237, 238, 261, 262, 263, 264, 265, 266, 272, 273, 318, 328, 329, 330, 336, 337, 347, 348, 351, 352, 355, 359, 369, 370, 377
    causing damages, obligations · 69
    definition · 67
spacecraft · 41, 42, 43, 73, 77, 81, 111, 291, 292, 317, 318, 319, 372, 373, 376
state of registry
    definition · 67
    obligation to furnish info · 68

T

territorial limits · 44, 66

U

unintended landing · 41, 42, 43, 47, 83

W

weapons
    nuclear weapons · 31, 77
    placing weapons on Moon orbit · 77
    states obligation regarding the Earth orbit · 31

DEFINITIONS

Aircraft

Definition
"[A] device that is used or intended to be used for flight in the air," as distinguished from a Spacecraft.
Source: Federal Aviation Regulations, 14 C.F.R. § 1.1 (2011).

Laws & Treaties
"Any machine that can derive support in the atmosphere from the reactions of the air other than the reactions of the air against the earth's surface."
Source: Convention on International Civil Aviation Annex 1, Annex 6 Part I, opened for signature Dec. 7, 1944, 61 Stat. 1180, 15 U.N.T.S. 295 (Chicago Convention).

"[M]eans aircraft as defined for the purposes of the Chicago Convention which are either airframes with aircraft engines installed thereon or helicopters."
Source: Protocol to the Convention on International Interests in Mobile Equipment on Matters Specific to Aircraft Equipment, Art. 1(2)(a), entered into force Jan. 3. 2006.

"[A]ny contrivance invented, used, or designed to navigate, or fly in, the air."
Source: 49 U.S.C. § 40102(a)(1) (2008).

Airplane: "[A]n engine-driven fixed-wing aircraft heavier than air, that is supported in flight by the dynamic reaction of the air against its wings."
Source: Federal Aviation Regulations, 14 C.F.R. § 1.1 (2011).

Example of Usage in the Space Treaties:

"A launching State shall be absolutely liable to pay compensation for damage cause by its space object on the surface of the earth or to an aircraft in flight."
Source: Liability Convention Art.II.

Legal dictionary

"Any contrivance used, or designed for navigation of or flight in the air, except a parachute or other contrivance designed for such navigation but used primarily as safety equipment. . . . [I]ncludes balloon, airplane, hydroplane and every other vehicle used for navigation through the air."
Source: Definition of Aircraft, Black's Law Dictionary 92 (4th ed. Rev. 1968).

Other U.S. Gov't

"Any structure, machine, or contrivance, especially a vehicle, designed to be supported by the air, being borne up either by the dynamic action of the air upon the surfaces of the structure or object, or by its own buoyancy; such structures, machines, or vehicles collectively, as, fifty aircraft. Aircraft, in its broadest meaning, includes fixed-wing airplanes, helicopters, gliders, airships, free and captive balloons, ornithopters, flying model aircraft, kites, etc., but since the term carries a strong vehicular suggestion, it is more often applied, or recognized to apply, only to such of these craft as are designed to support or convey a burden in or through the air."
Source: Dictionary of Technical Terms for Aerospace Use: NASA SP-7 (1965)

Aircraft Operations

Aircraft Operations means "the airborne movement of aircraft in controlled or noncontrolled airport terminal areas, and counts at en route fixes or other points where counts can be made. There are two types of operations: local and itinerant.

(1) Local operations mean operations performed by aircraft which:

(i) Operate in the local traffic pattern or within sight of the airport;

(ii) Are known to be departing for, or arriving from flight in local practice areas located within a 20-mile radius of the airport; or

(iii) Execute simulated instrument approaches or low passes at the airport.

(2) Itinerant operations mean all aircraft operations other than local operations.

Source: 4 CFR 170.3 [Title 14 Aeronautics and Space; Chapter I Federal Aviation Administration, Department of Transportation; Subchapter J Navigational Facilities; Part 170 Establishment and Discontinuance Criteria for Air Traffic Control Services and Navigational Facilities; Subpart A General]

Aircraft Piracy

Under special aircraft jurisdiction of the U.S., aircraft piracy means seizing or exercising control of an aircraft in the special aircraft jurisdiction of the U.S. by force, violence, threat of force or violence, or any form of intimidation, and with wrongful intent. An individual committing or attempting or conspiring to commit aircraft piracy will be imprisoned for at least 20 years; or if the death of another individual occurs from the commission or attempt of aircraft piracy, the person who committed piracy will be put to death or imprisoned for life. The punishments are same for aircraft piracy committed outside special aircraft jurisdiction.

Source: [49 USCS § 46502]

Other sources

Aircrafts exercise aeronautical capabilities while spacecrafts exercise astronautical capabilities.

Source: Marietta Benkö, Willem de Graff & Gijsbertha C.M. Reijnen, Space Law in the United Nations 121-122 (1985).

However, hybrid "aerospace vehicles" are possible; spaceplanes may have dual character as a space object and as an aircraft.

Source: Ricky J. Lee, Reconciling International Space Law with the Commercial Realities of the Twenty-First Century, 4 Sing. J. Int'l & Comp. L. 194, 211 (2000).

Astronaut

Definition
"A person trained to travel and work in space." *Related Terms*: Astronaut Wings, Personnel of a Spacecraft, and Space Flight Participant; also (not included in Guide) Cosmonaut and Taikonaut.
Source: Definition of Astronaut, NASA For Students

Laws & Treaties
"States Parties to the Treaty shall regard astronauts as envoys of mankind in outer space . . . . When astronauts make such a landing, they shall be safely and promptly returned to the State of registry of their space vehicle."
Source: Outer Space Treaty Art. V.

Although the Rescue and Return Agreement refers to "Personnel of a Spacecraft" in Articles 1-4, the Preamble states that the Agreement is designed to give further concrete expression to the duties of "rendering of all possible assistance to astronauts in the event of accident, distress or emergency landing, [and] the prompt and safe return of astronauts[.]"
Source: Rescue and Return Agreement Preamble.

States "shall regard any person on the moon as an astronaut within the meaning of Article V of" the Outer Space Treaty and the Rescue and Return Agreement.
Source: Moon Agreement Art. 10(1).

Standard English Dictionary
"[A] person who travels beyond the earth's atmosphere; also: a trainee for spaceflight."
Source: Definition of Astronaut, Merriam-Webster Online Dictionary

Other U.S. Gov't
"1. A person who rides in a space vehicle;

2. Specifically, one of the test pilots selected to participate in Project Mercury, Project Gemini, Project Apollo, or any other United States program for manned space flight."
Source: Dictionary of Technical Terms for Aerospace Use: NASA SP-7 (1965)

"[A] person trained to travel and work in space . . . In Greek, *astro* means star and *naut* means sailor. An astronaut is someone who sails among the stars."
Source: Definition of Astronaut, NASA For Students,

Other sources

"[D]esignation, derived from the Greek words for 'star' and 'sailor,' commonly applied to an individual who has flown in outer space. More specifically, astronauts are those persons who went to space aboard a U.S. spacecraft."
Source: Definition of Astronaut, Encyclopedia Britannica Online: Academic Edition 2011

"Astronauts are specifically selected and trained to achieve scientific, engineering, or political space goals. Like all professionals working for their national governments, they are also paid employees."
Source: Joanne Irene Gabrynowicz, One Half Century and Counting: The Evolution of U.S. National Space Law and Three Long-Term Emerging Issues, 37 J. of Space Law 41, 58 (Spring 2011).

"Any definition of an 'astronaut' for legal purposes would appear to require two elements, an element of training and an element of altitude. Correlatively there must also be an element of selection."
Source: Francis Lyall & Paul B. Larsen, Space Law: A Treatise 131 (2009)

"'Astronaut' cannot easily fit the non-professional that is likely to enter space in the coming years whether on a limited flight or in a space-hotel. We do not consider all those on a cruise-liner to be sailors, or passengers on aircraft to be pilots, flight engineers or cabin staff and there is a clear parallel between such cases and touristic space-flight."
Source: Id. at 129.

The passenger in a spacecraft isn't considered as astronaut: "The term 'astronaut' is already used colloquially and by the media for orbital tourists. However, it could be argued that a passenger in a spacecraft is not one of its personnel or that the proposed suborbital experiences do not qualify."
Source: Id. at 132 n.14

All personnel on board are astronauts: "...all on-board a space vehicle are astronauts, pointing out also that the term 'personnel' does not distinguish between civilian and military."
Source: W.D. Reed and R.W. Norris, Military Use of the Space Shuttle (1980) 13 Akron L. Rev. 665, 686-87

Mission specialist (astronaut)
The term Mission Specialist is "a career NASA astronaut trained and skilled in the operation of STS systems related to payload operations and thoroughly familiar with the operational requirements and objectives of the payloads with which the mission specialist will fly. The mission specialist, when designated for a flight, will participate in the planning of the mission and will be responsible for the coordination of overall payload/STS interaction. The mission specialist will direct the allocation of STS and crew resources to the accomplishment of the combined payload objectives during the payload operations phase of the flight in accordance with the approved flight plan."

Source: According to 14 CFR 1214.301 (e) [Title 14 Aeronautics and Space; Chapter V National Aeronautics and Space Administration; Part 1214 Space Flight; Subpart 1214.3 -- Payload Specialists for Space Transportation System (STS) Missions]

Language Terminology
"Those individuals who first traveled aboard a spacecraft operated by the Soviet Union or Russia are known as cosmonauts (from the Greek words for 'universe' and 'sailor'); China designates its space travelers taikonauts (from the Chinese word for 'space' and the Greek word for 'sailor')."
Source: Definition of Astronaut, Encyclopedia Britannica Online: Academic Edition 2011

Aerospace

Definition
"Space comprising the earth's atmosphere and the space beyond."
Source: Definition of Aerospace, Merriam-Webster Online Dictionary

Other U.S. Gov't
"Of, or pertaining to, Earth's envelope of atmosphere and the space above it; two separate entities considered as a single realm for activity in launching, guidance, and control of vehicles that will travel in both entities."
Source: Department of Defense Dictionary of Military and Associated Terms, Nov. 8, 2010

"1. Of or pertaining to both the earth's atmosphere and space, as in aerospace industries; 2. Earth's envelope of air and space above it; the two considered as a single realm foractivity in the flight of air vehicles and in the launching, guidance, and control of ballistic missiles, earth satellites, dirigible space vehicles, and the like."
Source: Dictionary of Technical Terms for Aerospace Use: NASA SP-7 (1965)

Outer Space

Definition:
"The known and unknown areas of the universe beyond airspace. The boundary between airspace and outer space is not fixed or precise."
Related Term: Aerospace, Airspace
Source: Definition of Outer Space, Black's Law Dictionary 1212 (9th ed. 2009).

Laws & Treaties:
Space Environment: "[T]he environment beyond the sensible atmosphere of the Earth."
Source: National Aeronautics and Space Act, 51 U.S.C. § 40302(5) (2010).

Space Station: A "station which is located on an object which is beyond, is intended to go beyond, or has been beyond the major portion of the Earth's atmosphere."
Source: ITU Radio Regulation 1.64, available at www.itu/int/terminology/index.html (last visited Sept. 21, 2011).

Legal dictionary:
"1. The known and unknown areas of the universe beyond airspace. The boundary between airspace and outer space is not fixed or precise. Cf. Airspace.

2. Int'l law. The space surrounding the planet that by United Nations treaty is not subject to claim of appropriation by any national sovereignty."
Source: Definition of Outer Space, Black's Law Dictionary 1212 (9th ed. 2009).

Other sources:
"Outer space lies beyond the currently undefined upper limit of a state's sovereign airspace. It was declared free for exploration and use by all states and incapable of national appropriation by a 1963 UN General Assembly resolution."
Source: Definition of Space Law, Encyclopedia Britannica Online: Academic Edition 2011

"The so-called von Karman line set the boundary at the point at which a vehicle traveling seven kilometers a second loses aerodynamic lift and becomes a 'spacecraft.' Such an event would occur about fifty-three miles up. Cooper and common law [] indicated that space simply stopped at that point below which an orbit could not be sustained."
Source: Glenn H. Reynolds & Robert P. Merges, Outer Space: Problems of Law and Policy 5 (2d ed. 1997).

"The basic division is between theories which concentrate on physical elements—the 'spatial' or 'spacialist' approach—and the idea that altitude is less important than the purpose or 'function' of the instrumentality involved—the 'functional' approach."
Source: Francis Lyall & Paul B. Larsen, Space Law: A Treatise 163 (2009).

Obtrusive space advertising
Means "advertising in outer space that is capable of being recognized by a human being on the surface of the Earth without the aid of a telescope or other technological device."
Source: 49 USCS § 70102 [Title 49. Transportation; Subtitle IX. Commercial Space Transportation; Chapter 701. Commercial Space Launch Activities]

Absolute Liability

Definition
Liability (i.e., a legal obligation to pay claims for bodily injury or property damage) imposed without regard to fault.

Absolute liability is a tortuous liability. Absolute liability can be imposed on a person even without proof of the person's negligence. Generally, owners, employers, and manufacturers are brought under the rule of absolute liability. Absolute liability is sometimes called strict liability. Absolute liability arises when a manufacturer of a non-defective product is held absolutely liable for the damage that resulted because of use of the product.

Related Terms: Liability, Fault-Based Liability, and Abnormally Dangerous.
Source: Derived From Definition of Strict Liability, Merriam-Webster Online Dictionary

Law & Treaties
"A launching State shall be absolutely liable to pay compensation for damage caused by its space object on the surface of the earth or to aircraft flight."
Source: Liability Convention Art. II.

Other U.S. Gov't
Strict Liability: "Liability without proof of fault (responsibility is assigned regardless of how careful the parties)."
Source: U.S. Department of Transportation, Federal Aviation Administration, Liability Risk-Sharing Regime for U.S. Commercial Space Transportation: Study
"By making the actor strictly liable . . . we give him an incentive, missing in a negligence regime, to experiment with methods of preventing accidents that involve not greater exertions of care, assumed to be futile, but instead relocating, changing, or reducing (perhaps to the vanishing point) the activity giving rise to the

accident . . . [t]he greater the risk of an accident and the costs of an accident if one occurs, the more we want the actor to consider the possibility of making accident-reducing activity changes; the stronger, therefore, is the case for strict liability."

"The 'strict liability' standard is less strict than that of absolute liability, although the two terms are frequently used interchangeably. Under the regime of strict liability, there may be several affirmative defenses a defendant may offer which may mitigate or even excuse liability. For example, if a plaintiff knowingly assumes the risk, either as a participant in the dangerous activity, or as an uninvolved party who deliberately moves into harm's way, the defendant may escape liability."
Source: Id., Ch. 5.2.

Other sources

"Strict liability is liability imposed without regard to the defendant's negligence or intent to cause harm . . . Strict liability does not signify absolute liability. Even in cases covered by this Section, various limitations on liability apply and various defenses are available[.]"

Source: Restatement (Third) of Torts: Liability for Physical and Emotional Harm § 20 Scope Note, cmt. a (2010).

Under the Liability Convention Article II, a launching State is absolutely liable for direct damages as well as all consequential damages that are proximately caused.
Source: Carl Q. Christol, Space Law: Past, Present and Future 222-23 (1991).

Air Traffic Control

Definition
The rules governing "the operation of aircraft in the air or in landing and takeoff."

Source: *Definition of Air Traffic Rules*, Ballentine's Law Dictionary 56 (3d ed. 1969)

Law&Treaties
"[A] service operated by appropriate authority to promote the safe, orderly, and expeditious flow of air traffic."
Aerial Navigation: "[A] method of navigation that permits aircraft operations on any desired flight path."

Source: *Federal Aviation Regulations, 14 C.F.R. § 1.1 (2011).*

Air Traffic Rules: "Statutes, rules and regulations prescribed by federal and state authority, or developed by way of application of common-law principles, which govern the operation of aircraft in the air or in landing and takeoff."

Source: *Definition of Air Traffic Rules, Ballentine's Law Dictionary 56 (3d ed. 1969)*

Standard English Dictionary Definition
"[A] government service that facilitates the safe and orderly movement of aircraft within and between airports by receiving and processing data from radar and devices that monitor local weather conditions and by maintaining radio contact with pilots."

Source: *Definition of Air Traffic Control, Dictionary.com,*

Other U.S. Gov't
"A service operated by appropriate authority to promote the safe, orderly and expeditious flow of air traffic."

Air Traffic Control Section: "In amphibious operations, the section of the Navy tactical air control center designed to provide initial safe passage, radar control, and surveillance for close air support aircraft in the operational area."

Source: NASA Thesaurus: Hierarchical Listing With Definitions 22 (2011).

Department of Defense Dictionary of Military and Associated Terms, Nov. 8, 2010 (as amended through May 15, 2011).

Other sources

"[P]reventing collisions between aircraft, preventing collisions on manoeuvring areas between aircraft and obstructions on the ground, and expediting and maintaining the orderly flow of air traffic."

Air Traffic Control Service: "A service provided for the purpose of: a. preventing collisions: 1. between aircraft; and 2. on the maneuvering area between aircraft and obstructions; and b. expediting and maintaining an orderly flow of air traffic."

Source: International Academy of Astronautics (IAA), Cosmic Study on Space Traffic Management 51 (2006). ICAO Recommended Practices and Procedures

Airspace

Definition
The Earth's atmosphere below the point where outer space begins; often measured up to 90-110 kilometers above mean sea level.

Related Term: Outer Space.

Laws&Treaties
Navigable Airspace: "[A]irspace above the minimum altitudes of flight prescribed by regulations . . . Including airspace needed to ensure safety in the takeoff and landing of aircraft."

Source: 49 U.S.C. § 40102(a)(1) (2008).

Example of Usage in International Law:

"The contracting States recognize that every State has complete and exclusive sovereignty over the airspace above its territory."

Source: Convention on International Civil Aviation, Art. 1, opened for signature Dec. 7, 1944, 61 Stat. 1180, 15 U.N.T.S. 295 (Chicago Convention).

Legal Dictionary
"The space lying above the earth or above a certain area of land or water; especially: the space lying above a nation and coming under its jurisdiction."

Source: Definition of Airspace, Merriam-Webster Online Dictionary

Other U.S. Gov't
"Specifically, the atmosphere above a particular portion of the earth, usually defined by the boundaries of an area on the surface projected upward."
Source: Dictionary of Technical Terms for Aerospace Use: NASA SP-7 (1965)

In the aviation context, airspace can be defined as any part of the earth's atmosphere that can be used by an aircraft. Airspace is a three-dimensional space, or volume, where aircraft (including rockets, balloons, gliders, etc) can operate.
Source: Civil Aviation Safety Authority - Australia

Other Sources
"The space above a particular national territory treated as belonging to the government controlling the territory. It does not include outer space, which, under the Outer Space Treaty of 1967, is declared to be free and not subject to national appropriation. The treaty, however, did not define the altitude at which outer space begins and air space ends."
Source: Definition of Airspace, Encyclopedia Britannica Online: Academic Edition 2011

The "Outer Space Treaty of 1967 established a new and quite different international legal status for 'outer space' based upon freedom of nonappropriation, without any definition of that term . . . The three-mile limit in traditional international law was based on the effective distance which could be covered by the normal cannon . . . As in maritime law, it has been suggested by the functionalists that only that area which can be effectively policed can be claimed to be subject to a country's sovereignty, i.e., the air space currently exploited and used by aircraft. This could mean that the air space up to sixty miles, or so, over a country can be claimed[.]"

Source: P. *Meredith, et. al, 1 American Enterprise, the Law, and the Commercial Use of Space: An Analysis of Treaties, Legislation, Regulation and the Political Scenario 92 (1986).*

"[C]onsensus may be gradually arising that . . . an altitude at 100 kilometers would be an appropriate altitude at which to separate the legally distinct areas."
Source: Frans G. von der Dunk, Passing the Buck to Rogers: International Liability Issues in Private Spaceflight, 86 Neb. L. Rev. 400, 525-27 (2007).

Other
Navigable Airspace
Navigable airspace is the airspace above a prescribed minimum altitude of flight. The following is an example of a federal statute defining navigable airspace.

According to 49 USCS § 40102 (32), "navigable airspace" means "airspace above the minimum altitudes of flight prescribed by regulations under this subpart and subpart III of this part [49 USCS §§ 40101 et seq., 44101 et seq.], including airspace needed to ensure safety in the takeoff and landing of aircraft."

Controlled airspace
Controlled airspace is an aviation term used to describe airspace in which Aviation traffic controller has the authority to control air traffic, the level of which varies with the different classes of airspace. Controlled airspace usually exists in the immediate vicinity of busier airports, where aircraft used in commercial air transport flights are climbing out from or making an approach to the airport, or at higher levels where air transport flights would tend to cruise. Some countries also provide controlled airspace almost generally, however in most countries it is common to provide uncontrolled airspace in areas where significant air transport or military activity is not expected.

Territorial Airspace of the United States
Pursuant to 19 CFR 122.49b [Title 19 -- Customs Duties Chapter I -- U.S. Customs And Border Protection, Department Of Homeland Security; Department Of The Treasury], the term Territorial Airspace of the United States means the airspace over the United States, its territories, and possessions, and the airspace over the territorial waters between the United States coast and 12 nautical miles from the coast. Territorial airspace of the United States means "the airspace over the United States, its territories, and possessions, and the airspace over the territorial waters between the United States coast and 12 nautical miles from the coast."

State authority of the airspace
The sovereign states' authority to control the airspace above their territories is an attribute of their sovereignty. To ensure the safety of sovereign states, the states must be given jurisdiction to control the airspace above their territories. Every government completely

sovereign in character must possess power to prevent those whom it determines to be undesirable from entering its confines.

In Erickson v. King, 218 Minn. 98 (Minn. 1944), the court observed that "it is essential to the safety of sovereign states that they possess jurisdiction to control the airspace above their territories. Every government completely sovereign in character must possess power to prevent from entering its confines those whom it determines to be undesirable. That power extends to the exclusion from the air of all hostile persons or demonstrations, and to the regulation of passage through the air of all persons in the interests of the public welfare and the safety of those on the face of the earth."

Common Heritage of Humankind

Definition

"The parts of the earth and cosmos that can be said to belong to all humanity . . . and that should be protected and administered for its benefit. The term embraces the ocean floor and its subsoil, and outer space." See also Province of all Humankind

Source: Definition of Common Heritage of Mankind, Black's Law Dictionary 313 (9th ed. 2009)

Related Terms : common heritage; common interest of all mankind; world heritage; common heritage of humanity; global commons; benefits to all mankind; benefits to all nations; equitable sharing; tragedy of the commons; common-pool resource.

Common heritage of mankind is a principle of international law that states that the elements of the earth and cosmos are common to humankind. Common heritage of mankind includes ocean floor and its subsoil and also outer space. The principle states that areas of Antarctica, the sea bed, and outer space cannot be monopolized for the benefit of one state or group of states alone, but should be treated as if they are to be used for the benefit of all mankind.

There are five core components of the common heritage of mankind concept:

1. There can be no private or public appropriation, ie; no one legally owns common heritage spaces;

2. Representatives from all nations must manage resources contained in such a territorial or conceptual area on behalf of all, because commons area is considered to belong to everyone;

3. All nations must actively share with each other the benefits acquired from exploitation of the resources from the common heritage region;

4. There can be no weaponry or military installations established in territorial commons areas.

5. The common space should be preserved for the benefit of future generations.

The concept of common heritage of mankind has been explained in various treaties and conventions adopted by the United Nations. Developing nations often see the principle as a means of protecting critical resources from exploitation by developed nations and their corporations.

Source: Ass'n for Molecular Pathology v. United States PTO, 2010 U.S. Dist. LEXIS 35418 (S.D.N.Y. Apr. 2, 2010).

Laws&Treaties

"The moon and its natural resources are the common heritage of Mankind."

"Recognizing the common interest of all mankind in the progress of the exploration and use of outer space for peaceful purposes . . ."

Source: Moon Agreement Art. 11.

"The exploration and use of outer space, including the moon and other celestial bodies, shall be carried out for the benefit and in the interests of all countries . . . And shall be free for exploration and use by all States without discrimination of any kind, on a basis of equality[.]"

Source: Outer of Space Treaty Preamble & Art. 1

"The Area and its resources are the common heritage of mankind." The Area "means the seabed and ocean floor and subsoil thereof, beyond the limits of national jurisdiction."

Source: U.N. Convention on the Law of the Sea, Art. 136 para. 1(1), Dec. 10, 1982, 1833 U.N.T.S. 397.

Legal Definition

"The parts of the earth and cosmos that can be said to belong to all humanity, without regard for geographic location, and that should be protected and administered for its benefit. The term embraces the ocean floor and its subsoil, and outer space."

Source: Definition of Common Heritage of Mankind, Black's Law Dictionary 313 (9th ed. 2009).

Other Sources:

Compare Law of the Sea: Romans "characterized the sea as commune omnium, the common property of all, both as to ownership and use, and they considered it as usus publicus, as a public utility . . . [Then the] early politics of freedom— not sovereignty—shaped the English concept . . . It was also established, even though never universally agreed, that all states possessed sovereign rights in those parts of the sea that touched their shores . . . a three-mile limit was regarded as the most practical extent."

Source: George P. Smith II, Restricting the Concept of Free Seas: Modern Maritime Law Re-Evaluated 13, 19 (1980).

NATIONAL REGULATORY FRAMEWORKS FOR SPACE ACTIVITIES

STATE	LEGISLATION
ALGERIA	- *Presidential Decree No 02-49 "Creation, organization and functioning of the Algerian Space Agency (ASAL)"* (16 January 2002)
	- *Presidential Decree No 06-225 "Ratifying the Convention for Damage Caused by Space Objects"* (24 June 2006)
	- *Presidential Decree No 06-468 "Ratifying the Convention on Registration of Objects Launched into Outer Space"* (11 December 2006)
ARGENTINA	- *National Decree No. 995/91, Creation of the National Commission on Space Activities (28 May 1991)*
	- *National Decree No. 125/95, Establishment of the National Registry of Space Objects Launched into Outer Space (25 July 1995)*
AUSTRALIA	- *Space Activities Act 1998 (No. 123, 1998)*
	- *Statutory Rules No. 186 Space Activities Regulations 2001*
AUSTRIA	-*Austrian Federal Law on the Authorisation of Space Activities and the Establishment of a National Space Registry (Austrian Outer Space Act, adopted by the National Council on 6 December 2011, entered into force on 28 December 2011)*
BELARUS	-*Decree 609 of the President of the Republic of Belarus of 22 December 2004*
BELGIUM	- *Law on the activities of launching, flight operations or guidance of space objects of 17 September 2005*
	- *Royal Decree implementing certain provisions of the Law of 17 September 2005 on the activities of launching, flight operations and guidance of space objects*
BRAZIL	- *Law 8.854 of February 10, 1994*
	- *Law 9.112 of October 10, 1995.*
	- *Decree 1.953 of*

STATE	LEGISLATION
	July 10, 1996.
	- Administrative Edit n. 27 of June 20, 2001
	- Administrative Edit n.5 of February 21, 2002
	- Administrative Edict n. 96 of 30 November 2011
	- RESOLUTION NO. 51 OF 26 JANUARY 2001.
CANADA	*- Canadian Space Agency Act (1990, c. 13)*
	- Canadian Aviation Regulations (SOR/96-433)
	- Civil International Space Station Agreement Implementation Act
	- Remote Sensing Systems Act and Regulations
	- Radiocommunications Act
CHILE	*- Supreme Decree No. 338, Establishment of a Presidential Advisory Committee known as Chilean Space Agency, amended by Supreme Decree No. 0144 of December 29, 2008, being now the Chilean Space Agency presided by the undersecretary of Economy*
CHINA	*- Measures for the Administration of Registration of Objects Launched into Outer Space of 8 February 2001*
	- Interim Measures on the Administration of Permits for Civil Space Launch Projects of 21 December 2002
	- Interim measures on Administration of Mitigation of and Protection against Space Debris
COLOMBIA	*- Decree 2442, of July 2006 on the creation of the Colombian Commission of Space (CCE)*
FINLAND	
FRANCE	*- French Space Operations Act, No 2008-518 (2008)*
	- Decree No.2009-644 of 9 June 2009, modifying Decree No.84-510 of 28 June 1984, relating to CNES
	- Decree No. 2009-643 of 9 June 2008
	- Decree No. 2009-640 of 9 June 2009

STATE	LEGISLATION
GERMANY	-*Act to give Protection against the Security Risk to the Federal Republic of Germany by the Dissemination of High-Grade Earth Remote Sensing Data (Satellite Data Security Act — SatDSiG), 2007*
ITALY	- *Liability, with Law No. 23, 25 January 1983, Norms for the implementation of the Convention on International Liability for Damage Caused by Space Objects (Official Gazette No.35, 5 February, 1983)* - *Registration of objects launched into outer space, by Law No. 153, 12 July 2005 (Official Gazette No. 177, 1 August 2005)*
JAPAN	- *Basic Space Law (Law No.43, 2008 of 28 May 2008)* - *The Law concerning Japan Aerospace Exploration Agency (Law No. 161 of 13th December 2002)*
NETHERLANDS	- *The Netherlands Space Agency was established by Government Gazette 2008, No. 500. by covenant of the Ministry of Foreign Affairs, the Ministry of Education, Culture and Science, the Ministry of Transport, Public Works and Water Management and the Netherlands Organization for Scientific Research.* - *Rules Concerning Space Activities and the Establishment of a Registry of Space Objects (Space Activities Act) of 24 January 2007* - *Decree containing rules with regard to a registry of information concerning space objects (Space Objects Registry Decree) of 13 November 2007* - *Order concerning licence applications for the performance of space activities and the registration of space objects of 7 February 2008, as amended by Order of 16 April 2010*
NIGERIA	- *Nationals Space Research and Development Agency Act (NASDRA) Act 2010*
NORWAY	- *Act on launching objects from Norwegian territory into outer space.* *(No. 38, 13 June. 1969)*

STATE	LEGISLATION
REPUBLIC OF KOREA	- *Space Development Promotion Act of 1 December 2005* - *Space Liability Act (Law 8714 of 21 December 2007)*
RUSSIAN FEDERATION	- *Law on Space Activity, Federal Law No. 5663-1 (1993, as amended)* - *Statute on Licensing Space Operations, Federal Government Decree No. 104 (1996)*
SOUTH AFRICA	- *Space Affairs Act, No. 84 (1993)* - *Space Affairs Amendment Act, No. 64 (1995)* - *South African National Space Act 36 of 2008*
SPAIN	- *Royal Decree 278/1995, dated 24th February 1995, establishing in the Kingdom of Spain the Registry foreseen in the Convention adopted by the United Nations General Assembly on 2nd November 1974*
SWEDEN	- *Act on Space Activities (1982:963)* - *Decree on Space Activities (1982:1069)*
UKRAINE	- *Law of Ukraine on Space Activity, No. 503/96-VR, 1996*
UNITED KINGDOM	- *Outer Space Act (1986)*
USA	- *Title 51 of the U.S.C.* - *14 C.F.R. 400-499* - *NPR 8715.6A* - *NASA-STD 8719.14* - *U.S. Government Orbital Debris Mitigation Standard Practices* *Title 47 of the U.S.C.* - *47 C.F.R. Parts 5, 25, and 97* - *Order, FCC 04-130* - *47 C.F.R. 25.160-162*
VENEZUELA (BOLIVARIAN REPUBLIC OF)	- *Law on the Establishment of the Bolivarian Agency for Space Activities (Official Gazette No.38.796 of 25 October 2007)* - *Decree number 3.389 of December 2004* - *Decree No.4.114 of 28 November 2005*

BIBLIOGRAPHY

Works Cited

1023 UNTS 15, 2. U. *Convention on Registration of Objects Launched into Outer Space*. the General Assembly in Resolution 3235 (XXIX).

1363 UNTS 3, 1. I.–1. *The Agreement Governing the Activities of States on the Moon* . the General Assembly in Resolution 34/68.

672 UNTS 199, 1. U. *Agreement on the Rescue of Astronauts, the Return of Astronauts and the Return of Objects Launched into Outer Space.*

961 UBTS 187, 2. U. *Convention on International Liability for Damage Caused by Space Objects*. the General Assembly in Resolution 2777 (XXVI).

Kerrest, A. (2009). L'appropriation de la lune et des corps célestes. *Droit de l'Espace* , 342.

Kopal, V. (2008). *Historical context of the Outer Space Treaty*. Retrieved May 25, 2012, from United Nations: http://untreaty.un.org/cod/avl/ha/tos/tos.html

UN Doc. A/AC.105/L.2, 1. S. (1962). *Draft Declaration of the Basic Principles Governing the Activities of States Pertaining to the Exploration and Use of Outer Space.*

UN General Assembly, P. M., & (XVIII), R. 1. (1963). *Declaration of Legal Principles Governing the Activities of States in the Exploration and Use of Outer Space.*

© 2013, 2014, 2015 Daniel-Eduard Rociu
All rights reserved.

ISBN: 1490995498
ISBN-13: 978-1490995496

Cover and book design by AGORA BOOKS

Printed in the United States of America

Revised on May 2014, November 2015
First Printing: July 2013

Printed in Great Britain
by Amazon